The Himalaya Clause

Bruno Zeller

PhD (Melbourne); MIntTradeL(Deakin); B Com
(Melbourne); B Ed, (Melbourne)

and

Contributor

Gabriël Moens AM

JD (Leuven); LLM (Northwestern); PhD (Sydney); GCEd
(Queensland); MBA (Murdoch)

CONNOR COURT PUBLISHING PTY LTD
PO Box 7257
Redland Bay QLD 4165
sales@connorcourt.com
www.connorcourt.com

ISBN: 978-1-925826-83-8 (pbk.)

Front Cover By Paolo Monti - Available in the BEIC digital library and uploaded in partnership with BEIC Foundation. The image comes from the Fondo Paolo Monti, owned by BEIC and located in the Civico Archivio Fotografico of Milan., CC BY-SA 4.0, https://commons.wikimedia.org/w/index.php?curid=48042278

Cover design by Maria Giordano

Printed in Australia

CONTENTS

FOREWORD

One imagines that Mrs Adler, as a passenger of the *SS Himalaya*, might have enjoyed one of the ship's lavish gala dinners. In that era, the gala dinners offered delicacies such as clear green turtle soup, and boiled scotch salmon with cucumber and sauce hollandaise. There was, naturally, more pedestrian fare on the menu, including seasonal salads and assorted nuts. Apart from the cuisine, the *SS Himalaya* was a truly impressive vessel in her own right – as P & O's first liner after World War II; she measured 710 feet long and 90 feet wide and boasted a service speed of 22 knots. Built in the English town of Barrow-in-Furness, the *SS Himalaya* was launched on 5 October 1948 and departed on her maiden voyage on 6 October 1949.

A few years later, on 16 July 1952, Mrs Adler stepped on a gangway to the *SS Himalaya*. The sequence of events which follows is now very well known: the gangway suddenly became adrift due to the negligence of the master and the boatswain, Mrs Adler fell to the wharf below, and she suffered serious injuries including a broken leg, broken pelvis and broken ribs. She sued in tort. It was, in this seminal case of *Adler v Dickson,* that the English Court of Appeal opened the door to drafting an exemption clause to protect third parties with no connection to the contract – known today as the Himalaya Clause.

This book enriches our collective understanding and appreciation of the Himalaya Clause in the context of maritime law. The particular value of this book is that it is an international comparative study, which illuminates how, in the 20th century, the Himalaya Clause developed across key jurisdictions: England, the United States, South Africa and Germany, as well as Canada, Singapore, Hong Kong, South Korea, and China. This book thus offers an insight into the common law, the civil law. and the mixed legal system.

This book is underpinned by an acute awareness of how commercial sensibilities have shaped the international acceptance of the Himalaya Clause. This is especially pertinent in our present time, given the demands of global trade and transport. In doing so, this book explains how – not only as a matter of principle, but also as a matter of practicality – the Himalaya Clause has led to the gradual erosion of the Privity Rule. Crucially, this book emphasises the radical nature of these reforms by tracing the origins of the Privity Rule, including relevant statutory reform and recent judicial consideration, placing us firmly in the 21st century.

The clarity and precision of this book is a testament to Dr Bruno Zeller, Professor of Transnational Commercial Law at the University of Western Australia, Adjunct Professor at Murdoch University, and Adjunct Professor at Victoria University. Dr Zeller is recognised as the leading academic in the field of unified international sales laws in Australia and has contributed widely to the areas of maritime law, international trade law, international arbitration, and conflict of laws. Dr Zeller is a fellow of the Australian Institute for Commercial Arbitrations, is a member of the panel of arbitrators of the Maritime Law Association of Australia and New Zealand (MLAANZ).

In addition, this book is enriched by the contribution of Professor Gabriël Moens AM, Emeritus Professor of Law at the University of Queensland (where I was privileged to have him, together with the late Emeritus Professor Kevin Ryan, supervise my doctoral thesis). Professor Moens is renowned for his work in constitutional law, legal philosophy, and business law, particularly in relation to international and comparative studies. In 2019, Professor Moens was awarded a Member of the Order of Australia; in 2003, awarded the Australian Centenary Medal; and in 1999, received the Australian Award for University Teaching in Law and Legal Studies. Professor Moens has served as Pro Vice Chancellor and Dean at Murdoch University, and as Head of the Graduate School of Law at the University of Notre Dame.

This book promises the prospective reader with a voyage through space and time – not a mere scenic cruise, like the *SS Himalaya* once offered, but a fully-fleshed exploration. I am pleased to recommend this book to any such reader, whether they be a contract drafter, academic, court, or even a casual interloper.

The Hon Justice Sarah C Derrington

Harry Gibbs Commonwealth Law Courts

Brisbane, May 2020.

1

THE 'PRIVITY RULE' AND THE HIMALAYA CLAUSE: THE LEGAL LANDSCAPE

1.1   Introduction

This book is essentially about risk allocations in a maritime adventure. Its core issue concerns an attempt by various legal systems to circumvent the 'Privity Rule' to achieve an outcome which is commercially sound and desirable.

The 'Privity Rule' was once considered to be a fundamental principle of law. The principle that a person who is not a party to a contract can neither enforce a contract by benefiting from it, nor incur any liability, was firmly established in English law in *Dunlop Pneumatic Tyre Co Ltd v Selfridge Co Ltd.*[1] However, the principle has been roundly criticised and is now subject to either significant exceptions or it is circumvented by the drafting of relevant clauses. The principle has also been abrogated in many jurisdictions, especially in civil law countries because the application of the 'Privity Rule' potentially results in gross injustices, some of which are described in the next Chapter. In this context, it is not surprising that Furmston and Tolhurst, in the preface[2] to their book, noted that, "of all the central doctrines

---

1   [1915] AC 847.
2   M. Furmston and G.J. Tolhurst, *Privity of Contract*, Oxford Press, 2015.

in the common law of contract that is the most fractured."

The 'Privity Rule' mandates that only parties to a contract can either profit or sue. The Himalaya Clause, the exemption clause named after the SS Himalaya in the seminal case of *Adler v Dickson*,[3] heralded the beginning of the end of the 'Privity Rule'. It is not surprising that numerous criticisms were directed at the 'Privity Rule'. The English Law Commission in 1996[4] noted, amongst other reasons, that the Rule thwarts the intention of parties, might cause injustice to third parties and the range of exceptions makes the law complex, artificial and uncertain. Nevertheless, some commentators continue to argue in favour of the retention of the Rule, and some courts have proffered reasons for its usefulness. These reasons are either based on practical or theoretical considerations.

This book does not analyse the theoretical considerations in depth as, ultimately, the 'Privity Rule' has been overruled or bypassed in many specialised areas such as shipping and insurance. However, to fully understand the Himalaya Clause and any further developments, some comments are made in the next Chapter regarding the abandonment, for practical and theoretical reasons, of the Rule. This book will concentrate on the shipping of goods by sea and, specifically, it will look at the effect of the Himalaya Clause in maritime law. In brief, the aim of a Himalaya Clause, properly drafted is to:

> wholly exempt a contractual carrier's or other contracting party's servants, agents or subcontractors from liability under a contract and/or to confer on such servants, agents and subcontractors all the rights, limits, defences and exemptions from liability enjoyed by the contractual carrier under that contract.[5]

A suitable Himalaya Clause has been recommended by the

---

3   [1955] 1 QB 158.
4   Privity of Contract: Contracts for the Benefit of Third Parties Law Com, No 242. 1996.
5   BIMCO, *Special Circular*, note 1.

Baltic and International Maritime Council (BIMCO). Arguably, the clause reflects the current thinking of carriers who take the development of the Himalaya Clause and other solutions into consideration. It is an excellent example of a clause which appears to be covering all the shortcomings found in the long and interesting history of exemption clauses. The clause will assist the reader in understanding the following chapters and in appreciating the development and thinking of courts and tribunals on this issue.

The importance of BIMCO is best described as follows on its website:

> BIMCO is the world's largest international shipping association, with 2,300 members in around 130 countries. We provide a wide range of services to our global membership – which includes shipowners, operators, managers, brokers and agents. BIMCO's core objective is to facilitate the commercial operations of our members by developing standard contracts and clauses, and providing quality information, advice and education. BIMCO promotes fair business practices, free trade and open access to markets and we are a strong advocate for the harmonisation and standardisation of all shipping related activity. BIMCO actively promotes the application of globally agreed regulatory instruments – we are accredited as a Non-Governmental Organisation (NGO) with all relevant United Nations agencies and other regulatory entities.[6]

The importance of BIMCO for maritime trade necessitates a detailed study in this book of its tested and successful clause which will protect all parties involved in a maritime adventure. Hence, it is useful to reproduce the clause here:

International Group of P&I Clubs/BIMCO Himalaya Clause for bills of lading and other contracts 2014

(a) For the purposes of this contract, the term "Servant"

---

6   http://maritime-executive.com/magazine/bimco.

shall include the owners, managers, and operators of vessels (other than the Carrier); underlying carriers; stevedores and terminal operators; and any direct or indirect servant, agent, or subcontractor (including their own subcontractors), or any other party employed by or on behalf of the Carrier, or whose services or equipment have been used to perform this contract whether in direct contractual Privity with the Carrier or not.

(b) It is hereby expressly agreed that no Servant shall in any circumstances whatsoever be under any liability whatsoever to the shipper, consignee, receiver, holder, or other party to this contract (hereinafter termed "Merchant") for any loss, damage or delay of whatsoever kind arising or resulting directly or indirectly from any act, neglect or default on the Servant's part while acting in the course of or in connection with the performance of this contract.

(c) Without prejudice to the generality of the foregoing provisions in this clause, every exemption, limitation, condition and liberty contained herein (other than Art III Rule 8 of the Hague/Hague-Visby Rules if incorporated herein) and every right, exemption from liability, defence and immunity of whatsoever nature applicable to the carrier or to which the carrier is entitled hereunder including the right to enforce any jurisdiction or arbitration provision contained herein shall also be available and shall extend to every such Servant of the carrier, who shall be entitled to enforce the same against the Merchant.

(d)

(i) The Merchant undertakes that no claim or allegation whether arising in contract, bailment, tort or otherwise shall be made against any Servant of the carrier which imposes or attempts to impose upon any of them or any vessel owned or chartered by any of them any liability whatsoever in connection with this contract whether or not arising out of negligence on the part of such Servant. The Servant shall also be entitled to enforce the foregoing covenant against the Merchant; and

(ii) The Merchant undertakes that if any such claim or allegation should nevertheless be made, he will indemnify the carrier against all consequences thereof.

(e) For the purpose of sub-paragraphs (a)-(d) of this clause the carrier is or shall be deemed to be acting as agent or trustee on behalf of and for the benefit of all persons mentioned in sub-clause (a) above who are his Servant and all such persons shall to this extent be or be deemed to be parties to this contract.

The BIMCO clause, reproduced above, contains two main parts which aim at achieving different results: the first one (letter (a)) aims at providing total protection by granting to all third parties involved in the carriage of goods an immunity for tort liability against the claims brought by cargo receivers; secondly, sub-clause (b) purports to extend the benefits that the carrier receives *ex lege* under the international uniform conventions on carriage of goods by sea.[7]

1.2   The Importance of the Himalaya Clause in International Commerce

The applicability of the Himalaya Clause is important in today's global economy involving increased trade and unceasing demands for international transport. In order to understand the changes in risk allocation fully, the underlying commercial landscape needs to be taken into consideration. It is in effect

---

7   Certain legal aspects of the Himalaya Clause in the contract of international carriage of goods by sea, University of Oslo, Faculty of Law, research paper, https://www.duo.uio.no/bitstream/handle/10852/38410/Thesis.

the framework in which contracts operate; this framework is changing rapidly.

At present, developments in global commerce have the potential to shift political and economic alliances. They also involve a new way of looking at transport and its associated legal aspects. For example, in late 2013, the President of P R China, Mr Xi announced the concept of the Silk Road Economic Belt, also referred to as the One Belt One Road Project (OBOR). The Project envisages a road and rail route to Europe via central Asia which also involves the strengthening of the shipping corridors, including routes via Africa. The fact that P R China is looking at Europe is not accidental as the EU is China's largest trading partner. Projects in Europe which are financed by P R China are increasing as noted in *The National Interest*:

> China is financing the upgrade of the Greek port of Piraeus and a $3 billion bullet train from Belgrade to Budapest. Another network of rails, roads and pipelines, starting in the Chinese central city of Xian, will stretch westward as far as Belgium. Beijing has already started building an eight-thousand-mile cargo rail route between the Chinese city of Yiwu and Madrid[8]

It does not take much imagination to understand that an increased seamless supply line from P R China into Europe requires an evaluation of new risks. This is especially so considering that countries, specifically in central Asia, have unfamiliar legal systems. In addition, there is a noticeable increase in multimodal transports which create new and possibly novel legal challenges. It is anticipated that sophisticated parties will include into their contracts of carriage, whether by rail or ship, exclusion clauses protecting their interests. Indeed, it can be reasonably anticipated that participants within the supply line need to carry the risk of having to cover possible damages emanating from the transport of goods. The law, over the centuries, has proposed

---

8   *The National Interest (*online) July 27, 2016. https://nationalinterest.org/feature/chinas-huge-one-belt-one-road-initiative-sweeping-central-17150.

many solutions but so far, the issue that somebody must carry the risk has not been properly resolved and is still developing. Ultimately, it is left to proper insurance cover to mitigate losses in relation to loss of, or damage to, goods while in possession of third parties.

Historically, the issue of liability in relation to international transport "has been regarded as one of the most international areas of law."[9] International conventions such as the International Convention for the Unification of Certain Rules of Law Relating to Bills of Lading ("The Hague Rules") in shipping established a liability regime as early as 1924. However, this regime only covered transport by sea from port to port. But goods also need to be transported inland and, to that end, relevant parties enter into multimodal contracts, involving different transport means. Hence, a contracting carrier must deal with performing carriers creating different liability rules. Liability for damage can either affect the carrier and also his sub-contractors or one of the contractual parties. The law has produced many solutions in shifting the risk from one party to another depending on the contract and the jurisdiction in which it is drafted. Initially, the 'Privity Rule' was applied and, accordingly, a third party could not profit from a contract between the shipper (or seller) of goods and the carrier. The early Conventions, such as the Hague Rules, did not disembowel the 'Privity Rule" but, instead, limited the damages of the carrier of the goods. Of course, it would also be possible for the seller of goods to protect themselves against any liability by simply incorporating a term similar to the INCOTERM 2010 ExW (Ex Works) into the carriage of goods contract. In accordance with Ex Works, the buyer bears the risk of loss of, or damage to. the goods carried and assumes the liability of the carrier or any subcontractors depending on the contractual terms.

---

9   V. Ulfbeck, Multimodal Transports in the United States and Europe--Global or Regional Liability Rules? 34 *Tul. Mar. L.J.* 37 2009-2010, 37.

Subsequently, however, the Himalaya Clause was used to protect third parties to a contract and has extended this protection past the sea leg into multimodal contracts. The goal of this development is to create international uniformity.[10] This book will trace this development and explain where we are now. This situation can be changed in relation to the carrier with the inclusion of exemption clauses into the bill of lading, which is evidence of the existence of the shipping contract. The carrier can also include an exemption which covers all parties who handle the goods along the supply line. Alternatively, a series of contracts can be devised where each function of the transport of goods is encapsulated in a contract; however, this is certainly not practical and is very time-consuming. In commerce, it has always been assumed that all players in a market are robust and informed, and hence, they can look after themselves. In general, and specifically because of exemption clauses, the burden of risk has always and still is properly shifted to an insurance company. Lord Steyn in *Marc Rich and Co AG and Others v Bishop Rock Marine Co Ltd and Others*[11] explains this relationship well when he noted:

> The dealings between shipowners and cargo owners are based on a contractual structure, The Hague Rules, and tonnage limitation, on which the insurance of international trade depends. ... Underlying it is the system of double or overlapping insurance of cargo. Cargo owners take out direct insurance in respect of the cargo. Shipowners take out liability risks insurance in respect of breaches of their duties of care in respect of the cargo. The insurance system is structured on the basis that the potential liability of the shipowners to cargo owners is limited under The Hague Rules and by virtue of tonnage limitation provisions. And insurance premiums payable by owners obviously reflect such limitations on the shipowner's exposure.[12]

---

10   Ibid., 40.
11   [1996] 1 AC 211.
12   Ibid., 239-240.

The question of insurance will not be pursued in this book, but the drafting of exemption clauses and the associated question whether a third party can be protected is the theme of this book. However, Tetley's arguments in relation to, what he terms, the 'fallacy of the commercial/insurance argument' needs to be addressed. He argues that a person causing damage to cargo ought to be held responsible otherwise he would continue to be negligent and will not alter their practices.[13] In effect, it is cost shifting from one party, the cargo owner, to the insurance company. However, it is misleading to characterise this as risk-shifting: insurance companies are not in the business to carry losses but to make a profit. Hence, from an insurance industry perspective. insurance is good business.

1.3   Outline of the issues

The liability system which is in force in the shipping industry is not new. It has occupied courts in various jurisdictions. The shipping industry has developed a liability system where the owners of cargo, which is damaged during the voyage, will only recover a small part of their loss. This is so even if the carrier negligently caused the loss and hence is liable for it. This limit of liability is found first in the Hague-Visby Rules[14] and, secondly, in the contract of carriage incorporating The Hague-Visby rules. The limitation of damage also includes "agents and servants" of the carrier.[15] If the damage is caused by an independent contractor of the carrier, the owner of the cargo might recover in full as the contractor is not covered by the Rules. However, this loophole has now been covered by a Himalaya Clause which extends the carrier's limitation of liability to anybody connected to the marine adventure.

---

13   W. Tetley, The Himalaya Cause – Revisited, 2003, 9 *JIML* 40, 42. Ibid., 41.
14   These rules are currently the most universally accepted rules. In this term, The Hague Rules as they are sometimes called are also included.
15   See Article IV of The Hague-Visby Rules.

This book will trace the development of exemption clauses in shipping from the 'Privity Rule' to the Himalaya Clause and beyond. The Himalaya clause not only protects the parties to a contract but extends the benefits of the contract to unconnected third parties such as stevedores. However, this book is not so much a critical analysis of the Himalaya Clause; rather it maps the development of the Clause in several important jurisdictions and states the law as noted by the courts. It will assist the reader in understanding the law as it applies to the drafting of exemption clauses. Simply put, an understanding of the development and current state of the law will assist contract drafters, courts and academics on how the Himalaya Clause, properly drafted, assists the carriers and all parties connected to the sea carriage document, including now beyond the sea leg. It will also inform the shipper of the importance of procuring the relevant insurance cover.

1.4   Where are we now?

The development of liability clauses in shipping has demonstrated that an international solution is possible. Sturley correctly observed that:

> International legal conflicts are not simply random occurrences.
> On the contrary, independent domestic legal concerns push
> national courts into differing interpretations of supposedly
> uniform laws. Each court considers itself bound to interpret
> and apply international uniform law in a manner that will avoid
> inconsistency or tension with its own domestic law.[16]

Various jurisdictions have recognised that a solution in one jurisdiction which is commercially sound could or should be incorporated into their own jurisdiction. It will be argued in this book that this is precisely the case with the Himalaya Clause.

---

16   M. Sturley, International Uniform Law in National Courts: The Influence of Domestic Law in Conflicts of Interpretation, 27 *Virginia Journal of International law*, 1987,729, 733.

It is obvious that exemption clauses as such are not a novel aspect of law. What is novel, and the theme of this book, is the development of the Himalaya Clause in the 20th century which revolutionised the effect and scope of exemption clauses. The Himalaya Clause, as noted above, allows a third party who has no connection to the contract to rely on the same benefits, namely an exemption of liability, as the original parties. The carrier subsequently engages a stevedore to unload the goods. Essentially, the third party (the stevedore) is protected by the contractual terms. This would not be the case if the 'Privity Rule' were to apply. To understand the changes that have occurred during the last century, it is important that the 'Privity Rule' be addressed in order to appreciate what exactly changed in the allocation of risk as addressed by the Himalaya Clause.

Much has been written by commentators in relation to the merits or otherwise of the Himalaya Clause. This book recognises that the "horse has bolted". Hence, this book provides an analysis of the views of commentators who have written for or against the Himalaya Clause. It will also be argued that the Himalaya Clause, in contrast to the 'Privity Rule', is based on a sound theoretical base and can be explained either through the will or economic analysis theory.

The purpose of this book is twofold. First, it will give an overview of the development of the Himalaya Clause in selected jurisdictions which have been chosen because (i) they are the most important shipping countries and (ii) there is enough jurisprudence available belonging to common law, civil law and mixed legal systems. Secondly, this book will discuss earlier seminal cases, the *ratio decidendi* of which were in some cases fundamentally incompatible with each other. It is also noteworthy that in later cases, and in several jurisdictions, very little deviation from the transnational understanding of the effect of the Himalaya Clause has been detected. This, in effect, demonstrates that the solution offered by the Himalaya Clause is internationally acceptable and, importantly, commercially desirable.

This book will assist commentators, academics and the judiciary in their interpretive task without having to read all the cases which can be lengthy. A further point needs to be added, namely that clauses in contracts need to be interpreted, hence, the interpretive tool also needs to be considered. This is important because it is argued that in common law the development of/or circumventing the parol evidence rule is still a work in progress. A further reason is to show that global reform is not necessarily driven by international bodies such as the United Nations Commission on International Trade Law ("UNCITRAL") or UNIDROIT but by domestic courts looking at each other and recognising that a solution such as the Himalaya Clause is a commercially sound development, the introduction of which in their own legal system should be facilitated.

This book does recognise that the Himalaya Clause is not the only option to circumvent the 'Privity Rule' in shipping. It will demonstrate that the Himalaya Clause cannot be properly understood without understanding the evolution of the 'Privity Rule' which, despite still being relevant today, has become in terms "of substantive coverage and effect, relatively hollow."[17] In effect, the Himalaya Clause has assisted in almost eradicating the Rule itself.[18]

In summary, this book will trace the "warfare" between traditionalists supporting the Privity of contract rule, on one hand, and the reformers who moulded the law to reflect modern commercial reality in shipping, in particular, and drafting of exemption clauses, in general. The case law of England, Australia, the United States, South Africa and Germany as well as to a lesser degree Canada, Singapore, Hong Kong and South Korea is examined. A comment in relation to the Chinese

---

17   V. Palmer, *The Paths to Privity*, Austin & Winfield, 1992, 244.
18   Ibid.

attitude and treatment of the Himalaya Clause is also noted. It allows the reader to understand the transnational development and treatment of Himalaya clauses.

The civil law aspect is restricted to German law. The Münchener Vertrags-Handbuch does mention Himalaya clauses in their treatment of Shipping law (Seefrachtrecht).[19] The commentary specifically draws on English case law in the creation of the Himalaya Clause, but unfortunately jurisprudence referring to Himalaya clauses is not plentiful.

In addition to jurisprudence, academic writing is used to discuss the various points of view in relation to the utility and, importantly, the understanding of the reach of the Himalaya Clause.

This book will also trace the development of clauses which rely on both the agency theory and the trust theory of a third-party benefit and by adding a circular indemnity provision which will be discussed in a further Chapter. The issue is that the historical development of the Himalaya Clause over the past 50 years, mainly in England and the United States will assist drafters and interpreters of contracts to understand the proper process in protecting relevant parties in a maritime adventure.

1.5   Structure of the book

Chapter 2 will analyse and explain the 'Privity Rule' as it developed. not only in common law but also in civil law. The discussion will highlight the fact that in civil law the Privity Rule' has been abandoned since the late 19th century in favour of contracting for the benefit of third parties. Two examples, namely *Trident v McNiece*[20] as well as how the 'Privity Rule' is still dominant in India will be referred to in the discussion.

---

19   Band 4, Wirschaftsrecht III 5. Auflage Beck Munchen, 2002, 1031-32.
20   (1988) 165 CLR 107.

Chapter 2 will also deal with the right of an aggrieved party to sue.

Chapter 3 will examine the efforts of national parliaments in introducing statutory reforms in relation to the 'Privity Rule'. In essence, it will be argued that the reforms amount to the introduction of mere exceptions to the 'Privity Rule'. Most common law jurisdictions are represented in the brief overview and includes international efforts to overcome the 'Privity Rule' by the Principles of International Commercial Contract Law drafted by UNIDROIT.

Chapter 4 will describe problems associated with the application of the 'Privity Rule' as noted by the English judiciary. The specific focus is on the early attempts by courts to depart from the Rule. The relevant seminal case of *Elder Dempster & Co. Ld. v. Paterson, Zochonis & Co. Ltd*[21] assists in the explanation of the development of the Himalaya Clause.

Chapter 5 discusses the seminal cases which were important in the development of the Himalaya Clause specifically *Brandt v. Liverpool*[22], *Brazil and River Plate Steam Navigation Co. Ltd*[23], *Elder Dempster & Go. Ld. v. Paterson, Zochonis & Co. Ltd*[24]. *and Adler v Dickson*[25], where the phrase 'Himalaya Clause' was coined.

Chapters 6 to 10 are dedicated to the analysis and further development of the Himalaya Clause in selected legal systems. To that end, jurisprudence in England, Australia, the United States and Canada as the major common law exponent, Germany as the civil law representative and South Africa as the mixed legal system are discussed. In addition, other, significant jurisprudence in a variety of countries such as Singapore, South

---

21   [1924] 18 LI,I Rep, 69.
22   [124] G1 K. B. 575.
23   [1924] 1 K.B.575.
24   [1924] 18 LI>I Rep. 69.
25   [1955] 1 QB 158.

Korea and P R China are also included in Chapter 10.

Chapter 11 is devoted to the discussion of the Himalaya Clause. The further development of the Clause and its possible alternatives will also be explored in this Chapter. Finally, the question will be asked whether the end of the road has been reached. The book concludes in Chapter 12 with an evaluation of the Himalaya Clause jurisprudence.

2

AN AGGRIEVED PARTY'S RIGHT TO SUE

2.1   Introduction

This Chapter will describe the contractual documents in which an exemption clause can be embedded, namely the charter party and the bill of lading. Besides contractual rights, an aggrieved party has several rights of action in relation to claim damages from non-contractual parties which will only be discussed as far as it is relevant to this book.

The right to sue can be based on contractual and non-contractual actions of which the following will be analysed as far as necessary.

- Contractual action
- Charter party
- Bill of lading
- Interpretative methodology as informed by The Ardennes26
- Bailment27 as explained in The Pioneer Container28
- Sub-bailment exceptions as illustrated by Gadsden Pty Ltd
  v Australian Coastal Shipping Commission.29

---

26   [1951]1 KB 55.
27   It is recognised that bailment can also exist in a non-contractual relationship
      but for convenience it has been put into contractual sub-heading.
28   [1994] 2 A.C. 324.
29   [1977] 1 NSWLR 575.

- Non-contractual action
- Agency
- Trust
- Tort
- Letters of Credit

In every maritime venture, someone needs to conclude a carriage of goods by sea contract if the buyer or consignee is eventually to receive the goods.[30] Carriage of goods by sea is defined in article 1(b) in The Hague-Visby ("Amended Hague Rules") Rules:

> "Contract of carriage" means a contract of carriage covered by a sea carriage document (to the extent that the document relates to the carriage of goods by sea), and includes a negotiable sea carriage document issued under a charterparty from the moment at which that document regulates the relations between its holder and the carrier concerned.

Two points need to be understood; first a contract must be one that is related to a carriage by sea as defined in The Amended Hague Rules. Secondly, the document which is defined as being a sea carriage document is also defined in article I(g):[31]

> "Sea carriage document" means:
>
> (i) a bill of lading; or
>
> (ii) a negotiable document of title that is similar to a bill of lading and that contains or evidences a contract of carriage of goods by sea; or
>
> (iii) a bill of lading that, by law, is not negotiable; or
>
> (iv) a non-negotiable document (including a consignment note and a document of the kind known as a sea waybill or the kind known as a ship›s delivery order) that either contains or evidences a contract of carriage of goods by sea.

---

30   Simon Baughen, *Shipping Law*, 2004, 3rd ed. Cavendish Publishing, 19.
31   This definition relates to the Australian Rules and especially part (iv). Waybills might not be in other Rules.

It is obvious that the parties to a sea carriage document need to be ascertained. It will *prima facie* determine who has standing in any legal action in a carriage dispute. *Pyrene Co Ltd v Scindia* Navigation Co Ltd[32] is instructive as the court explained the importance of a sea carriage document and, hence, the document determines who will enter into, or is part of, the contract with the carrier. The court held that:

> the rights and liabilities under the rules did not attach to a period of time but attached to a contract or part of a contract, their operation being determined by the limits of the contract of carriage by sea, and however restricted a meaning were given to the words "carriage of goods by sea" the loading of the goods related to the carriage.[33]

However, *Pyrene Co Ltd v Scindia* Navigation Co Ltd[34] is also important in understanding the route of recovery. The court distinguished between contractual and non-contractual rights to sue that is in tort or bailment. The court noted that express terms can and are supplemented by implied terms which are not to be found in the four corners of the contract. In addition, civil law countries do not recognise the parol evidence rule nor do international conventions and model laws.

2.2   Interpretive methodology

It is helpful to be aware of different methods of interpretation as in the end a contract is never clear and relies on interpretive assistance by courts and tribunals. Civil law countries do not rely to a great extent on jurisprudence but rather follow academic writing and commentaries. The reason is mainly because civil law countries rely on codes and, hence, judicial law making, unlike in common law countries, is not present.

---

32   [1954] 2 QB 402.
33   Ibid., 403.
34   [1954] 2 QB 402.

This is different to the approach taken by common law countries where jurisprudence takes on a great role, to not only interpret statutes, but also to create new laws as seen in the case of the Himalaya Clause which is the subject of this book. However, as already indicated, shipping in particular does not follow exactly the classic parol evidence rule but takes the intent of the parties into consideration. The question which the courts have asked is: what did the parties know or ought to have known taking customary practices and knowledge into consideration?

In relation to shipping law, changes have taken place since *Leduc v Ward*[35] where Lord Esher stated that once the contract has been reduced to writing "parol evidence to alter or qualify such writing is not admissible, and the writing is the only evidence of the contract."[36] In Australia this approach appears to be still standing as noted in *Codelfa Construction Pty Ltd v State Rail Authority (NSW)*.[37]

However, *Leduc v Ward* has not been followed as seen in *The Ardennes*.[38] In *Leduc v Ward* the facts indicated that it was a case between a shipowner and an endorsee of the bill of lading. In these cases, the Bills of Lading Act 1855 mandates that the terms of the bill of lading are conclusive so that no evidence was admissible to contradict or vary its terms between those parties listed int the contract.[39] Hence, in *Leduc* the court stated the law as it stood then, namely that the "writing is the only evidence of the contract."[40]

One hundred years later in the *Ardennes* the approach had changed. The bill of lading was between the shipper and the carrier. The issue was that the shipper relied on an oral promise that the ship will directly sail to London. In fact, it went via

---

35   (1888) 20 QBD 478.
36   Ibid., 480.
37   (1982) 149 CLR 337.
38   [1951]1 KB 55.
39   Ibid., 60.
40   *Leduc v Ward* (n35) 480.

Antwerp, hence, causing the shipper damages as he could not sell the oranges at a favourable price. The bill of lading contained a liberty or deviation clause. The question which occupied the court was whether the oral promise "trumped" the liberty clause in the bill of lading. Lord Goddard C.J noted that "it is well settled that a bill of lading is not in itself the contract between the shipowner and the shipper of goods, though it has been said to be excellent evidence of its terms."[41] He continued:

> The contract has come into existence before the bill of lading is signed; the latter is signed by one party only, and handed by him to the shipper usually after the goods have been put on board. No doubt if the shipper finds that the bill contains terms with which he is not content, or does not contain some term for which he has stipulated, he might, if there were time, demand his goods back; but he is not, in my opinion, for that reason, prevented from giving evidence that there was in fact a contract entered into before the bill of lading was signed different from that which is found in the bill of lading or containing some additional term. ... He is no party to the preparation of the bill of lading; nor does he sign it.[42]

The court treated the promise as a warranty and in effect "it was a promise that the shipowner would not avail himself of a liberty which otherwise would have been open to him."[43]

In a more recent decision in *Evans (J.) Ltd. v. Andrea Merzario Ltd. (C.A.)*[44] Lord Denning reinforced the decision in the *Ardennes*. The facts were that an English importer of machines from Italy used a forwarding agent and the machines - to protect them from rusting – were always put in crates and shipped under deck while at sea. In 1967 the forwarding agent proposed to ship the machines in containers instead of as previously in crates.

---

41   Ardennes, 59.
42   Ibid., 59-60.
43   Ibid, 60.
44   [1976] 1 W.L.R., 1078.

The English manager agreed to the change after the agent gave him an oral assurance that the containers would still be carried under deck and not on deck and with that knowledge agreed on the written terms. The written terms in essence stated:

> condition 4 which gives the company complete freedom in respect of means, route and procedure in the transportation of goods; condition 11 which says that the company will not be liable for loss or damage unless it occurs while in their actual custody and then only if they are guilty of wilful neglect or default; condition 13 which says that their liability shall not exceed the value of the goods or a sum at the rate of £50 per ton of 20 cwt.[45]

However, the container was shipped on deck and fell overboard. The court at first instance noted that the carrier was not liable as he issued a bill of lading containing the words "Shipped on deck at shippers' risk"[46] and hence the English importer initiated an action against the forwarding agent.

The result of the original trial was that:

> The forwarding agents denied liability, relying on the exemptions in their printed conditions of carriage. Kerr J. held that the oral assurance was not a legally binding warranty such as would operate collaterally to the contract and override the standard conditions, and dismissed the action.[47]

In the appeal Lord Denning – in his judgment – was quick to note that:

> I must say that much of what was said in that case is entirely out of date. We now have the Misrepresentation Act 1967 under which damages can be obtained for innocent misrepresentation of fact. This Act does not apply here because we are concerned with an assurance as to the future. But even in respect of promises as to

---

45   Ibid. 1081.
46   Ibid 1080.
47   Ibid 1078.

the future, we have a different approach nowadays to collateral contracts. When a person gives a promise or an assurance to another, intending that he should act on it by entering into a contract, and he does act on it by entering into the contract, we hold that it is binding.[48]

Lord Denning also noted that cases where oral promises overrode written exempting conditions are numerous and he repeated what he said in *Mendelssohn v. Normand* that, "The printed condition is rejected because it is repugnant to the express oral promise or representation."[49]

Other judgments expressed the same views as Lord Denning. As an example, Roskill L.J. did note that usually parol evidence cannot be given to contradict the terms of a written contract but he noted that in this case

> one is not concerned with a contract in writing (with respect, I cannot accept Mr. Hallgarten's argument that there was here a contract in writing) but with a contract which, as I think, was partly oral, partly in writing, and partly by conduct. In such a case, the court does not require to have recourse to lawyer's devices such as collateral oral warranty in order to seek to adduce evidence which would not otherwise be admissible. The court is entitled to look at and should look at all the evidence from start to finish in order to see what the bargain was that was struck between the parties.[50]

Geoffrey Lane L.J. in the same case states the argument succinctly when he noted:

> It seems to me that whether the test is an objective or a subjective one, whether one takes the view of the officious invisible bystander, or the view of Mr. Spano or the view of Mr. Leonard himself as to the effect of the meeting in autumn 1967,

---

48   Ibid., Evans 1081.
49   *Mendelssohn v. Normand [1970] 1 Q.B. 177*, 184.
50   *Evans (J.) Ltd. v. Andrea Merzario Ltd. (C.A.) (n144)* 1083.

the answer would be the same. The effect of their agreement was to remove from the new term the restrictions or exemptions contained in those trading conditions. Any other conclusion would be to destroy the business efficacy of the new agreement from the day it started.[51]

Simply put, the interpretive approach has taken commercial reality into consideration which in effect inquires what the parties intended to be bound to in the first instance – that is the subjective approach. In addition, courts tended also to interpret the relevant writings with commercial rather than strict legal eyes.

A further point needs to be taken into consideration, namely that domestic law also contains conventions such as the CISG which were ratified as well as model laws which were introduced into domestic statutes such as the model law on cross border insolvencies. The instruments generally also contain interpretative articles which on occasions can clash with the parol evidence rule. Most instruments such as the UNIDROIT Principles 2016 also followed the civil law approach; it is instructive to examine in brief the interpretative approach taken by international instruments.

2.3   International interpretation of contracts

The best two examples are the CISG, article 8 and the UNIDROIT Principles of International Commercial Contracts, articles 4.1 to 4.8. These articles assist the court in the interpretation of the conduct of, and statements made by, the parties. The CISG, a convention, applies by force of law and the UNIDROIT Principles, a model law, need to be included into the contract to be applied, or alternatively the courts can use the Principles to assist in the interpretation of contracts. Several courts have indeed referred to the Principles on interpretive issues. In

---

51   Ibid., 1085.

Australia, the Principles were quoted seven times, once in the High Court, three times in the Federal Court and three times in the New South Wales Supreme Court. Of interest is the context in which the Principles have been noted.[52] The High Court in 2007, as a representative example, had to look at the claim whether a breach of a "non-essential" term gives rise to a breach of contract. The Court comparatively addressed this issue with other laws and noted that this issue:

> finds no reflection in the relevant parts of the United States Restatement of the law. Nor is it adopted in the Uniform Commercial Code of the United States. There is nothing like it in the United Nations Convention on Contracts for the International Sale of Goods 1980. Nor does it appear in the UNIDROIT Principles of International Commercial Contracts 2004.[53]

This passage indicates that the court did not simply rely on domestic interpretative tools but that international instruments, speaking on this issue, have gained the attention of the judiciary and, hence, cannot be ignored. In addition, the international principles align themselves with the way the Himalaya Clause is interpreted.

As far as the UNIDROIT Principles are concerned, two articles are to be noted: article 4.1 and 4.2[54]. Article 4.1 states:

(1) A contract shall be interpreted according to the common intention of the parties.

(2) If such an intention cannot be established, the contract shall be interpreted according to the meaning that reasonable persons of the same kind as the parties would give to it in the same circumstances.

---

52   See B. Zeller,*The Development of a Global Contract Law. Still a Dream?* in Eppur si muove: The age of Uniform Law – Festschrift for Michael Joachim Bonell, to celebrate his 70th birthday, UNIDROIT (ed.), 2016.

53   *Koompahtoo Council v Sanpina P/L/ (2007)* 233 CLR 115. 157 referring to articles 7.3.1 and 7.3.3.

54   UNIDROIT Principles 2016, 138-139.

The common intention of the parties prevails at all times. This has also been paramount in the understanding in shipping contracts that every party in the supply chain knows that the carrier will need to involve on occasion several third parties unconnected to the main contract to complete the process of delivering goods to their final destination. As far as sub-paragraph (2) is concerned, a common intention can be found by considering all the relevant circumstances of the case, the most important of which are listed in Article 4.3:

> In applying Articles 4.1 and 4.2, regard shall be had to all the circumstances, including
>
> (a) preliminary negotiations between the parties;
>
> (b) practices which the parties have established between themselves;
>
> (c) the conduct of the parties subsequent to the conclusion of the contract;
>
> (d) the nature and purpose of the contract;
>
> (e) the meaning commonly given to terms and expressions in the trade concerned;
>
> (f) usages.

The same comment applies again in relation to the closeness of the UNIDROIT Principles and the application of the Himalaya Clause. The "commercial reality check", essentially, needs to look at least to some of the circumstances listed in article 4.3. Of controversy and rejected by the common law is article 4.2 as the subjective intent is very much of importance in the interpretive process. The article states:

> (1) The statements and other conduct of a party shall be interpreted according to that party's intention if the other party knew or could not have been unaware of that intention.
>
> (2) If the preceding paragraph is not applicable, such statements and other conduct shall be interpreted according to the meaning that a reasonable person of the same kind as the other party

would give to it in the same circumstances.

"In practice the principal field of application of this Article, which corresponds almost literally to Article 8(1) and (2) CISG, will be in the process of the formation of contracts where parties make statements and engage in conduct the precise legal significance"[55] of which may have to be established when determining the scope and validity of the Himalaya clause.

Considering that several interpretive principles are used by various domestic legal systems, it certainly is of value to keep the purpose and scope of the UNIDROIT Principles in mind when drafting a contract. It might even assist to include the interpretative articles into the contract to ensure that the common intent of both parties will be taken into consideration when interpreting the contract.

2.4   Contractual Actions

Essentially, the shipping contract can be contained in two basic forms, the charter party or the bill of lading, or the waybill. Charter party terms can also be included into the bill of lading, hence, the relationship between the charter party terms and the bill of lading needs to be understood.

The waybill is similar to the bill of lading except that it is not negotiable and, depending on the Carriage of Goods by Sea legislation, might not be a sea carriage document. However, recently it has been brought into the Australian Carriage of Goods by Sea Act (COGSA) regime and is now a sea carriage document.

1.1.1 The Charter Party

---

55   Ibid., 2016.

As noted above, two contracts are of importance: first the charter party contract between the shipowner and the charterer and secondly, the bill of lading which will be issued in due course which is a contract between the shipper and the carrier. A charterer, whether time or voyage charter, can also take on board goods which belong to other shippers to fill the vessel. An important point to consider is whether the charter party agreement is a sea carriage document under the Carriage of Goods by Sea Act 1991 (COGSA). In Australia, this is not the case, as noted finally in *Dampskibsselskabet Norden A/S v Gladstone Civil Pty Ltd*.[56] The case relies on s 11 of the enabling legislation of the Australian COGSA which is a mandatory rule. It provides in the relevant part:

> Construction and jurisdiction
>
> (1) All parties to:
> (a) a sea carriage document relating to the carriage of goods from any place in Australia to any place outside Australia; or
> (b) a non-negotiable document of a kind mentioned in subparagraph 10(1)(b)(iii), relating to such a carriage of goods; are taken to have intended to contract according to the laws in force at the place of shipment.

The importance of this article lies in the fact that once a voyage starts in Australia the governing law is the one in force in Australia. Section 11 will only apply if the document containing the contract is a sea carriage document.

The Amended Hague Rules define sea carriage document in article 1(g) as follows:

> "Sea carriage document" means:
>
> (i)   a bill of lading; or

---

56   [2013] FCAFC 107, [2013] 216 FCR, 469.

(ii) a negotiable document of title that is similar to a bill of lading and that contains or evidences a contract of carriage of goods by sea; or

(iii) a bill of lading that, by law, is not negotiable; or

(iv) a non-negotiable document (including a consignment note and a document of the kind known as a sea waybill or the kind known as a ship's delivery order) that either contains or evidences a contract of carriage of goods by sea.

The court took note of article 1(1)(b) where a clear distinction has been drawn between a charter party and a sea carriage document. A negotiable instrument can be issued under a charter party which does not make the charter party a sea carriage document.

The court noted: "Those matters [as indicated in the legislative history] indicate that the amended Hague Rules preserve the distinction between a charter party including a voyage charter party, and a sea carriage document."[57]

Once a bill of lading includes charter party terms, the usual contractual rules apply. This includes third parties such as consignees who might be surprised to learn that terms other than the one contained in the bill of lading might apply.[58] However, the innocent third party holding a valid and enforceable bill of lading is entitled to the rights, and is burdened by the obligations, of the terms of the contract between the carrier and the predecessor which can include terms of the charter party.[59\]

1.1.2 The Bill of Lading

---

57   Ibid., 475.
58   See Generally Melis Özel, "Incorporation of Charterparty Clauses into Bills of Lading: Peculiar to Maritime Law" in Malcolm Clarke (ed) *Maritime Law Evolving: Thirty Years at Southampton*, Hart Publishing, 2013, 181.
59   Michael White, *Australian Maritime Law* (3rd ed),The Federation Press, 2014, 193.

Shippers normally will book space through an agent on a vessel and the contract of affreightment is normally executed at this stage. Care must be taken when a freight forwarder is engaged. He might act as an agent of the shipper or as the principal himself. If he acts as the principal, he will be held personally liable.

The shipping documents, namely the bill of lading bestows rights to the holder which are legislated in the relevant COGSA. As an example, in Australia the enabling legislation in s 2 states:

S 2 Rights under shipping documents..

(1) Subject to the following provisions of this section, a person who becomes—

(a) the lawful holder of a bill of lading;

(b) the person who (without being an original party to the contract of carriage) is the person to whom delivery of the goods to which a sea waybill relates is to be made by the carrier in accordance with that contract; or

(c) the person to whom delivery of the goods to which a ship's delivery order relates is to be made in accordance with the undertaking contained in the order, shall (by virtue of becoming the holder of the bill or, as the case may be, the person to whom delivery is to be made) have transferred to and vested in him all rights of suit under the contract of carriage as if he had been a party to that contract.[60]

The bill of lading essentially fulfils three functions. First, it is a receipt for goods shipped. The bill will note whether the goods have been received by the carrier in good order or not and is *prima facie* evidence in favour of anybody else who purchases the bill of lading. Of importance is that the bill of lading must be clean: the carrier testifies that the goods are in good order. If there are any doubts in the mind of the carrier, he will note on the

---

60   http://www.legislation.gov.uk/ukpga/1992/50.

bill of lading the defects he observed such as "steel shows rust" or the master's protest which is also noted on the bills of lading. With this notation, the carrier is not liable to the consignee and, hence, the responsibility rests with the shipper. Secondly, the bill of lading is evidence of the existence of the contract of carriage. The terms are usually on the reverse side of the bill of lading. However, as already noted the courts have adopted also external evidence: they will imply terms into a contract as seen in *the Ardennes*.[61] Thirdly, the bill of lading is also a document of title. Simply put, the bill of lading represents the goods and possession of the bill equates to possession of the goods. As Bowen LJ noted *in Sanders v McLean*:

> A cargo at sea while in the hands of the carrier is necessarily incapable of physical delivery. During this period of transit and voyage the bill of lading, by the law merchant, is universally recognized as its symbol and the indorsement and delivery of the bill of lading operates as a symbolic delivery of the cargo. Property in the goods passes by such indorsement and delivery of the bill of lading whenever it is the intention of the parties that the property should pass, just as under similar circumstances the property would pass by an actual delivery of the goods ... it is the key which, in the hands of the rightful owner, is intended to unlock the door of the warehouse, floating or fixed, in which the goods may chance to be.[62]

The problems associated with the title to sue have been resolved, in general, through the relevant COGSA. However, the common law device of implied terms is still available. Courts have been prepared to imply a contract between an endorsee and the carrier separate from the original contract between shipper and carrier. Consideration was the payment of the freight charges and delivery against the bill.

---

61   [1951]1 KB 55.
62   (1983) 11 QBD 327, 341.

1.1.3 Bailment

It is obvious that the legal possession in goods is transferred along the supply chain of a maritime adventure. Hence, the person in possession of the goods is a bailee and if goods are passed further down the supply chain, sub-bailees. There are two situations where the shipper has to rely on bailment. First, where he contracts directly with the carrier and receives a charterer's bill of lading and he intends to sue the shipowner, and secondly, where the bill of lading allows for transhipment and the shipper wishes to sue the second shipowner. The reason is that the charterparty is not a sea carriage document, hence, bailment is a better option if not the only one to attempting to sue under contract.

It is useful to remember what the court noted in *Barclays Bank Ltd v Commissioners of Customs and Excise*[63] that a contract of affreightment is "a combined contract of bailment and transportation."[64] Furthermore, in *The Pioneer Container* it was stated that bailment is formed independent of a contract.[65] Simply put, the bailee promises to redeliver the goods to the owner or other person in accordance with the owner's instruction[66] and, hence, owes a duty of care to the bailor. Courts have established that it is not necessary to be in physical possession of goods as noted in *Spectra International plc v Hayesoak Ltd.*[67] The freight forwarder had the authority to place the goods into a bonded warehouse and then arrange for inland transport. Of importance on this issue is also *The Innes*[68] where bailment ceased once the time charterer had procured the issue of a shipowner's bill of lading.

Furthermore, in any sea venture goods are passed on to other

---

63   [1963] 1 Lloyd's Rep 81.
64   Ibid., 88.
65   *The Pioneer Container* [1994] 2 A.C. 324.
66   *Wincanton Ltd v P & O Trans European Ltd* [2001] C.L.C. 962.
67   [1997] 1 Lloyd's Rep. 153.
68   [1995] 2 Lloyd's Rep. 144.

companies within the supply chain, thereby creating sub-bailments.[69] In most cases a sub-bailee will rely on defences within the contract and it is known as a sub-bailment on terms.[70] This particular issue is of interest because contractual issues are at play.

Cases concerning bailment on terms can be categorised into two types;

1. Where the third party relies on the terms in the bill of lading issued by the contracting carrier,[71]

2. Where the third party relies on the terms in the contract between the contracting carrier and the sub-bailee. (Sub-bailment on terms).[72]

In cases where reliance is placed on the main contract, the breaching party has to show that the bailor was aware of sub-bailments and that the terms in the bill of lading are incorporated in the sub-bailment.[73]

This feature allows a third party to rely on terms contained in a sub-contract. It could possibly be argued that sub-bailment on terms is sometimes superior to Himalaya clauses and hence the judgment in *The Pioneer Container* is of interest.

---

69   See *The Winson* [1982] A.C. 939.

70   S. Baughen, *Shipping Law*, 4th edn (Oxon: Routledge-Cavendish, 2009), 51.

71   See for example: *Elder Dempster & Co Ltd v Paterson, Zochonis & Co Ltd* [1924] A.C. 522, *The Forum Craftsman* [1985] 1 Lloyd's Rep. 291, *The Mahkutai* [1996] A.C. 650.

72   See for example*: Morris v C W Martin & Sons Ltd* [1966] 1 Q.B. 716, *Singer Co (UK) Ltd v Tees and Hartlepool Port Authority* [1988] 2 Lloyd's Rep. 164, *The Captain Gregos (No.2)* [1990] 2 Lloyd's Rep. 395, *The Pioneer Container* [1994] 2 A.C. 324, *Spectra International Plc v Hayesoak Ltd* [1997] 1 Lloyd's Rep. 153.

73   G. Treitel, F.M.B. Reynolds, Thomas Gilbert Carver, Carver on Bills of Lading, 3rd ed., London: Sweet & Maxwell, 2011, 447.

2.5 The Pioneer Container[74]

In the *Pioneer Container*[75] the judicial committee considered that:

> if the sub-bailment is for reward, the obligation owed by the sub-bailee to the owner must likewise be that of a bailee for reward, notwithstanding that the reward is payable not by the owner but by the bailee. It would, they consider, be inconsistent in these circumstances to impose on the sub-bailee two different standards of care in respect of goods so entrusted to him. But the question then arises whether, as against the owners, the sub-bailees can invoke any of the terms on which the goods were sub-bailed to them, and in particular the exclusive jurisdiction clause.[76]

The facts were that:

> no direct contractual relationship has been created between the owner and the sub-bailee, the only contract created by the sub-bailment being that between the bailee and the sub-bailee. Even so, if the effect of the sub-bailment is that the sub-bailee voluntarily receives into his custody the goods of the owner and so assumes towards the owner the responsibility of a bailee, then to the extent that the terms of the sub-bailment are consented to by the owner, it can properly be said that the owner has authorised the bailee so to regulate the duties of the sub-bailee in respect of the goods entrusted to him, not only towards the bailee but also towards the owner.[77]

The court noted that case law specifically in *Morris v C. W. Martin & Sons Ltd. [1966] 1 Q.B. 716* and *the Gilchrist Watt* case[78] led to the conclusion that:

---

74   [1994] 2 A.C. 324.
75   [1994] 2 A.C. 324.
76   Ibid., 338.
77   Ibid., 339.
78   [1970] 1 W.L.R. 1262.

... a sub-bailee can only be said for these purposes to have voluntarily taken into his possession the goods of another if he has sufficient notice that a person other than the bailee is interested in the goods so that it can properly be said that (in addition to his duties to the bailee) he has, by taking the goods into his custody, assumed towards that other person the responsibility for the goods which is characteristic of a bailee. This they believe to be the underlying principle. Moreover, their Lordships do not consider this principle to impose obligations on the sub-bailee which are onerous or unfair, once it is recognised that he can invoke against the owner terms of the sub-bailment which the owner has actually (expressly or impliedly) or even ostensibly authorised. In the last resort, the sub-bailee may, if necessary and appropriate, be able to invoke against the bailee the principle of warranty of authority.[79]

The court did dismiss the appeal "that where goods had been sub-bailed with the authority of the owner, the obligation of the sub-bailee towards the owner was that of a bailee for reward and the owner could proceed directly against the sub-bailee under the law of bailment without having to rely on the contract of sub-bailment."[80]

A further point is of importance which has been touched upon above, namely the question of consent. Lord Goff eloquently explained the issue when he said:

In truth, [there is] a doctrinal dispute of a fundamental nature, which is epitomised in the question; is it a prerequisite of a bailment that the bailor should have consented to the bailee's possession of the goods? An affirmative answer to this question leads to the conclusion that, if the owner seeks to hold a sub-bailee responsible to him as bailee, he has to accept all the terms of the sub-bailment, warts and all; for either he will have consented to the sub-bailment on those terms or, or if not, he will be held to have ratified all the terms of the sub-bailment.[81]

---

79   Ibid 342.
80   Ibid.
81   Ibid 341-2.

However, Lord Goff also agreed that a further analysis is possible in respect to consent which appears to have been adopted by English law:

> On this approach, a person who voluntarily takes another person's goods into his custody holds them as bailee of that person (the owner) and he can only invoke, for example, terms of a sub-bailment under which he received the goods from a intermediate bailee as qualifying or otherwise affecting his responsibility to the owner if the owner consents to them.[82]

The *Pioneer Container* furthermore established that a sub-bailee might invoke the terms of the sub-bailment as a defence against an action brought by the owner of the goods, but courts have been reluctant to allow the sub-bailee to rely on terms contained in the head contract between the shipper and the head bailee. The reason is that the sub-bailee is not a party to the contract.[83] This issue is well illustrated in an Australian case namely *Gadsden Pty Ltd v Australian Coastal Shipping Commission.*[84]

2.5 Gadsden Pty Ltd v Australian Coastal Shipping Commission[85]

A cargo of tinplate suffered water damage in transit. The bills of lading were issued by the charterer and not signed on behalf of the ship or its owner. Furthermore, the bills of lading provided that the bills were to have effect subject to the provisos of The Hague Rules set out in the Schedule to the *Sea-Carriage of Goods Act* 1924-1973 (Cth.).[86] The consignee sued the shipowner, firstly, on the basis of bailment and, secondly, in tort for negligence.

---

82   Ibid.
83   *Wilson v. Darling Island Stevedoring*, (1956) 95 L. L. R. 43, 149.
84   [1977] 1 NSWLR 575.
85   Ibid.
86   Ibid., 575.

Moffitt P. stated his concern with the submission. He noted:

> There is, in my view, a fundamental difficulty in these submissions ... They ignore the subject matter of the rules, particularly the subject matter expressly defined by Art. 11. As I will seek to show, that subject matter is contract, the contract alone and, indeed, a particular class of contract. It is in respect of that contract that the rules compulsorily apply various obligations, rights, liabilities and immunities.[87]

The particular contract in this case, as the court noted, was the bill of lading as defined in article I (b) of The Amended Hague Rules. The question was whether the shipowner was included as being covered by these rules. The court indicated that in this case it is not so:

> Despite the use of the word "includes" in the definition of "carrier", this definition, in its context and taken with the definition of "contract of carriage" and the controlling provision made in Art. II, makes it clear that the owner is brought within the rules, and in particular Art. III, dealing with responsibilities and liabilities, only when he is a party to the relevant contract, that is, he enters into a contract of carriage covered by a bill of lading or a similar document of title.[88]

In addition, to be covered by the exemptions and limitations accorded under The Amended Hague Rules, only the terms in a contract of carriage are relevant and the protections do not extend to liabilities in tort. This is so as the tortfeasor is not a party to the contract.[89] Moffit P. went on to explain the purpose of several of The Amended Hague Rules as they were relevant to this matter. He argued:

> An examination of the content of Art. III, particularly rr. 1 to 5 confirm what Art. II expressly says, namely that the subject matter is a contract of carriage as defined and nothing else.

---

87   Ibid., 578.
88   Ibid., 579.
89   Ibid., 579.

> Rules 1 to 3 impose, by statute, obligations upon the carrier in relation to his contract of carriage, being that covered by the bill of lading. The owner can have no liability under these provisions, unless he is the carrier within the meaning of the rules and as I have already discussed. Rule 4 is directed to the prima facie evidence against the carrier provided by the bill of lading. Rule 5 deals with the responsibility of the shipper, but in relation to the carrier.[90]

Samuels J.A. specifically noted that the appellant put its arguments relying on *Elder Dempster* and, hence, is entitled to the protections contained in the bill of lading.[91] He rejected that argument as did Sheppard J in the original trial. *Elder Dempster* was distinguished and the court applied the Privity rule. The court held that, "The shipowner, not being a party to the bill of lading, was not entitled to the benefit of r. 6 of Art. III of The Hague Rules, as being a term thereof."[92] In effect the court followed the decision in *Wilson v Darling Island Stevedoring and Lighterage Co. Ltd*[93] which is discussed in Chapter X.

In summary, the duty of a bailee, as noted above, depends on the contractual terms between the bailor and the bailee. Lord Denning, in the earlier case of *Morris v C. W. Martin & Sons Ltd.*,[94] stated that, "The answer to the problem lies, I think, in this: the owner is bound by the conditions if he has expressly or impliedly consented to the bailee making a sub-bailment containing those conditions, but not otherwise".

However, the issue will arise where the shipper has a contract of carriage with the carrier. In such circumstances, there is no need to seek compensation on bailment. In these situations, a cause of action under bailment becomes superfluous. However, if possession has passed to a new holder of the bill of lading

---

90   Ibid., 580.
91   Ibid., 582.
92   Ibid., 576.
93   (1956) 95 C.L.R. 43.
94   [1966] 1 Q.B. 716, 729.

pursuant to the English COGSA under s 2(5) - (there is no equivalent section in the Australian Hague Rules) - the right to sue in bailment is not extinguished as noted in *East West Corp v DKBS 1912*.[95]

S 2(5) notes in the relevant parts:

> Where rights are transferred by virtue of the operation of subsection (1) above in relation to any document, the transfer for which that subsection provides shall extinguish any entitlement to those rights which derives—
>
> (a) where that document is a bill of lading, from a person's having been an original party to the contract of carriage; or
>
> (b) in the case of any document to which this Act applies, from the previous operation of that subsection in relation to that document;
>
> but the operation of that subsection shall be without prejudice to any rights which derive from a person's having been an original party to the contract contained in, or evidenced by, a sea waybill and, in relation to a ship's delivery order, shall be without prejudice to any rights deriving otherwise than from the previous operation of that subsection in relation to that order. [96]

As s 2(5) has no counterpart in the Amended Hague Rules, arguably a court in Australia could refer to *East West Corp v DKBS 1912* in order to reach the same result.

2.6   Non-contractual Actions

The two most important non-contractual actions are founded on agency, or negligence. This is not to say that there are other avenues such as collateral contracts, Public Policy, Restitution and Assignment, but these will not be discussed as they are not relevant to the main theme of this book.

---

95   [2003] 1 Lloyd's Rep 239.
96   http://www.legislation.gov.uk/ukpga/1992/50.

2.6.1 Agency

If a principal appoints another person to act on his behalf, the principal is bound to a third party if the agent transacted with the third party within his actual or ostensible authority. The effect is that Privity has been created between the principal and the person who would otherwise be a third party.[97] Obviously if no agency has been created, Privity is trumped by the Himalaya clause. These issues were, among others, also discussed in *The Eurymedon.*

However, if Privity has been created, agency can still create exceptions to the Privity rule. The most important one is, if there is an undisclosed principal. This situation arises when the agent contacts on his behalf with a third party but does act within the authority given to him by his principal. It creates certain problems as the third party can sue the agent who in turn is protected by the principal or, alternatively, the principal can disclose the agency and, pursuant to the construction of the contract, enforce a contract.

In shipping another situation might arise where there is no agency, but one will be created through necessity. The obligation is placed upon the principal with or without his consent. Examples are accidents and emergencies at sea where the master can enter into contract with a third party and it will bind all cargo owners. The situation extends to a carrier which is carrying perishable goods by land.[98]

1.1.2 Trust[99]

In shipping, and generally in common law, it has been recognised that a party to a contract can declare that they hold a benefit under contract on trust for some third parties.[100] Fullagar J, despite the

---

97   Furmston and Tolhurst, (n1), 64.

98   See *Sims @ Co v Midland Railway Co* [1913] 1 KB 103 at 112.

99   See generally Furmston. (n1) at 66 ff.

100   See *Wilson v. Darling Island Stevedoring and Lighterage Co. Ltd.* 95 C.L.R. 43, [1956] 1 Lloyd's Rep. 346.

defendant not relying on the trust argument, nevertheless stated:

> the common law rule was a rule which could operate unjustly in some circumstances may be conceded, but equity could and did intervene in many cases by treating the promisee as trustee of a promise made for the benefit of a third party, and allowing the third party to enforce the promise, making the promisee-trustee, if necessary, a defendant in an action against the promisor. A well-known example is Lloyd's v Harper. It is difficult to understand the reluctance which courts have sometimes shown to infer a trust in such cases.[101]

All that is required is that a clear intention exists between the parties to create a trust. As early as 1880 it was contended that a simple contract between two people making a third party a beneficiary does not create a trust. Jessell MR stated that, "A mere agreement between A and B that B shall pay C (an agreement to which C is not a party either directly or indirectly) will not prevent A and B from coming to a new agreement the next day releasing the old one."[102]

The approach that an express intention to create a trust must be present has been established in *Re Schebsman* in the following terms: "Unless an intention to create a trust is clearly to be collected from the language used and the circumstances of the case, I think that the court ought not to be astute to discover indications of such an intent."[103]

A further development took place in *Wilson v Darling Island Stevedoring and Lighterage Co. Ltd* (as noted above) where the implied terms or conduct are also taken into consideration. Mason CJ and Dawson J commented on the statement by Fullagar J in Australia. [104] Their view was:

---

101   Ibid., 67.
102   *Re Empress Engineering Co*, (1880) 16 Ch D 125, 129.
103   [1943] 1 Ch. 83, 104.
104   *Trident General Insurance Co. Ltd. v. McNiece Bros. Pty. Ltd* (1988) 165 C.L.R. 107.

In equity, "intention alone will not constitute a trust obligation (and) ... mere conduct without such intention is ineffectual to impose it, or, as Lewin, 12th ed., at p.88, says, to 'impute' it." The requisite intention to create a trust of a contractual promise to benefit a third party can, however, be formed and carried into effect (either by the contract itself or some other act) by a promisee who would be bemused by the information that the chose in action constituted by the benefit of a contractual promise is property and uncomprehending of the distinction between law and equity. ... In the context of such a contractual promise, the requisite intention should be inferred if it clearly appears that it was the intention of the promisee that the third party should himself be entitled to insist upon performance of the promise and receipt of the benefit and if trust is, in the circumstances, the appropriate legal mechanism for giving effect to that intention. A fortiori, equity's requirement of an intention to create a trust will be at least prima facie satisfied if the terms of the contract expressly or impliedly manifest that intention as the joint intention of both promisor and promisee.[105]

Deane J, in relation to reforms of the Privity rule, suggested that the criticisms were

flawed by an incomplete perception of the extent to which the practical effect of the rule of Privity is confined and qualified, and to which the injustice which the rule might otherwise cause is precluded by the application and development of other principles.[106]

In particular, he suggested that a trust would be such an instrument. However, looking at the developments of the Himalaya Clause, it can be suggested that the Privity rule has been further reformed and that the trust issue is a further tool assisting the Himalaya Clause. In addition, with the enactment of the Contracts (Rights of Third Parties) Acts, it is not likely

---

105   Ibid, para 10.
106   Ibid., 143- 44.

that the technique of trust will be often used in the future.[107] However, this is not to say that in commercial practice the end of the trust is imminent. There will be situations specially if the results or parts of the results are kept separate from those of the promise; in such case there is strong evidence that a trust has been intended. Importantly, it will turn on the construction of the contract and, obviously, the parol evidence rule that objective intent is applied. It is unfortunate that the common law still rejects the subjective approach like it is used in many international instruments such as the CISG as it can inform the court of the real intention of the parties and not what the court thought the intention of the parties was.

1.1.3 Tort

Tort could be an issue when a promisor might have a lability to a third party. It is not a feature of Privity as there is never a third party. The seminal cases of *Donoghue v Stevenson*[108] in the House of Lords and *Macpherson v Buick*[109] in the United States marked the breaking away of tort from the restrictions cast on common law liability by the Privity rule.[110]

It is the duty of care under the broad heading of negligence which is applicable. An example would be a stevedore who negligently damages goods. However, the problem is that in cases where a third party merely suffers economic loss proving the duty of care is not straightforward. The Australian and Canadian courts are not as cautious in applying the duty of care as the English courts. The problem is that courts are not content to merely look at the foreseeability test and, hence, assume that the duty of care has been established.[111] Lord Bridge in *Caparo Industries Plc v*

---

107   Furmston and Tolhurst, (n1) 73.
108   [1932] AC 562.
109   (1916) 217 NY 382.
110   Furmston and Tolhurst, (n1) 45.
111   Ibid., 46.

Dickman[112] put forward a three-way approach. He said:

> What emerges is that, in addition to the foreseeability of damage, necessary ingredients in any situation giving rise to a duty of care are that there should exist between the party owing the duty and the party to whom it is owed a relationship characterised by the law as one of 'proximity' or 'neighbourhood' and that the situation should be one in which the court considers it fair, just and reasonable that the law should impose duty of a given scope upon the one party for the benefit of the other. But it is implicit ... that the concept of proximity and fairness embodied in these additional ingredients are not susceptible of any such precise definition as would be necessary to give them utility as practical tests, but amount in effect to little more than convenient labels to attach to the features of different specific situations which, on a detailed examination of all the circumstances, the law recognises pragmatically as giving rise to a duty of care of a given scope. Whilst recognising, of course, the importance of the underlying principles common to the whole fields of negligence, I think the law has now moved in the direction of attaching greater significance to the more traditional categorisation of distinct and recognisable situations as guides to the existence, the scope and the limits of the varied duties of care which the law imposes. ... One of the most important distinctions always to be observed lies in the law's essential different approach to the different kinds of damage ... It is one thing to owe a duty of care to avoid causing injury to the person or property of others. It is quite another to avoid causing others to suffer purely economic loss.

Furmston puts it succinctly by noting that, "the aversion to allowing damages for purely economic loss necessarily limits the impact of tort law."[113]

However, in relation to shipping contracts, *Elder Dempster*

---

112   [1990] 2 AC 605, 617-18.
113   Furmston and Tolhurst, (n1) 50.

noted that, "the contractual exclusion of liability for bad stowage in the bill of lading could not be circumvented by reliance on a liability in tort where the act or omission complained of was one connected with the performance of the contract."[114] In effect relying on tort in contracts of affreightment appears to be of little utility.

1.1.4 Letters of Credit (L/C)

This area is mainly covered by the Uniform Customs and Practice for Documentary Credits (UCP600) drafted by the International Chamber of Commerce (ICC). It derives the force of law once it is included into the contract. The letter of credit is independent of the underlying contract and the bank is only concerned with the compliance of the documents with the terms and conditions of the letter of credit.[115] The doctrinal question is how to find the presence of a consideration moving from the seller. However, the real point is that the obligation of the bank is enforceable by the beneficiary[116] and in practice the issue whether consideration has moved from the seller or whether it is an exception to the Privity rule is at best theoretical. As far as the exemption clause in the underlying sales contract is concerned, letters of credit do not affect the sale and transportation of goods and, hence, are purely a financial matter in relation to the payment of the price.

2.7   Conclusion

This Chapter has demonstrated that not only contractual terms are decisive in framing a legal action but also non-contractual principles such as bailment. However, the importance of this Chapter is to demonstrate that contractual terms need to be

---

114   *London Drugs Ltd. v. Kuehne & Nagel International Ltd., 1992 CarswellBC* 315 (1992). para 250.
115   See UCP600, article 15.
116   Ibid., article 7.

carefully drafted but also the relevant document, namely a sea carriage document must contain the terms. The importance of the bill of lading as the most likely instrument to contain exemption clauses has been highlighted.

It is also important to note that contractual liabilities are not always the solution to the problem of who is responsible to pay for damages to goods while being transported. The choice of the legal principle in framing a claim is crucial and decisive in the outcome.

In addition, the interpretive tool which is employed by courts can and has played an important role. The fact that extrinsic material and customary practices are often used by courts in deciding the issues indicates that a total reliance on the parol evidence rule is not warranted and has not been adhered to in all cases as demonstrated in this Chapter.

3

REFORMING THE 'PRIVITY RULE'

3.1 Introduction

This Chapter will describe the statutory reforms which were introduced in common law countries to overcome the uncertainty, caused by exemption clauses included in contracts to avoid the applicability of the Privity Rule. This description reveals that statutory reforms have not effectively clarified the legal situation but, instead, may have contributed to confusion surrounding the applicability of the Rule. Statutory attempts to reform the Privity Rule were problematic because these legislative reforms, in general, created general rules which covered, not the whole field, but individual circumstances.

The following jurisdictions will be briefly looked at: England, Australia, Canada, Singapore and the United States. In addition to these jurisdictions, the relevant part in the UNIDROIT Principles of International Commercial Contracts ("UNIDROIT Principles"), a soft law, will also be examined because it might be a useful tool for the drafters of contracts who do not want to incorporate exemptions to the Privity Rule in their contracts.

The United States was the first country where legislative attempts were made in the 1930s to reform the Privity Rule. The attempts were followed by similar developments in England. Other countries followed suit, however, at a much later time, except civil law countries where the Rule did not exist.

It will be argued in this Chapter that the statutory reforms, except perhaps in the United States, failed to provide certainty to the courts and the commercial players to finally settle the argument as to the retention of the Privity Rule in relation to third party benefits.

3.2   England

In 1937, the Law Revision Committee, which was critical of the Privity Rule, proposed that a third party can enforce a contract.[117] The Committee indicated that the Rule was only followed by a small number of legal systems.[118] However, the recommendations of the Committee on the Privity Rule were never implemented.

In 1965, a permanent English and Scottish Law Commission was established. The Scottish Law Commission withdrew from the discussions and its report was never published, but it was taken up by Italy. It contained a provision to give rights to third parties.[119] However, in England, in 1973, work on the contract code was suspended "although the draft had got as far as to provide for the creation of third party rights."[120]

Law Lords criticised the lack of progress; as an example Lord Scarman in 1980 stated that "cases which stand guard over this unjust rule" [would be reviewed] "now, not forty years on".[121] The topic was again considered in 1991 and it resulted in publication of the Law Commission's Report in 1996. The Law Commission presented a report which resulted in the House of Commons passing the *Contracts (Rights of Third Parties) Act*

---

117   Law Reform Committee, Sixth Interim Report (Statute of Frauds and the Doctrine of Consideration) (HMSO, London, 1937), para 48.
118   Ibid., para 41.
119   Furmston and Tolhurst, (n1) 266.
120   M. Dean, Removing a blot on the landscape - the reform of the doctrine of Privity. *Journal of Business law*, 2000, 143, 144.
121   *Woodar Investment Development Ltd v. Wimpey Construction U.K. Ltd* [1980] 1 W.L.R. 277, 300 and 301.

1999. Section 1 contains the central purpose of the Act:

> Subject to the provisions of this Act, a person who is not a party to a contract (a "third party") may in his own right enforce a term of the contract if—
>
> (a) the contract expressly provides that he may, or
>
> (b) subject to subsection (2), the term purports to confer a benefit on him.
>
> (2) Subsection (1)(b) does not apply if on a proper construction of the contract it appears that the parties did not intend the term to be enforceable by the third party.
>
> (3) The third party must be expressly identified in the contract by name, as a member of a class or as answering a particular description but need not be in existence when the contract is entered into.
>
> (6) Where a term of a contract excludes or limits liability in relation to any matter references in this Act to the third party enforcing the term shall be construed as references to his availing himself of the exclusion or limitation.[122]

Section s 1(6) which states that a third party enforcing a term in a contract can avail "himself of the exclusion or limitation" is not in line with section s 6(5)(b) which states:

> Section 1 confers no rights on a third party in the case of—
>
> (a) a contract for the carriage of goods by sea, or
>
> (b) a contract for the carriage of goods by rail or road, or for the carriage of cargo by air, which is subject to the rules of the appropriate international transport convention, except that a third party may in reliance on that section avail himself of an exclusion or limitation of liability in such a contract.[123]

---

122   http://www.legislation.gov.uk/ukpga/1999/31/section/1.
123   http://www.legislation.gov.uk/ukpga/1999/31/section/6.

Section s 6(5)(b), in effect, contains an exception (the Himalaya Clause) to an exception. Tetley in relation to s 6(5)(b) explains the issue well. He noted:

> There is however one major exception to this exception, permitting the third-party beneficiary, in reliance on section 1, to 'avail himself of an exclusion or limitation of liability in such contracts' (section 6(5)(a)). It is this exception to an exception in the Contracts (Rights of Third Parties) Act 1999 which, in effect puts the Himalaya clause on a statutory footing in the United Kingdom. (Referring to the explanatory note)[124]

The Explanatory Note to s 6(5) states:

> Subsection (5), which excludes certain contracts relating to the carriage of goods, nevertheless does not prevent a third party from taking advantage of a term excluding or limiting liability. In particular, this enables clauses which seek to extend an exclusion or limitation of liability of a carrier of goods by the sea to servants, agents and independent contractors engaged in the loading and unloading process to be enforced by those servants, agents or independent contractors (so called 'Himalaya' clauses).[125]

Despite some uncertainties, this Act has been described as removing one of the most universally disliked and criticised blots on the legal landscape.[126] As noted on occasions by some courts – an example is *Trident v McNiece*[127] – the removal or reform of the Privity Rule was not universally noted as a being unjust.

What can be said is that the Act has reformed certain aspects of the Privity Rule but has not removed the Rule. Indeed s 7(1) confirms that the Act does not "repeal existing statutory

---

124   Tetley, (n13) 49.
125   http://www.legislation.gov.uk/ukpga/1999/31/notes/division/4/6.
126   Dillon J. referred to the doctrine of Privity as "a blot on our law and most unjust", *Forster v. Silvermere Golf & Equestrian Centre* (1981) 125 *S.J.* 397.
127   (1988) 165 CLR 197.

and common law exceptions to the Privity doctrine, such as the exceptions of agency, assignment and trust of a promise."[128] However, the legislation still represents, in legal fiction, a remarkably quick transition from a pipe dream to the statute book. But it may unwittingly have created a few black holes."[129]

3.3 Australia

In Australia the Privity Rule still exists and legislation merely created some exceptions to the Rule but never abolished it. The most important exceptions included marine insurance[130] and bills of lading.[131] To complicate matters, as Australia is a Federation, exceptions to the Privity Rule only exist in Queensland, Western Australia and the Northern Territory. It is sufficient to note that the Queensland *Property Law Act* 1974 in s 55 notes in the relevant part:

Contracts for the benefit of third parties

(1) A promisor who, for a valuable consideration moving from the promisee, promises to do or to refrain from doing an act or acts for the benefit of a beneficiary shall, upon acceptance by the beneficiary, be subject to a duty enforceable by the beneficiary to perform that promise.

(2) Prior to acceptance the promisor and promisee may, without the consent of the beneficiary, vary or discharge the terms of the promise and any duty arising from it.

(3) Upon acceptance—

(a) the beneficiary shall be entitled in the beneficiary's own name to such remedies and relief as may be just and convenient for the enforcement of the duty of the promisor, and relief by

---

128 Tetley, (n13) 49.
129 http://www.legislation.gov.uk/ukpga/1999/31/notes/division/416.
130 *Insurance Contracts Act* 1984 (Cth) s 48.
131 Eg *Sea-Carriage Documents Act* 1997 (NSW) sub-s 8, 10.

way of specific performance, injunction or otherwise shall not be refused solely on the ground that, as against the promisor, the beneficiary may be a volunteer; and

(b) the beneficiary shall be bound by the promise and subject to a duty enforceable against the beneficiary in the beneficiary's own name to do or refrain from doing such act or acts (if any) as may by the terms of the promise be required of the beneficiary; and

(c) the promisor shall be entitled to such remedies and relief as may be just and convenient for the enforcement of the duty of the beneficiary; and

(d) the terms of the promise and the duty of the promisor or the beneficiary may be varied or discharged with the consent of the promisor and the beneficiary.

Of importance is the fact that there is no requirement that the consideration moves from the promisee. It should also be noted that the Western Australian legislation was modelled on the English Law Revisions Committee's 1937 report and recommendations.[132] In addition the Western Australian Supreme court in *The Bell Group (in liq) Ltd v Westpac Banking Corporation (No 9)* held that the Act only applies to formal written contracts.[133] The reason is that the contract must benefit the third partly directly and an incidental or indirect benefit is not sufficient to enliven the Act.[134]

3.4   Canada

In Canada, like in Australia, the Privity Rule still applies subject

---

132   Furmston and Tolhurst, (n1) 293.
133   (2008) WASC 239, at [3351-[3361].
134   Ibid., [3362]-[3364].

to a general exception under the common law and some judicial modifications. *The Law Reform Act RSNB* 2011 in s 4 of Chapter 184 provides:

Privity of contract

4(1) Unless the contract provides otherwise, a person who is not a party to a contract but who is identified by or under the contract as being intended to receive some performance or forbearance under it may enforce that performance or forbearance by a claim for damages or otherwise.

4(2) In proceedings under subsection (1) against a party to a contract, any defence may be raised that could have been raised in proceedings between the parties.

4(3) The parties to a contract to which subsection (1) applies may amend or terminate the contract at any time, but if by doing so, they cause loss to a person described in subsection (1) who has incurred expense or undertaken an obligation in the expectation that the contract would be performed, that person may recover the loss from any party to the contract who knew or ought to have known that the expenses would be or had been incurred or that the obligation would be or had been undertaken.

4(3.1) For the purposes of subsection (1), a person who is identified by or under a contract as being intended to receive some performance or forbearance under it includes

(*a*)a person who is intended to receive the performance or forbearance only in certain circumstances, if those circumstances occur, and

(*b*)a person who is not named in the contract but is a member of a class of persons intended to receive the performance or forbearance.[135]

---

135   https://www.canlii.org/en/nb/laws/stat/rsnb-2011-c-184/latest/rsnb-2011-c-184.html.

Subsection 4(3.1) was an amendment which arose due to the ruling in *Manderville v Goodfellow's Trucking Ltd.*[136] The facts are simple. A trucking company subcontracted its duty to another company at a lower rate than they received under the head contract. The subcontractor, Manderville argued that they could rely on s 4(1) of *The Law Reform Act RSNB* 2011 and claim the benefits. The court decided that Manderville was not covered under s 4(1) and, hence, could only claim the lower rate of haulage. The effect of the amendment was that the generic term of 'beneficiary' also includes employees and subcontractors belonging to the class of persons.

3.5   Singapore

Singapore has enacted a number of exceptions to the Privity Rule such as the *Bill of Lading Act*[137] and the *Bill of Exchange Act*[138] and only in 2001 enacted a general statutory exception.[139] In essence it mirrors the English Act and states in the relevant section:

Right of third party to enforce contractual term

2.(1) Subject to the provisions of this Act, a person who is not a party to a contract (referred to in this Act as a third party) may, in his own right, enforce a term of the contract if —

(*a*) the contract expressly provides that he may; or

(*b*) subject to subsection (2), the term purports to confer a benefit on him.

(2) Subsection (1)(*b*) shall not apply if, on a proper construction of the contract, it appears that the parties did not intend the term to be enforceable by the third party.

---

136   (1999) 44 CLR (2d) 10.
137   1994 Rev ed., s 2(1).
138   2004 Rev ed., sub ss 27 to 38.
139   *Contracts (Rights of Third Parties) Act* 2001.

(3) The third party shall be expressly identified in the contract by name, as a member of a class or as answering a particular description but need not be in existence when the contract is entered into.

(4) This section shall not confer a right on a third party to enforce a term of a contract otherwise than subject to and in accordance with any other relevant terms of the contract.

(5) For the purpose of exercising his right to enforce a term of the contract, there shall be available to the third party any remedy that would have been available to him in an action for breach of contract if he had been a party to the contract (and the rules relating to damages, injunctions, specific performance and other remedy shall apply accordingly) and such remedy shall not be refused on the ground that, as against the promisor, the third party is a volunteer.

(6) Where a term of a contract excludes or limits liability in relation to any matter, references in this Act to the third party enforcing the term shall be construed as references to his availing himself of the exclusion or limitation.

(7) In this Act, in relation to a term of a contract which is enforceable by a third party —

"promisee" means the party to the contract by whom the term is enforceable against the promisor;

"promisor" means the party to the contract against whom the term is enforceable by the third party.

Interestingly, the Act [was] brought into force essentially in two stages. In the first stage, from 1 January 2002 until 30 June 2002, the Act [was] operating on an opt in basis and therefore did not apply unless the contract expressly provides otherwise. In the second stage, from 1 July 2002 onwards, the Act applies on an opt out basis and, therefore, applies unless the contract expressly or by implication provides otherwise.[140]

Arguably, therefore, many counsels will advise their clients to opt out of the Act as it appears to be the case with many pieces of legislation which include an opt out formula as exemplified by the Convention on Contracts for the International Sale of Goods (CISG). It is routinely excluded in many cases because counsels are not fully aware of its implications or simply prefer the law with which they are familiar. It should also be noted that Singapore and Hong Kong essentially included the same legalisation in relation to third party rights.[141]

3.6   The United States

The Restatement (Second) of Contracts and Third-Party Beneficiaries is the major source of legislation governing the exceptions to the Privity Rule. It needs to be kept in mind that the Restatement is only a commentary or a summary and not what the law is or should be. The law is stated in the Uniform Commercial Law (UCC). When the *Restatement Second* was drafted it was evident that case law demonstrated "that a categorical approach was too simplistic to deal with novel and complex factual situations; courts were often forced to place new cases into old categories. This lack of flexibility precluded an expanded categorical approach."[142]

In the end, the "intent to benefit" test was adopted in s 302 of *Restatement Second* which provides:

> (1) Unless otherwise agreed between promisor and promisee, a beneficiary of a promise is an intended beneficiary if recognition of a right to performance in the beneficiary is appropriate to effectuate the intention of the parties and either

---

140   http://www.lawgazette.com.sg/2002-1/Jan02-feature.htm.
141   Contracts (Rights of Third Parties) Bill 2014 Hong Kong.
142   Sumners, (n144) 890.

(a) the performance of the promise will satisfy an obligation of the promisee to pay money to the beneficiary; or

(b) the circumstances indicate that the promisee intends to give the beneficiary the benefit of the promised performance.

(2) An incidental beneficiary is a beneficiary who is not an intended beneficiary.[143]

The provisions of the *Restatement Second* were less restrictive and gave courts the ability to "eliminate the automatic vesting provisions applicable to donee beneficiaries under the first Restatement."[144]

As with many statutory texts the prescribed tests are not sufficiently defined and, hence, the "intent to benefit" test is left to courts to apply and define. The inevitable result is that the test is either too restrictively or too broadly interpreted. A further problem is the fact that the *Restatement Second* gives no clear guidelines as to whose intent should govern a third-party contract. Courts, in general, have disagreed on this issue and conflicting judgments can be found. Summers notes the following example:

> *Compare* Spires v. Hanover Fire Ins. Co., 364 Pa. 52, 56-57, 70 A.2d 828, 830 (1950) ("To be a third party beneficiary entitled to recover on a contract it is not enough that it be intended by one of the parties to the contract and the third person . . . but both parties to the contract must so intend and must indicate that intention in the contract. . . .") (emphasis in original) and Pennsylvania Liquor Control Bd. v. Rapistan, Inc., 472 Pa. 36, 42,371 A.2d 178, 182 (1976) ("[T]here must still be evidence, sufficient to permit reasonable reliance, that the promisee and promisor intended to confer a right on a third party.")

---

143   Restatement (Second) of Contracts § 302 (1979).
144   D. M. Summers, Third Party Beneficiaries and the Restatement (Second) of Contracts, 67 *Cornell Law Review*, 1982, 888 Available at: http://scholarship. law.cornell.edu/clr/vol67/iss4/12..890.

with Hamill v. Maryland Cas. Co., 209 F.2d 338, 341 (10th Cir. 1954) ("[I]t is the intent or purpose of the promisee who pays for the promise that has been generally looked upon as governing.") *and* McCulloch v. Canadian Pac. Ry., 53 F. Supp. 534, 542 (D. Minn. 1943) ("[T]he courts look primarily to the intent of the promisee."). *See also* 45 VA. L. REv. 1226, 1228 (1959) ("Depending upon the jurisdiction, it is the intent of the promisee, promisor, or both of the parties that governs.").[145]

Black's Law dictionary defines the word "intent" as being "the state of mind with which an act is done or omitted."[146] The comparison between *state of mind* and *good faith* comes to mind as both terms defy definition and only take on substance if applied to a set of facts. It could be argued that courts simply ought to apply the principle of good faith and ask the question what the parties' subjective intentions were when entering into a contract.

Summers in the end argues that:

> Courts should focus on the promisee's intent to benefit the third party and the promisor's assent to that intent. Finally, courts should consider all the circumstances surrounding the making of the contract. By adopting these further guidelines, courts using the Restatement Second will promote greater predictability and clearer analysis of third party beneficiary claims.[147]

Arguably the United States, despite an attempt at defining third party rights in the *Restatement Second*, have not eliminated the problems in interpretation of terms and, hence, problems still persist and exceptions to the Rule have not decreased.

3.7 The UNIDROIT Principles of International Commercial Contracts

UNIDROIT stands for the International Institute for the

---

145   Ibid., 895 fn 86.
146   Black's Law Dictionary 727 (5th ed. 1979).
147   Summers, (n144) 899.

Unification of Private Law (*Institut international pour l'unification du droit privé*). It was founded in 1926 and is a survivor of the League of Nations. It has 63-member states and has produced conventions and soft laws or model laws.

The UNIDROIT Principles are included into this part because the text deals with third parties' rights. It is a soft law or model law, but contracts incorporating the UNIDROIT Principles may include terms dealing with third party rights. These provisions are contained in Chapter 5, under the title of "Content, third party rights and Conditions" which are detailed in articles 5.2.1 ff. Chapter 5 has been introduced in the 2004 edition and has been retained in all editions, the latest being the 2016 edition.

It is useful to briefly explain the function and purpose of the UNIDROIT Principles as they set forth general rules for international commercial contracts. In effect, the rules have been used by courts and tribunals to interpret and supplement domestic law specifically in the areas of good faith and interpretation of the conduct of parties. The Principles have also been used as a model for legislators for drafting or modernising legislation in the field of general contract law. Importantly, the UNIDROIT Principles can be used as a guide for drafting contracts as they identify the crucial issues which need to be addressed in a contract. In addition, as noted above, the UNIDROIT Principles might be introduced into a contract and, subject to mandatory laws, become the governing law of the contract.

The section on third party rights is of interest to this book. Article 5.2.1 states:

(1) The Parties (the "promisor" and the "promisee") may confer by express or implied agreement a right on a third party ("the beneficiary").

(2) The existence and content of the beneficiary's right against the promisor are determined by the agreement of the parties and are subject to any conditions or other limitations under the

agreement.

The underlying principle is that of autonomy which means that, if parties intend to confer rights on a third party, they can do so if they wish.[148] Compared to legislation, the text is simple but essentially contains the same general functions as found in many jurisdictions. It also stipulates that a promise can be conferred by implication and, hence, it makes the contract the centrepiece in determining the rights or obligations of third parties.

A further novel approach is contained in Article 5.2.2 which notes that the beneficiary must be identifiable but need not be in existence at the time the contract is made.[149] For example, a person can make a contract of insurance benefitting grandchildren who are not yet born.

Article 5.2.3 notes that, "The conferment of rights in the beneficiary includes the right to invoke a clause in the contract which excludes or limits the liability of the beneficiary." This Article spells out exactly the very purpose of an exemption clause. The purpose of including a third party such as a stevedore is to confer the same rights and obligations upon the third party as enjoyed by the contractual parties. As will be seen below, this clause, such as the Himalaya Clause, is of importance in a contract of carriage.

Of importance in this context is also Article 5.2.5 which states that, "The parties may modify or revoke the rights conferred by the contract on the beneficiary until the beneficiary has accepted them or reasonably acted in reliance on them." This Article resolves many of the varied responses of national systems in relation to the power of the promisee and promisor to change their minds. In the commentary on the Principles the extreme positions which are possible are laid out, namely that revocation can be undertaken any time or not at all once the contract has

---

148   UNIDROIT Principles of International Commercial Contracts, 2016 ed., 167.
149   Ibid., 169.

been formed. Few systems have adopted either of the two extreme positions.[150] The UNIDROIT Principles takes the middle road but leave it open for parties to include a different clause into their contract.

Any casual glance at the style of the Principles, namely a combination of simple provisions followed by a commentary and examples, indicates that Professor Farnsworth, a member for the first two editions and a rapporteur of the American Restatements of contract, assisted in the drafting of the Principles.[151] This style has persisted in all the editions.

3.8   The Privity Rule and Maritime Conventions

The Hague-Visby Rules or Amended Hague Rules do not offer any protection to independent contractors. Protection is limited to servant and agents of the carrier under contract and tort.[152] Much has been written on The Amended Hague Rules and, hence, the Rules are not discussed here. For completion sake, a brief comment will be made below in relation to the Hamburg and Rotterdam Rules. They are not yet ratified by important maritime nations and are of little significance at this stage.

However, of interest to this book is the question of who qualifies as a carrier under COGSA. This is an important question as exemption clauses need to be contained in a contract between the carrier and the shipper. The Bill of Lading is evidence of the existence of a contract of carriage. To that end *Fortis Corp. Ins., SA v Viken Ship Mgmt.*[153] is instructive. The facts are simple: rust damaged steel coils by exposure to seawater. The central issue in this appeal was "whether a ship manager charged with providing a Master, officers and crew, and performing

---

150   Ibid., 172.
151   Furmston and Tolhurst, (n1) 352.
152   Article IV bis (1) and Article IV bis (2) of The Hague-Visby Rules.
153   AS, 597 F.3d 784.

various other ship-management tasks for the shipping vessel qualifies as a "carrier" under the Carriage of Goods by Sea Act (COGSA)."[154] COGSA defines a carrier as follows: "The term 'carrier' includes the owner or the charterer who enters into a contract of carriage with a shipper." The defendant asked the court not to interpret the definition of carrier in a formalistic way but to endorse a functional approach. The problem in relation to this issue is whether the entity in question performed "a function traditionally carried out by a carrier even if, due to the advances in the shipping industry in the seventy-plus years since COGSA was enacted, it does not meet the traditional view of what qualifies as a carrier under the Act.[155] This approach did have some academic support as "It could be argued that interpretation of the Act should reflect the policy behind it and evolve to cover vessel management companies acting in the role traditionally played by carriers."[156]

In the end, the court noted, relying on *Herd & Co. v Krawill Machinery Corp*, [157] that the functional approach is foreclosed and that the manager is not a carrier under COGSA. However, this does not mean that managers are not protected or cannot be protected under COGSA as shipping parties may simply extend the coverage of COGSA by adding provisions to the bill of lading such as "extending the COGSA regime to any and all agents or independent contractors who participate in the shipment of goods under a particular contract."[158] Another option is to expand the definition of a COGSA Carrier.[159] This is not possible by attempting to change the definition within a convention as it would require new ratification processes. The best solution, as noted above, is simply to take note of this issue and adjust the Himalaya clause accordingly

---

154   Ibid., 786.
155   Ibid., 790.
156   K. Baldwin, 35 *Tulane Maritime Law Journal*, 2010-2011, 398.
157   359 U.S. 297, 79 S.Ct. 766 (1959).
158   Ibid., 792.
159   See K. Baldwin, (n156) 389.

3.8.1 The Hamburg Rules

The Hamburg Rules provide the same protection, but the only variation is that the Rules do not specifically exclude independent contractors.[160] The position of the independent contractor therefore is not clear. Article 1(2) defines "Actual carrier" as meaning "any person to whom the performance of the carriage of the goods, or of part of the carriage, has been entrusted by the carrier, and includes any other person to whom such performance has been entrusted." This leads to the suggestion that any third party could potentially be included in the definition of 'carrier'. However, the Hamburg Rules do make a distinction between an actual carrier and carrier under article X which notes:

> 1. Where the performance of the carriage or part thereof has been entrusted to an actual carrier, whether or not in pursuance of a liberty under the contract of carriage by sea to do so, the carrier nevertheless remains responsible for the entire carriage according to the provisions of this Convention. The carrier is responsible, in relation to the carriage performed by the actual carrier, for the acts and omissions of the actual carrier and of his servants and agents acting within the scope of their employment.

> 2. All the provisions of this Convention governing the responsibility of the carrier also apply to the responsibility of the actual carrier for the carriage performed by him. The provisions of paragraphs 2 and 3 of Article 7 and of paragraph 2 of Article 8 apply if an action is brought against a servant or agent of the actual carrier.

It will be of interest to discover how courts will apply the Hamburg Rules in connection to the protection of third parties.

---

160   Article VII(2) of the Hamburg Rules.

Although 34 countries have ratified the Hamburg Rules, none of the important shipping countries are parties to the Rules.

3.8.2 The Rotterdam Rules[161]

The latest Convention, The Rotterdam Rules, dealt in more detail with the issues of liability.

In relation to the limitation of liability, Article 4 notes:

> **Article 4 Applicability of defences and limits of liability**
> - **1.** Any provision of this Convention that may provide a defence for, or limit the liability of, the carrier applies in any judicial or arbitral proceeding, whether founded in contract, in tort, or otherwise, that is instituted in respect of loss of, damage to, or delay in delivery of goods covered by a contract of carriage or for the breach of any other obligation under this Convention against:
> **(a)** The carrier or a maritime performing party;
> **(b)** The master, crew or any other person that performs services on board the ship; or
> **(c)** Employees of the carrier or a maritime performing party.
> - **2.** Any provision of this Convention that may provide a defence for the shipper or the documentary shipper applies in any judicial or arbitral proceeding, whether founded in contract, in tort, or otherwise, that is instituted against the shipper, the documentary shipper, or their subcontractors, agents or employees.

As Backden[162] noted:

> It was the aim of the drafters of the Rotterdam Rules that this

---

161   http://www.dutchcivillaw.com/legislation/rotterdamrules.htm.
162   P. Backden, Will Himalaya Bring Class Down from Mount Olympus? - Impact of the Rotterdam Rules, 42 *Journal of Maritime Law & Commerce*, 115 2011, 115, 118.

provision would avail any person who assists the carrier in performing his duties under the Rules the full protection of rights, defences and limits of liability available to the carrier in the event that such agent or sub-contractor was faced with a claim directly against it.[163]

Importantly, the term "performing party" has been clarified in Article 1(6) which appears to be broad enough to include the independent contractors. "It can be presumed that the drafters sought to give this provision a scope similar to the standard Himalaya clause used in the trade."[164] Article 1.6 states:

Performing party" means a person other than the carrier that performs or undertakes to perform any of the carrier's obligations under a contract of carriage with respect to the receipt, loading, handling, stowage, carriage, care, unloading or delivery of the goods, to the extent that such person acts, either directly or indirectly, at the carrier's request or under the carrier's supervision or control.

Importantly, the obligation is not centred on the carrier but the goods; the performing party is responsible for the goods before the carrier arrives or departs from the docks. In essence, anybody within the supply chain that is dock-to-dock is a performing party. Hence, no distinction is drawn between the contractual parties and the independent contractors. Article 18 to that end notes:

Liability of the carrier for other persons

The carrier is liable for the breach of its obligations under this Convention caused by the acts or omissions of:

(a) Any performing party;

(b) The master or crew of the ship;

---

163   Ibid., quoting Report of the Working Group mI (Transport Law) on the work of its nineteenth session. (A/CN.9/621), page 21.

164   Backden, (n162) 119.

(c) Employees of the carrier or a performing party; or

(d) Any other person that performs or undertakes to perform any of the carrier's obligations under the contract of carriage, to the extent that the person acts, either directly or indirectly, at the carrier's request or under the carrier's supervision or control.

Furthermore, the period of responsibility of the carrier begins "when the carrier or a performing party receives the goods for carriage and ends when the goods are delivered."[165]

As with The Amended Hague Rules, the Rotterdam Rules also included in Article 59 a limit to the liability of the carriers and the limitation period of two years has also been preserved in Article 62.

Backden correctly notes:

> In all maritime legal areas affected by the new Rotterdam Rules, scholars as well as practitioners are considering the changes that the rules may bring about. It is obvious that the systemic alterations such as the omission of the nautical fault, the continuous obligation of the carrier to keep the ship seaworthy and the extension of the carrier's defences to independent contractors will bring consequential changes in the liability of parties under the maritime legal system as we know it.[166]

In summary, Himalaya clauses may be redundant as Articles 4.1 and 19.1 of the Rules provide remedies and limitations sought under the Himalaya Clause. However, pursuant to Article 79, Himalaya clauses will not be rendered void as they do not lessen any liability provided by the Rules.[167] In contrast, Article 79 will render Circular Indemnity clauses[168] void since they result in

---

165   Rotterdam Rules article 12(1).
166   Backden, (n162) ++122.
167   Theodora Nikaki, 'Himalaya clauses and the Rotterdam Rules', *Journal of International Maritime Law*, 17(1) 2011, 20-40, 37.
168   In brief a circular indemnity clause attempts to indemnify the carrier against all consequences of breaking its undertaking not to sue such third parties.

the exclusion of the third parties from liabilities regulated by the Rules.[169] However, this has not yet occured because, at this stage, the Rotterdam Rules have not been implemented.

3.9　Conclusion

This review of legislation in various jurisdictions reveals that the Privity Rule has been modified but not replaced. The exception are the UNIDROIT Principles which clearly and concisely spelled out the middle road in that it has recognised the commercial aspect of exemption clauses.

As far as jurisprudence is concerned, the Statutory reforms in all but the United States have achieved very little and courts simply had to reform the law as far as third-party rights are concerned in a statutory vacuum. However, it is obvious that reforms have taken place driven by courts with a keen eye on commercial reality. But, changes of a magnitude such as the abolition or containment of the Privity Rule have not been achieved quickly. It takes time for these changes to occur and it requires the existence of disputes which lend themselves to the development of new principles by courts.

169　Richard Williams, *The Overall Impact of the Rotterdam Rules on the Liability of Multimodal Carriers and their Sub-contractors*, p.9 (unpublished paper submitted to the Eighth Annual International Colloquium held by the Institute of International Shipping and Trade Law, Swansea University), 2012.

4

THE ESTABLISHMENT OF THE HIMALAYA CLAUSE

4.1   Introduction

This Chapter will discuss the willingness of courts to imply terms into contracts, thereby assisting in the development of the Himalaya Clause.

In maritime matters, clauses to protect contractually unconnected third parties were developed by decisions of the House of Lords and the Supreme Court of the United States.[170] Tetley did not think that the Himalaya Clause was or is beneficial to the shipping industry. In his view permitting stevedores and other third parties not connected to the contract to benefit by the contract between the carrier and the shipper leaves open the door to "incongruity, abuse and, at times, injustice to persons who have contracted in good faith."[171] However, the counter argument is that both parties, namely the carrier and shipper, are aware of the contractual clause and ought to take relevant precautionary steps, such as insurance into consideration.

Exemption clauses have been used before the seminal case of *Adler v Dickson*[172] was decided; this case is deemed to be the

---

170   Tetley, (n13) 42.
171   Ibid., 41.
172   [1955] 1 Q.B. 158.

origin, at least in name, of the Himalaya Clause. The use of exemption clauses has occupied courts before the shift away from the Privity of Contract Rule occurred. This was not a sudden shift and decisions of an evolutionary, and not a revolutionary, change in contract law contributed to this shift. Indeed, courts did refer in *Adler* to *Brandt v Liverpool, Brazil and River Plate Steam Navigation Co. Ltd*[173] as well as *Elder Dempster & Go. Ld. v Paterson, Zochonis & Co. Ld.*[174] It is noteworthy that both cases were before the courts in the same year but the judges presiding over the cases were not the same. Arguably, the conclusion can be reached that a change in thinking, centred on particular judges was occurring, and not the judiciary in general.

4.2   Brandt v Liverpool, Brazil and River Plate Steam Navigation Co. Ltd[175]

In *Brandt,* the question was whether an endorsee of a bill of lading can sue the carrier under the clauses contained in the bill of lading. This case does not deal directly with the question of the problems associated with the Privity Rule. However, it represents a different and more businesslike approach in the application of exemption clauses. The facts were as follows:

Bags of zinc ashes were shipped from Buenos Aires to Liverpool. Some of the bags were wetted by rain before shipment and as a result the upper layers of bags in one of the holds became heated. The master of the vessel, fearing damage to the ship and other cargo, discharged most of the bags at Buenos Aires and placed them in a warehouse; and after unnecessary delay they were reconditioned and reshipped on another vessel and forwarded to their destination at extra costs.[176] However, the shipowners issued a bill of lading indicating that the goods were received

---

173   [1924] G 1 K.B. 575.
174   [1924] A.C. 522; 40 T.L.E. 464.
175   [1924] G 1 K.B. 575.
176   Ibid. 575.

in apparent good order and condition. The bill of lading was endorsed, and the endorsees were asking for damages and delay.

The relevant clause in the bill of lading reads:

1. The ship shall not be liable for any delay, loss or damage caused by the act of God, perils of the seas, ports, rivers, or navigation of what nature or kind soever and howsoever caused .... land damage .... prolongation of the voyage, loss or damage arising directly or indirectly in store, on wharf, in craft, or on board, before, during, or after loading or until delivery is completed, rain, insufficiency of strength of packages, causes beyond shipowners' control.... effects of climate, sweating, heat of holds, evaporation, contact with goods, the ship, or anything in the ship .... latent or other defects, whether existing at the time of shipment or during the voyage .... whether or not all or any of the matters or things above-mentioned arise or be caused by the act, negligence or default or errors in judgment of agents, pilots, masters, engineers, stevedores, surveyors .... mariners or others whether on board the vessel carrying the goods, or any craft employed, or any other person or persons whose acts owners might otherwise be responsible or liable for, nor by unseaworthiness or unfitness of hull machinery or equipment, whether when loading sailing or arising during the voyage.

2. .... The ship will not be responsible for anything that may occur after the cargo or any part thereof has come within the control of any public authorities, dock, railway, warehouse or other carrier, or reached a custom house, nor for any consequences arising from sanitary or other regulations of authorities which may prevent or delay the discharge or removal of cargo "

Bankes L.J. put the problem as to whether there was a contract between Brandt & Co. and the shipowners.[177] He went on the state that:

---

177   Ibid., 589.

> it is quite true that there is no authority expressly covering the question how far, that is to what extent, the shipowner is bound by the contract which may be inferred from the offer made by the holder of a bill of lading to take delivery of the goods, which offer is accepted by the shipowner.[178]

The issue was that the court first searched for the existence of a contract between Brandt, the endorsee, and the Shipowner. Once Privity of Contract was established the court examined and interpreted the clauses in the bill of lading. The court accepted the proposition that the holder of the bill accepts the delivery and the carrier agrees that "the contract so made by that offer and acceptance covers, so as to include, the terms of the bill of lading."[179] However, the court found that the only condition upon "which [the ship] can rely is delay caused by prolongation of the voyage"[180] but not a postponement which was the case. The court noted: "I do not think it can reasonably be said that there was here any prolongation of this voyage at all. What happened was that the voyage referred to in the bill of lading did not commence."[181] Furthermore, as the bill of lading stated that bags were received in good order:

> The result, according to a well-known decision, which has been repeatedly followed since, was that persons taking a bill with that statement in it could in any complaint against the shipowner who had issued it rely on that statement and prevent the ship from proving the true fact which had not been correctly stated in the bill.[182]

The defence argued that the plaintiff was not a party to the contract and could not rely on its terms, in this case, the estoppel. Scrutton L.J. observed:

---

178   Ibid.
179   Ibid., 589.
180   Ibid., 601.
181   Ibid., 592.
182   Ibid., 593.

> This raises a novel point which has not in terms been considered in the authorities, as far as I know. Before the Bills of Lading Act, 1855, was passed, by the custom of merchants the indorsement of the bill of lading passed the property in the goods contained therein, but it did not assign the contract contained therein, and therefore the person who by indorsement became the owner of the goods did not by the same indorsement acquire a right to sue the shipowner upon his contract.[183]

The court observed that when the Bill of Lading Act 1855 "was passed this difficulty was so far remedied that when the whole property passed by the indorsement to the indorsee, the contract also passed."[184] However, the fact is that the Privity Rule still would not allow the contract to pass to a third party.

The court expanded on the passing of rights under the bill of lading and noted:

> When a holder of a bill of lading, who has some property in the goods, presents the bill of lading and accepts the goods, can there be inferred a contract on each side to perform the terms of the bill of lading? The view that Greer J. has taken is that such a contract can and ought to be implied in this case, and I take the same view. It follows, therefore, that Brandt & Co. may enforce the terms of the bill of lading and are entitled to the benefit of the estoppel which is contained in the statement, "In apparent good order and condition." ... The shipowners might be able to plead that they were protected by an exception, but in this case, they are in the difficulty that they cannot prove what has caused the delay; they cannot prove that it was caused by damage to the goods before shipment, because they have stated that they were shipped " in apparent good order and condition and are estopped from disproving it." [185]

The court in the end held that:

---

183   Ibid., 594.
184   Ibid., 595.
185   Ibid., 596.

although the plaintiffs, not being indorsees of the bill of lading to whom the property in the goods passed within the meaning of s. 1 of the Bills of Lading Act, 1855, could not sue on the contract contained therein, yet from the acts of presentation of the bill of lading, payment of the freight, and delivery and acceptance of goods specified in the bill of lading, there might and ought to be inferred a contract between the parties to deliver and accept the goods according to the terms of the bill of lading.[186]

It is interesting to speculate whether the court had in mind to extend the Privity Rule but found another way to connect an unconnected party to the contract. What can be said is that the court left the door slightly ajar to extend or change the Privity Rule. In this context, it is also interesting to note that 50 years later the court in *Cremer v General Carriers*[187] cited with approval the decision in *Brandt*. Kerr J noted that, "A contract incorporating the terms of the bill of lading was to be implied between the plaintiffs and the defendants by reason of the payment of freight by the plaintiffs and the delivery of the goods by the defendants against the bill of lading."[188]"

The essential part of the payment of freight is that it constitutes the consideration necessary to imply a contract. In other words, the importance of *Brandt* is the recognition by the court that upon presentation of the bill of lading and the giving of delivery an implied contract incorporating the terms of the bill of lading has formed.

The doctrine of implied terms is a matter of fact, and not of law, and it is driven by the willingness of the courts to give business reality to the transaction as seen in *The Captain Gregos (No 2)*.[189] The court found "very powerful grounds for concluding that it is necessary to imply a contract between them and create the

---

186   Ibid., 575.
187   [1973] 2 Lloyds Rep. 366.
188   Ibid., 371.
189   [1990] 2 Loyd's Rep. 395.

obligations which, we think, both parties believed to exist."[190]

The next step in "uncoupling" the Privity Rule was the bold decision in the House of Lords in *Elder Dempster & Go. Ld. v Paterson, Zochonis & Co. Ld.*[191] The complete change in the law was achieved in *Adler v Dickson*[192] where the court accepted the invitation to extend the protection of the exemption clauses past the strict Privity Rule.

The conclusion is that the state of laws in this area is sufficiently advanced but not completely harmonised in an international sense to have overcome the problems of showing a contractual relationship between those who are bound to, and can, take advantage of contractual clauses either in the bill of lading or in a charter party contract.

Arguably the attention of courts to protect parties from liability uncoupled from the Privity of contract was first discussed in the House of Lords in *Elder Dempster & Co. Ld. v Paterson, Zochonis & Co. Ld.*[193] (*Elder Dempster*)

4.3   Elder Dempster

The Privity Rule, in effect, stood uncontested until the court in *Elder Dempster & Co. Ld. v Paterson, Zochonis & Co. Ltd*[194] departed from the traditional Privity of Contract principle and started the protection of unconnected third parties.

The facts were that a time charterer loaded palm oil at a West African port to be shipped to Hull in the steamship *Grelwen*. The ship also loaded palm kernels on top of the barrels. The kernels being heavy crushed the barrels and upon arrival in England the

---

190   Ibid., 403.
191   [1924] A.C. 522; 40 T.L.E. 464.
192   [1955] 1 Q.B. 158.
193   Elder Dempster (n191).
194   Ibid.

greater part of the palm oil was lost. The bill of lading protected the charterers from damage due to bad stowage. The shipper sued the charterer and the shipowner for damage for breach of contract or, alternatively, for negligence or breach of duty.

Viscount Cave in the House of Lords posed the question whether the damage was due to unseaworthiness or bad stowage. If it was due to unseaworthiness the charterers were not protected by the conditions in the bill of lading. The court of appeal stated:

> The ship must be fit at loading to carry the cargo the subject of the particular contract. If she is so fit, and the cargo when loaded does not make her unseaworthy .... the fact that other cargo is so stowed as to endanger the contract cargo, is bad stowage on a seaworthy ship, not stowage of the contract cargo on an unseaworthy ship.[195]

Lord Sumner agreed and added: "For my part I neither think that the alleged defects in the ship and her equipment amount in law to unseaworthiness, nor that the damage to the puncheon of oil was due to them. No structural defect in the *Grelwen* caused this damage, nor was her equipment defective."[196]

The next question was whether the shipowner is protected by the clause in the bill of landing. The court noted that, "There is nothing in the charter to bind the shipowners towards the respondents at all. Their contract with the plaintiffs is in the bill of lading, if anywhere."[197] Viscount Cave argued that the shipowners are protected because:

> It may be that the owners were not directly parties to the contract; but they took possession of the goods (as Scrutton L.J. says) on behalf of and as the agents of the charterers, and so can claim the same protection as, their principals.[198]

---

195   *Elder Dempster* (n191) 530.
196   Ibid., 549.
197   Ibid., 552.
198   Ibid., 534.

Viscount Finlay, in essence, agreed with Viscount Cave but added:

> If the act complained of had been an independent tort unconnected with the performance of the contract evidenced by the bill of lading, the case would have been different. But when the act is done in the course of rendering the very services provided for in the bill of lading, the limitation on liability therein contained must attach whatever the form of the action and whether owner or charterer be sued.[199]

Lord Sumner also agreed with the finding that:

> ... in the circumstances of this case the obligations to be inferred from the reception of the cargo for carriage to the United Kingdom amount to a bailment upon terms, which include the exceptions and limitations of liability stipulated in the known and contemplated form of bill of lading. ... I cannot find here any such bald bailment with unrestricted liability or such tortious handling entirely independent of contract, as would be necessary to support the contention.[200]

Elder Dempster certainly created discussions and subsequent courts (as will be seen later) had some difficulties ascertaining the ratio within the case. Furmston and Tolhurst argue that the case was decided on the basis that both the owner and charterer were in the same position and the case was rightly decided.[201] In agreeing with Treitel and Reynolds,[202] they argue that the most satisfying explanation was that there was "a bailment to the shipowner of the goods on the terms to be contained in the bill of lading ... but that arguments of agency or implied contracts ... do not so easily fit the facts of Elder Dempster."[203]

It should also be remembered that Lord Denning LJ later in

---

199   Ibid., 548.
200   Ibid., 564-5.
201   Furmston and Tolhurst, (n1) 146.
202   See Carver on Bills of Lading (3rd ed) Sweet and Maxwell, 2010, Ch 7.
203   Furmston and Tolhurst, (n1) 146.

Smith and Snipes Hall Farm Ltd v River Douglas Catchment Board[204] stated:

> The [Privity] principle is not nearly as fundamental as it is sometimes supposed to be. It did not become rooted in our law until the year 1861 (Tweddle v Atkinson) and reached its full growth in 1915 (Dunlop v Selfridge). It has never been able to entirely to supplant another principle whose roots go much deeper. I mean the principle that a man who makes a deliberate promise which is intended to be binding, that is to say, under seal or for good consideration, must keep his promise; and the court will hold him to it, not only at the suit of the party who gave the consideration, but also at the suit of one who was not a party to the contract, provided that it was made for his benefit and that he has a sufficient interest to entitle him to enforce it subject of course always, of course, to any defences that may be open on its merits ... Throughout the history of the principle the difficulty has been, of course, to say what is sufficient interest to entitle the third person to recover.[205]

The court concluded that the exemption clause contained in the Bill of Lading also protected the owner of the vessel. Hallebeek commented that, "The reasoning of the judges is not at all clear, and it is easy to suppose that they were as much influenced by the commercial absurdity of reaching the contrary conclusion as by any doctrinal nicety."[206] It should be noted that *Elder Dempster* did not explore the possibilities that the law of agency or bailment could also have reached a similar result. However, the law as it was stated was problematic as it failed to recognise the emerging realities of complex commercial transactions specially in supply line contracts, such as construction and shipping contracts. In addition, in the second half of the 19th century, changes occurred in that "Common law judges began to

---

204   [1949] 2KB 500.
205   Ibid., 514.
206   Jan Hallebeek and Harry Doudorp (eds.), *Contracts for a Third-Party Beneficiary: A Historical and Comparative Account* (2008) Brill, 122.

take control over the rules relating to the measure of damages"[207] as best noted in *Hadley v Baxendale*.[208]

To put the shortcoming of the Privity Rule and the rule of consideration in simple terms:

> The problems of twentieth-century contract law did not stem from either of these on its own, but from the fact that they existed together. There was a "legal black hole", where the person who had suffered the loss could not sue and the person who could sue had suffered no recoverable loss. [209]

However, *Elder Dempster* was not followed in all circumstances until the seminal case of *Adler v Dickson*[210] was decided where the term 'Himalaya Clause' was coined. It was the name of the ship. This and other seminal cases are analysed in subsequent chapters. In brief, the important point which emerged was whether the exempting clause, the Himalaya Clause, was effectively drafted to allow a third party to take advantage of the protection.

Lord Roskill in an article summarised the changes from the Privity Rule to the Himalaya Clause succinctly. He wrote:

> The importance of these various decisions is this. They show a fundamental change in the attitude of our courts and a welcome determination to give effect to the intention of the parties where that intention has been clearly expressed in their contract and not to allow technical rules like the doctrine of consideration to stand in the way of so doing. This route is a different route from that which appealed to Lord Denning in his dissenting speech in the Midlands Silicones case, and I venture to think is, with all respect, very much more soundly based in legal principle.[211]

---

207 Ibid., 119.
208 (1854) 9 Ex 341.
209 Hallebeek, (n206) 117.
210 Adler (n192) 158.
211 Lord Roskill, *Half-A-Century of Commercial Law 1930–1980*, Birmingham, 1981, 11.

It is not surprising that many statutory exceptions were drafted in order to give clarity in important commercial subject areas such as the *Insurance Contracts Act* 1985 (Cth), s 48, *Bills of Exchange Act* 1909 (Cth), ss 36-43, *Cheques Act* 1986 (Cth), s 73 and the *Motor Vehicles (Third Party Insurance) Act* 1942 (NSW), s 10(7)

Some common law countries do not seem to have the same issue with the Rule and created relevant statutes to give the third party a right to demand performance. As an example, the United States already in 1889[212] eroded this principle. In 1932 "the first Restatement of Contracts further fostered this development and sounded the death knell for the Privity requirement by formally recognizing that certain third parties had independent rights in some contracts."[213] The important next step was taken in *Adler v Dickson*.[214]

4.4   Adler v Dickson[215]

The issue of the application of exemption clauses favouring third parties was refined in *Adler*. The facts are simple. The plaintiff was injured when mounting the gangway of the ship at a port of call. It was due to the negligent fastening of the gangplank by the master and the boatswain. The exemption clause was contained in the ticket:

> This ticket is issued by the company and accepted by the passenger subject to the following conditions and regulations. The company will not be responsible for and shall be exempt from all liability in respect " of any . . . injury whatsoever of or to the person of any passenger . . . whether such injury of

---

212   *Gifford v. Corrigan*, 117 N.Y. 257, 22 N.E. 756 (1889).
213   D. M. Summers, Third Party Beneficiaries and the Restatement (Second) of Contracts, 67 Cornell Law Review, 1982, 880 Available at: http://scholarship. law.cornell.edu/clr/vol67/iss4/12. 881.
214   [1955] 1 Q.B. 158.
215   Ibid.

or to the person of any passenger . . . shall occur on land, on shipboard or elsewhere . . . and whether the same shall arise from or be occasioned by the negligence of the company's servants on board the ship or on land in the discharge of their duties, or while the passenger is embarking or disembarking, or whether by the negligence of other persons directly or indirectly in the employment or service of the company, or otherwise, or by the act of God . . . dangers of the seas ... or by accidents . . . or any acts, defaults or negligence of the . . . master, mariners ... company's agents or servants of any kind under any circumstances whatsoever..[216]

The plaintiff sued under Tort, namely negligence. The issue was whether the clause was wide enough to not only limit the liability in contract but also in tort. Pilcher J commented that it is "established that the plaintiff's accident and injuries were caused by the negligence of one or other or both of the defendants, neither of whom was, on the face of any document, in direct contractual relationship with the plaintiff."[217]

He also made the comment that, "It is perhaps remarkable that the particular point which I am asked to decide never appears to have engaged the attention of the court in a claim for personal injuries,"[218] This is not surprising as at this stage the Privity Rule was still in command but subject to judicial questioning.

The plaintiff did acknowledge that the exemption clause protected the company, but the question was whether it also protected the master and the boatswain under tort. Lord Denning did refer to *Cosgrovc v Horsfal*[219] and observed that nobody is protected by a contractual clause if they are not a party to it; this observation complies with the Privity Rule.

However, the defence noted that this conclusion was inconsistent

---

216   Ibid., 159.
217   Ibid., 168.
218   Ibid.
219   (1945) 62 T.L.E. 140.

with the decision in *Elder Dempster*[220] where it was held that is was well established in cases of carriage of goods by sea, that the master and crew are entitled to the protection of the exemption clauses "and that there is no reason why they should not also be so entitled in the carriage of passengers."[221]

One of the questions whether the principle in *Elder Dempster* can also be extended to include passengers was answered in the affirmative as seen in *Hall v North Eastern Railway Co*.[222] The facts were that a drover was given a railway ticket by the Scottish rail company to travel from Scotland to England. While on the English line he was injured. The English rail company was not a party to the contract. Lord Denning commented in relation to *Hall v North Eastern Railway Co*:

> The reason was, in Blackburn J.'s words, that the drover "must be taken to have assented that the ticket should "protect the North Eastern Company just as well as the North "British." In short, it was a necessary implication that the English company should be protected.[223]

It can be argued that, already in 1875 a small crack in the application of the Privity Rule must have occurred. However, the commercially sound reasoning did not bear fruit at that time but was recognised in *Adler* as being persuasive.

The next point which was brought up by the defence was that the decision in *Elder Dempster* hinged on the issue of seaworthiness as well as contractual exemptions. The facts were that the court, after finding that the ship was seaworthy, looked at the exemption clause in the bill of lading which stated: "The Company shall not be liable .... for any damage arising from other goods by stowage or contact with the goods shipped

---

220   [1924] A.C. 522; 40 T.L.E. 464.
221   *Adler v Dickson,* (n 192) 181.
222   (1875) L.E. 10 Q.B. 437.
223   *Adler v Dickson,* (n192) 183.

hereunder."[224] The court dismissed the argument and Lord Denning, for the purpose of this case, summarised the decision in *Elder Dempster* as follows:

> They undoubtedly show that when a carrier issues a bill of lading for goods, the exception clauses therein enure for the benefit, not only of the carrier himself, but also for the benefit of the shipowner, the master, the stevedores and any other persons who may be engaged in carrying out the services provided for by the contract. Such persons are not parties to the contract of carriage, but, nevertheless, when they are rendering their services they are protected by the exceptions contained therein; and this is so, even though the clauses are not expressed to be made for their benefit, at any rate not in so many words. It follows that if they are guilty of negligence in rendering their services and are sued in tort, they can nevertheless rely on the exceptions to relieve them from liability. These propositions have been established in England by *Elder Dempster v Paterson.*[225]

Lord Denning stated correctly that, "the speeches in the House of Lords in the *Elder Dempster* case are so compressed on this point that we have a variety of reasons to choose from."[226] Arguably the issue reconciling the proposition that nobody can claim a benefit from a contract except the parties, and the coverage of an exemption clause has not been properly resolved in *Elder Dempster*. Lord Denning argued that:

> One suggestion, which was much canvassed, was that, in addition to the contract of carriage between the goods owner and the carrier (which was evidenced by the bill of lading), there were a number of collateral contracts between the goods owner and all the various persons concerned in the carriage.[227]

It is obvious that the argument in relation to collateral contracts

---

224   *Elder Dempster* (n191) 537.
225   *Adler v Dickson*, (n192) 181.
226   Ibid., 182.
227   Ibid.

was not correct as the contract was between the goods owner and the carrier and nobody else. The only point is whether other persons, for example subcontractors, are also able to benefit from its terms. In this case Lord Denning suggested that they are able to benefit from it because "they participated in so far as it affected them and can take those benefits of it which appertain to their interest therein."[228] In effect, an implied term was applied, namely that the shipper knew that subcontractors were involved. He effectively consented to their involvement hence they are protected, despite the fact they were not direct parties to it. Lord Denning, however, made an important distinction when he stated:

> The injured party must assent to the exemption of those persons. His assent may be given expressly or by necessary implication, but assent he must before he is bound: for it is clear law that an injured party is not to be deprived of his rights at common law except by a contract freely and deliberately entered into by him; and all the more so when the wrongdoer was not a party to the contract, but only participated in the performance of it.[229]

There is no doubt that, at the time when *Adler* was decided, this was the prevalent rule in case of shipment of goods. As early as in *Elder Dempster* the court was of the opinion that without the protection of subcontractors it would "otherwise … be an easy way round the bill of lading."[230] In any case the exemption clause in *Adler* only protected the steamship company and Lord Denning stated that, "servants or agents are therefore not excused from the consequences of their personal negligence."[231] He also observed that even if the steamship company intended to cover their servants, he saw nothing whatever to suggest that Mrs. Adler knew of their intention or assented to the inclusion

---

228   Ibid., 183.
229   Ibid., 184.
230   *Elder Dempster (n191)* 441.
231   *Adler v Dickson*, (n192) 185.

of the servants.[232]

The court therefore concluded that "since the contract neither expressly nor by necessary implication deprived the plaintiff of her right to sue the defendants in tort, she was entitled to pursue her claim against them."[233]

4.5   Conclusion

The challenge in changing the Privity Rule was taken up by the seminal case of *Elder Dempster* where both Lord Sumner and Scrutton LJ were leading commercial lawyers of their generation "and that their intuitive perception of the right answer had a good chance of being correct."[234]

The interesting issue which emerges from this decision is that courts were prepared to take commercial practices into consideration and go beyond simply looking at express terms but were prepared to look for, and find, implied terms to interpret the contract.

Adler took up the challenge and exposed the lacuna. The challenges were first, the exemption clause available to the carrier needs to extend to every servant, agent or independent contractor of the carrier acting as such. Secondly, the clause needs to establish that the carrier is, for purposes of all the foregoing provisions of the clause, acting on behalf of all such servants, agents and independent contractors.

Interestingly, the court was divided when the question was asked what the result would be if the liability of the crew was contained in the contract. Denning LJ would have held it effective whereas Jenkins and Morris LJJ did not see it that way. Jenkins and Morris took a narrow view of what *Elder Dempster*

---

232   Ibid.
233   Ibid., 158.
234   Furmston and Tolhurst, (n1) 146.

stood for: bailment on terms.[235]

Denning LJ interpreted and, hence, read the ratio in *Elder Dempster* differently and he noted:

> The truth is that there was only one contract, namely, the contract evidenced by the bill of lading: and the reason why the stevedores and others are protected is because, although they were not parties to the contract, nevertheless they participated in the performance of it, and the exception clause was made for their benefit whilst they were so performing it. The clause was not made expressly for their benefit, it is true, but nevertheless it was by necessary implication, which is just as good: and they have a sufficient interest to entitle them to enforce it. Their interest lies in this: they participated in so far as it affected them and can take those benefits of which appertain to their interest therein.[236]

As time went on, the position taken by Denning LJ has also been implemented not only in England but also in Australia[237] and the United States[238] as well as in the *Carriage of Goods by Sea Act*, 1924 Article IV (2). Specifically, the Carriage of Goods by Sea Act, pointing to a protection of all participants in the supply chain, caused the courts to examine the clash between the Act and the well-established principle that no one can claim the benefit of a contract except a party to it.

The main issue in the discussion of establishing a shift away from the Privity Rule is whether and how independent contractors can take advantage of exemption clauses against the cargo owners. Therefore, courts needed to develop a "fully fledged exception to the doctrine of Privity of contract, thus escaping from all the technicalities with which courts [were] faced in English law."[239]

---

235   Ibid., 199-200.
236   Ibid., 182.
237   *Gilbert Stokes & Kerr Pty. v. Dalgety & Co.* (1948) 81 Ll.L.E. 337.
238   *Collins v. Panama*, (1952) 197 Fed.Rep. 983.
239   Ibid., 665.

As will be seen in the following chapters, another milestone in the development of the Himalaya Clause was the decision in the *Mahkutai*[240] where the court stated that, "the bold step taken by the Privy Council … has been widely welcomed. But it is legitimate to wonder whether that development is yet complete".[241]

Three issues need to be resolved. First, what consideration are third parties rendering, secondly, where is the authority of third parties to act on behalf of the shipowner and thirdly, how are consignees of the cargo bound to the terms within the bill of lading?

---

240   (1996) AC 650.
241   Ibid., 664.

5

ENGLISH JURISPRUDENCE ON THE HIMALAYA CLAUSE

5.1   Introduction

This Chapter will analyse what might be considered the most important cases that have contributed to the development of the Himalaya clause. Special attention is directed to the actual exemption clauses in each case, and the analysis of the courts of the clauses are an important aspect of the solutions as highlighted in this Chapter. The jurisprudence is arranged in chronological order to appreciate the changes and refinements over time. It should also be noted that, although each case appears to reach the same conclusions, an incremental change in the development of the Himalaya clause has taken place.

As noted above, it is now recognised that the principle of the Himalaya clause was first established in *Adler v Dickson* in 1955. However, the full extent of what an exemption clause can achieve was not developed fully in *Adler*. It was only the first tentative step away from the implementation of the Privity Rule.

Since *Adler,* courts have worked out how far a Himalaya clause can protect third parties. The first flirtation of establishing a basis on which stevedores can claim protection under the clauses in a bill of lading can be found in *Midland Silicones Ltd v Scruttons Ltd*.[242] Two points need to be made First, national laws promote distinct national interests Secondly, an interesting point is that in shipping, countries are commonly identified as "carrier" nations or "cargo" nations. This means that a carrier nation tends to favour the carrier and a cargo nation arguably ought to be more disposed towards the interests of the cargo owners. Despite this classification the distinction in relation to cargo or carrier interests seemed to be irrelevant. Sturley argued:

> England is a leading carrier nation, but the House of Lords' initial response to the "Himalaya clause" problem" was strongly pro-cargo. The United States is a cargo nation, but its Himalaya clause jurisprudence favors the carrier. The primary judicial interest is in reconciling a technical legal convention with national law, not with national policy.[243]

The early start in the development of the Himalaya Clause has not followed the initial view that distinct national interests inform judicial decision making. Subsequent cases have added and refined the clause to an extent that today non-contractual parties are protected by the clause contained within the Bill of lading or the charter party. English case law, as will be seen in later chapters, has also influenced not only other common law countries but also civil law countries, such as Germany and mixed legal systems, such as South Africa. Essentially, it can be argued that the English development has influenced most courts that had to deal with carriage of goods by sea irrespective of whether they are cargo or carrier nations.

---

242   *Midland Silicones Ltd. v. Scruttons Ltd.* [1962] A.C. 446.
243   M. Sturley, International Uniform Law in National Courts: The Influence of Domestic Law in Conflicts of Interpretation, 27 *Virginia Journal of International Law*, 1987, 729, 743.

5.2 Jurisprudence

5.2.1 Midland Silicones Ltd v Scruttons Ltd[244]

This case is of significance as it is, using the words of Lord Denning, "the first case ever recorded in our English books where the owner of goods has sued a stevedore for negligence."[245] The stevedores negligently damaged a drum of chemical while loading it onto a lorry and they attempted to rely on the exceptions and limitations contained in the bill of lading. The stevedores did admit liability but relied on the limitation of damage clause in the bill of lading. In effect, the carrier engaged the stevedore under a separate contract stating in brief that the stevedore was fully responsible for any damage to or loss of cargo "while being handled or stowed, unshipped or delivered, or while in stowage, if damage caused by any negligence or themselves or their servants. The stevedores to have such protection as are afforded by the terms, conditions and exceptions of the bills of landing westbound and eastbound."[246]

The plaintiff relied on the principle of bailment on terms as explained in *Elder Dempster*. Furthermore, they also relied on an implied contract as contained in the Bill of Lading. The court re-asserted the doctrine of Privity of contract; in effect rejecting the decision in *Elder Dempster* giving weight to what Viscount Haldane had to say in *Dunlop Pneumatic Tyre*:

> My Lords, in the law of England certain principles are fundamental. One is that only a person who is a party to a contract can sue on it. Our law knows nothing of a *jus quaesitum tertio* arising by way of contract.[247]

In addition, the court gave the issue of bailment on terms a very restrictive treatment. The court explained:

---

244   [1962] A.C. 446.
245   Ibid., 491.
246   Ibid., 449.
247   [1915] A.C.847, 853.

> It is a fundamental principle that only a person who is party to a contract can sue upon it, and a stranger to a contract cannot in question with either of the contracting parties, take advantage of provisions of the contract even where it is clear from the contract that some provision in it was intended to benefit him.[248]

Viscount Simonds (relying on Viscounts Haldane's passage in *Dunlop Pneumatic Tyre*) commenced his judgment by noting that in the exemption clause the word carrier is used and the word stevedore is not a carrier in the ordinary use of language.[249] He relied on the textual approach of interpretation and also relied on clause 17 of the" bill of lading which authorises the carrier or master to appoint stevedores."[250] In effect the stevedores were independent contractors and not included in the exemption clause. The question of implied terms was raised which, as the court noted, has the purposes of given "business efficacy" to a contract.

This argument was dismissed as the court correctly noted that the shipper has a contract with the carrier but does not care how the carrier discharges his contractual duties. If the carrier contracts with a stevedore that would be entirely within the carrier's responsibility and the shipper is not included in this transaction. The issue of extending the contractual relationship to an undisclosed principal or beneficiary prompted Viscount Simonds to state that: "For me heterodoxy, or, as some might say, heresy is not the more attractive because it is dignified by the name of reform."[251]

Furthermore, the court made it clear that, "If the principle of *jus quaesitum tertio* is to be introduced into our law, it must be done by Parliament after a due consideration of its merits and demerits."[252] It is very interesting how the court dealt with

---

248   *Midlands*, (n244) 447.
249   Ibid., 466.
250   Ibid.
251   Ibid., 467.
252   Ibid., 468.

analysing *Elder Dempster*. Viscount Simonds commenced his discussion by noting:

> When, therefore, it is urged that the Elder Dempster case decided that, even if there is no general exception to what I have called the fundamental rule that a person not a party to a contract cannot sue to enforce it, there is at least a special exception in the case of a contract for carriage of goods by sea, an exception which is to be available to every person, servant or agent of the contracting party or independent contractor.[253]

The importance of this statement lies in the fact that the court did at least acknowledge the view that in cases of shipping the strict contract rule is not supported or reflects the realities of carriage of goods by sea.

He observed that it was undeniable that the facts in *Elder Dempster* are not the same as found in the present case.

The next question was whether there is a clear principle of law which can be extracted from the *Elder Dempster* Case in order to change the law on the Principle of contractual obligations. The answer was no and, in doing so, he relied on *Wilson v Darling Island Stevedoring and Lighterage Co. Ltd.*[254]

Lord Reid acknowledged that this case was brought to the court as a test case. He was of the view that:

> Although I might regret it I find it impossible to deny the existence of the general rule that a stranger to a contract cannot in a question with either of the contracting parties take advantage of provisions of the contract, even where it is clear from the contract that some provision in it was intended to benefit him.[255]

Instead Lord Reid relied on *Tweddle v Atkinson*[256] and *Dunlop*

---

253   Ibid., 469.
254   95 C.L.R. 43, [1956] 1 Lloyd's Rep. 346.
255   *Midlands*, (n244) 473.
256   (1861) 1 B. & S. 393.

Pneumatic Tyre Co. Ltd. v Selfridge & Co. Ltd[257] where the rule of Privity of contract was firmly established in the first case and followed in the latter.

The court left open situations where one of the parties' contracts as agent for the third person. Lord Reid made this position clear when he laid out four principles:

> I can see a possibility of success of the agency argument if (first) the bill of lading makes it clear that the stevedore is intended to be protected by the provisions in it which limit liability, (secondly) the bill of lading makes it clear that the carrier, in addition to contracting for these provisions on his own behalf, is also contracting as agent for the stevedore that these provisions should apply to the stevedore, (thirdly) the carrier has authority from the stevedore to do that, or perhaps later ratification by the stevedore would suffice, and (fourthly) that any difficulties about consideration moving from the stevedore were overcome.[258]

This passage proved to be the essential argument in the development of the Himalaya clause as fist noted in *Adler*. However, in the present case the problem was that Lord Reid could not elicit the fact that the carrier was contracting as agent for the stevedore in addition to contracting on his own behalf, hence, the Privity rule still applies. However, from a practical point of view it would be extremely unlikely that the carrier would be an agent of a stevedore as in practice it is the other way around and hence viewing it from Lord Reid's point of view the Privity rule always applies. In relation to reading implied terms into the clause Lord Reid noted:

> ... from the consignees' angle, they would know that stevedores would be employed to handle their goods, but if they read the bill of lading they would find nothing to show that the shippers had agreed to limit the liability of the stevedores. There is

---

257 [1915] A.C. 847.
258 *Midlands*, (n244) 474.

nothing to show that they ever thought about this or that if they had they would have agreed or ought as reasonable men to have agreed to this benefit to the stevedores.[259]

As courts are bound by precedents Lord Reid found it necessary to explain why the *Elder Dempster* case was not a precedent. He observed:

> I would certainly not lightly disregard or depart from any *ratio decidendi* of this House. But there are at least three classes of case where I think we are entitled to question or limit it: first, where it is obscure, secondly, where the decision itself is out of line with other authorities or established principles, and thirdly, where it is much wider than was necessary for the decision so that it becomes a question of how far it is proper to distinguish the earlier decision. The first two of these grounds appear to me to apply to the present case. It can hardly be denied that the *ratio decidendi* of the Elder Dempster decision is very obscure.[260]

It is also of interest to note that Lord Keith of Avonholm said:

> It may be difficult to discover any common ratio decidendi in the speeches of their Lordships who decided the *Elder Dempster* case in favour of the owners of the Grelwen. But I take the preferred view of Lord Sumner, which had the support of Lord Dunedin and Lord Carson, as meaning that in the circumstances of that case, including the fact that the bills of lading were signed by the master of the ship, the cargo was received by the ship and its owners, with the assent of the shippers, on the same condition as regards immunity in respect of stowage as had been obtained by the charterers under their contract of carriage.[261]

Simply put, the court could not extract a *ratio decidendi* from previous cases and hence the rule of Privity of contract was still the deciding factor.

---

259   Ibid., 474-475.
260   Ibid., 476-477.
261   Ibid., 481.

Of real importance is the dissenting judgment of Lord Denning. He commenced his analysis by pointing out that two contracts are of importance. He stated:

> Now, there are two principal questions in this case which need separate consideration: The first is whether the stevedores can rely on the limitation clause in the bill of lading to which they were not parties: The second is whether they can rely on the protection given by the stevedoring contract to which they were parties.[262]

Lord Denning, unfortunately dissenting, points to the exact problem namely if the Privity principle is applied the exemption clause cannot flow from contract one to contract two as described above. The issue, of course, is how can the two contracts be linked, that is how can the limitation clause flow from contract one to contract two. *Elder Dempster* decided that it is possible by implication when it stated that "servants or agents who act under that contract have the benefit of the exemption clause."[263]

Lord Denning argued that one "cannot understand the *Elder Dempster* case without some knowledge of the previous law and I would draw the attention of your Lordships to it."[264] He noted that the Privity rule is an invention of the nineteenth century and is not rooted in legal history at all. The importance of *Elder Dempster*, as Lord Denning argued, was that they viewed the contract from a point of view of principal and agent, hence "the charterers and their agents " were not liable and as a second reason through bailment upon terms, which "include the exceptions and limitations stipulated in the known and contemplated form of bill of lading."[265]

> But if you look at the Elder Dempster case with the spectacles of 1961, then there is a way in which it can be supported. It is this:

---

262   Ibid., 482.
263   Ibid., 483.
264   Ibid.
265   Ibid., 487.

Even though negligence is an independent tort, nevertheless it is an accepted principle of the law of tort that no man can complain of an injury if he has voluntarily consented to take the risk of it on himself. This consent need not be embodied in a contract. Nor does it need consideration to support it. Suffice it that he consented to take the risk of injury on himself. So, in the case of through transit, when the shipper of goods consigns them "at owner's risk" for the whole journey, his consent to take the risk avails the second carrier as well as the first, even though there is no contract between the goods owner and the second carrier. Likewise, in the Elder Dempster case the shipper, by exempting the charterers from bad stowage, may be taken to have consented to exempt the shipowners also. But I am afraid that this reasoning would not avail the stevedores in the present case: for the simple reason that the bill of lading is not expressed so as to protect the stevedores but only the "carrier." [266]

Lord Denning held for the stevedores on another ground, namely the stevedores' contract with the shipowner under which liability was limited. He said:

The question is: Did the owner of the goods impliedly authorise the carrier to employ the stevedores on the terms that their liability should be limited to $500? I think they did.[267]

Arguably, Lord Denning was instinctively aware that the wording of the clause ultimately will decide who is protected and who is not once the hurdle of Privity of contract has been overcome. In addition, Lord Denning also took the view that the Privity doctrine has been modified by the emergence of negligence as an independent tort.[268]

Midland did indicate that *Elder Dempster* in essence has "shown a light" in relation to overcoming the Privity concept. Lord Denning recognised it in dissenting to the arguments

266   Ibid., 488.
267   Ibid., 489-490.
268   Ibid., 488.

of the majority of the House. Considering that *Midlands* was decided after *Adler* it is arguable that the Himalaya clause was first thought of in *Elder Dempster* and not *Adler*. *Adler* was only mentioned once in passing by their Lordships whereas great discussions were constructed why *Elder Dempster* was wrong and should not be followed. The question is; did *Elder Dempster* provide the impetus or *Adler* in the "birth" of the Himalaya clause? The answer arguably is both cases did and, importantly, the Lords in *Midland* ought to have put more faith in the decision reached in *Adler*.

In addition, it is not surprising that commentators at that time thought that:

> For the result reached by the House of Lords in *Midlands Silicones Ltd. v. Scruttons* Ltd. is hardly consistent with the expectations of the parties and may, in fact, cause considerable commercial inconvenience because of the difficulty of allocating liability in transactions where numerous parties are involved.[269]

This is exactly, as Halstead predicted, what happened in the following cases.

5.2.2 The *Eurymedon*[270]

The court affirmed, from an appeal of a decision in New Zealand, the protection granted to subcontractors by the Himalaya clause against claims of tort. In this case the stevedores acted negligently in damaging a drilling machine.

In the *Eurymedon* the important and necessary part of the exemption clause on the Bill of Lading notes:

> It is hereby expressly agreed that no servant or agent of the

---

269   Halstead, R T, Privity of Contract and Bills of Lading: Midland Silicones Ltd v Scruttons Ltd, 1964, 4(3) *Sydney Law Review* 464, 470.

270   *New Zealand Shipping v. Satterthwaite Ltd. (P.C.) the Eurymedon* [1975] A.C. 154.

carrier (including every independent contractor from time to time employed by the carrier) shall in any circumstances whatsoever be under any liability whatsoever to the shipper, consignee or owner of the goods or to any holder of this bill of lading for any loss or damage or delay of whatsoever kind arising or resulting directly or indirectly from any act neglect or default on his part while acting in the course of or in connection with his employment and, without prejudice to the generality of the foregoing provisions in this clause, every exemption, limitation, condition and liberty herein contained and every right, exemption from liability, defence and immunity of whatsoever nature applicable to the carrier or to which the carrier is entitled hereunder shall also be available and shall extend to protect every such servant or agent of the carrier acting as aforesaid and for the purpose of all the foregoing provisions of this clause the carrier is or shall be deemed to be acting as agent or trustee on behalf of and for the benefit of all persons who are or might be his servants or agents from time to time (including independent contractors as aforesaid) and all such persons shall to this extent be or be deemed to be parties to the contract in or evidenced by this bill of lading.[271]

The court agreed that the "exemption is designed to cover the whole carriage from loading to discharge, by whomsoever it is performed: the performance attracts the exemption or immunity in favour of whoever the performer turns out to be."[272] The court referred to Lord Reid's comments in the *Midland Silicones* case, specially the four criteria set out above.[273] Lord Wilberforce was convinced that the first three criteria were satisfied; the only issue remaining whether the fourth one, namely the question of consideration, was also satisfied.[274]

Lord Wilberforce stated:

271   Ibid., 165.
272   Ibid., 167.
273   *Midlands*, (n244) 474.
274   Eurymedon, (n270) 167b.

The question in this appeal is whether the contract satisfies these [requirements]. Clause 1 of the bill of lading, whatever the defects in drafting, is clear in its relevant terms. The carrier, on his own account, stipulates for certain exemptions and immunities: among these is that conferred by art III(6) of the Hague Rules which discharges the carrier from all liability for loss or damage unless suit is brought within one year after delivery. In addition to these stipulations on his own account, the carrier as agent for (*inter alias*) independent contractors stipulates for the same exceptions.

Much was made of the fact that the carrier also contracts as agent for numerous other persons; the relevance of this argument is not apparent. It cannot be disputed that among such independent contractors, for whom, as agent, the carrier contracted, is the appellant company which habitually acts as stevedore in New Zealand by arrangement with the carrier and which is, moreover, the parent company of the carrier. The carrier was, undisputedly, authorised by the stevedore to contract as its agent for the purposes of clause 1. All of this is quite straightforward and was accepted by all the learned judges in New Zealand. [275]

However, the question was whether consideration was provided. The court answered this question in the affirmative by suggesting:

[The] initial unilateral bargain was capable of becoming mutual between the shipper and the appellant, made through the carrier as agent. The performance of these services for the benefit of the shipper was the consideration for the agreement by the shipper that the appellant should have the benefit of the exemptions and limitations contained in the bill of lading. [276]

In essence, the court followed *Scotson v Pegg*[277] where it was stated that "The performance of an act which a person has agreed with another to perform, is a good consideration to support – a

---

275   Ibid., 1091.
276   Ibid., A.C. 168.
277   [1861] EWHC Exch J2.

contract with a third person if the latter derives a benefit from the performance."[278]

The court made it clear that the consignee is entitled to the benefit of the bill of lading by his acceptance and, hence, is also bound by the stipulations in the bill of lading including the Himalaya clause.[279] The court saw no problems arguing that the exemption clause "brought into existence a bargain initially unilateral but capable of becoming mutual between the shipper and the stevedore"[280] and "this became a full contract when the stevedore performed the services by discharging the goods".[281]

Lord Wilberforce also noted that a United States District Court[282] came to the same conclusions. Interestingly, the court noted:

> it is no doubt true that the law in the United States is more liberal than ours as regards third party contracts, their Lordships see no reason why the law of the Commonwealth should be more restrictive and technical as regards agency contracts. Commercial considerations should have the same force on both sides of the Pacific.[283]

Arguably, Lord Wilberforce's rationale for his decision is best explained by the following passage:

> In the opinion of their Lordships to give the appellant the benefit of the exemptions and limitations contained in the bill of lading is to give effect to the clear intentions of a commercial document, and can be given within existing principles. They can see no reason to strain the law or the facts in order to defeat

---

278   Ibid., 121.
279   Ibid.
280   Ibid., 167-168.
281   Ibid., 168.
282   *Carle & Montanari Inc. v. American Export Isbrandtsen Lines Inc.* [1968] 1 Lloyd's Rep. 260.
283   Eurymedon, (n276) 169.

these intentions. It should not be overlooked that the effect of denying validity to the clause would be to encourage actions against servants, agents and independent contractors in order to get around exemptions (which are almost invariably and often compulsorily accepted by shippers against carriers, the existence, and presumed efficacy, of which is reflected in the rates of freight. They see no attraction in this consequence. [284]

The court recognised that shipping is an international adventure requiring a harmonised approach. However, this is unfortunately not always the case as some courts are still compelled to follow the principle of the law of contract or of agency.[285]

Furmston[286] suggested that, importantly, the consent argument was put to the Privy council by Michael Mustill QC indicating:

These three propositions are based on contract and are alternative to one another and mutually exclusive. The fourth proposition is independent of contract and stands by itself. It involves that the benefit of the exemption can be conferred without a contract. Whether or not there was a contract, the bill of lading evidenced the consent of the shipper to the performance of services in relation to the goods upon terms that the stevedores should have the benefit of every exemption from, and limitation of liability contained in the bill of lading. The consent nullified the duty of care which stevedores would otherwise have owed at common law. Alternatively, the consent excluded or qualified the liability of stevedore for breaches of that duty. This does not amount to volenti non-fit injuria, which doctrine destroys the duty of care, not merely excludes liability for negligence. Consent *inter partes* can effectively exclude liability with contract [*reference was made to leading cases*] The principles to be extracted from the cases are; (1) that it makes no difference whether the consent of the plaintiff is contained in a direct communication between

---

284   Ibid., 169.
285   See comments in the Mahkutai, (n71) 664.
286   See Furmston and Tolhurst, (n1) 143.

himself and the defendant or in a document passing through a third party; (2) that the basis for the operation of non-contractual exemption from liability can be on a condition imposed by a licence; (3) that a true defence of volenti non fit injuria may destroy and exclude the duty and (4) that certain forms of disclaimer as in *Hedley Byrne* prevent a duty from arising at all. It follows that if a defendant can exclude his liability altogether he can also limit it.[287]

Lord Wilberforce sidestepped the argument put by Mustill QC and said.

> The appellant submitted, in the alternative, an argument that, quite apart from contract, exemptions from, or limitations of, liability in tort may be conferred by mere consent on the part by the party who might be injured. As their Lordships consider that the appellant ought to succeed in contract, they prefer to express no opinion upon this argument; to evaluate it requires elaborate discussions.[288]

What can be said is that this case clearly demonstrated that the Himalaya clause contained in a bill of lading, a contractual document, expresses the commercial reality of shipping as, in effect, it gives a "clear intention of a commercial document, and can be given within existing principles."[289] The court did not see any reason to strain the law or the facts in order to defeat these intentions specifically as the exemption clauses have been accepted by shippers against carriers, the existence, and presumed efficacy, of which is reflected in the rates of freight.[290]

---

287   Eurymedon, (n276) 158.
288   Ibid., 168.
289   Ibid., 169.
290   Ibid.

5.2.3 *Nippon Yusen Kaisha v International Import and Export Co (The Elbe Maru)*[291]

This case is not really a solution or judgment in relation to a Himalaya clause, rather it runs on the question whether a circular indemnity clause is valid. The reason this is of importance is the fact that often indemnity clauses have become part and parcel of the Himalaya clause and, hence, is in a sense an alternative to it. In effect, it can be argued that if the court rejects the function of the Himalaya clause it will not entertain the validity of the indemnity clause either. Unfortunately, none of the leading cases on the Himalaya clauses, whether decided in England or the United States, were consulted or referred to in this case.

The facts are that the shipper Court International Ltd shipped goods to England on board the vessel *The Elbe Maru*. The carrier subcontracted the carriage of the goods from Southampton to Liverpool to a haulier, SC. While the goods were in the custody of SC, some of the goods were stolen. The carrier applied for an order to stay the proceedings as the indorsee of the bills of lading on the ground that the respondent had become a party to the bill of lading and were bound by cl. 4(2).

Two clauses in the bill of lading are of significance. namely clause 1 and 4.

> cl. 1, Definitions: "'merchant' includes … the receiver of the goods, any person owning or entitled to the possession of the goods or this bill of lading," … and,

> cl. 4, Subcontracting: … (2) The "merchant" undertakes that no claim … shall be made against any sub-contractor of the carrier which imposes or attempts to impose any of them any liability whatsoever in connection with the goods, and, if any claim should nevertheless be made, to indemnify the carrier against all consequences thereof …[292]

---

291   [1978] 1 Lloyd's Rep. 206.
292   Ibid., 206.

Ackner J.J agreed with the parties that the respondents became a party to the bill of lading by reason of being endorsees of the bill. The applicant relied on *Brandt & Co*[293] on this fact. Furthermore, it was clear that the action by the respondent is against the haulier in an action of tort as he was grossly negligent and as bailee he was also liable. However, SC relies on clause 4(2) as a defence. Ackner J.J. noted that the court has discretion to stay proceedings, but he would only do so if the claimant could establish that there is a real possibility of being prejudiced.

Ackner J.J. noted in particular that:

> [The claimant] relies of course upon the very existence of the express undertaking in cl. 4(2) and he says: here is a contractual obligation not to make the claim which is being made by the respondents. Accordingly, it should follow that the relief which he seeks, namely, the stay of those proceedings, should be granted. I do not think it follows that merely by establishing the contract he ipso facto obtains his relief because the matter is one for the discretion of the Court, but I accept that his ability to point to a clear right being infringed should prima facie entitle him to the relief he claims.[294]

Hence the court granted the relief as asked for by the claimant.

5.2.4 The New York Star[295]

This was an appeal from the High Court of Australia[296] to the Privy Council. This case turned on the issue whether the stevedores were protected under tort as they allowed persons to remove goods without the presentation of a bill of lading. The

---

293   (1923) 17 Ll.L. Rep. 143, specifically on 147.
294   Elbe Maru, (n291) 210.
295   *Port Jackson Stevedoring Pty Ltd v Salmond & Spraggon (Australia) Pty Ltd* (The New York Star) [1981] 1 W.L.R. 138.
296   *Port Jackson Stevedoring Pty Ltd v Salmond & Spraggon (Australia) Pty Ltd* (1980) 144 CLR 300.

outcome was in favour of the stevedores.

The question which occupied the court was whether the bill of lading was still operative while the goods were already off loaded after they had crossed the ship's rail. When the loss occurred, the goods were discharged and were no longer in the custody of the carrier. The court in the first instance noted that the stevedore was not acting as a subcontractor under the bill of lading but rather as a bailee. It follows that the liability of the stevedores was independent of, and not governed by, the clauses of the contract.[297]

In the appeal to the Privy Council Lord Wilberforce again delivered the judgment. The initial comments were that the significance of the *New York Star* was not that a legal principle has been established but rather "in the finding that in the normal situation involving the employment of stevedores by carriers, accepted principles enable and require the stevedore to enjoy the benefit of contractual provisions in the bill of lading."[298]

It was agreed that the relationship between carriers and stevedores might vary from case to case, however, "the decision does not support ... a search for fine distinctions which would diminish the general applicability in the light of established commercial practice of the principle."[299] The observation was made that the factual situation is typical and similar to the one in New *Zealand Shipping Company Ltd v A. M Satterthwaite & Co. Ltd.*[300] The court then looked at the facts closely and proceeded with the construction of the clauses in the bill of lading Clause 8 stated that, "delivery of the goods shall be taken by the consignee or holder of the bill of lading from the vessel's rail immediately the vessel is ready to discharge, berthed or not berthed ...".[301]

---

297   New York Star, (n295) 145.
298   Ibid., 143.
299   Ibid., 144.
300   [1975] A.C. 154.
301   Ibid.

The court commented that this phrase needs to be understood in the context of what practically happens, namely that consignees are rarely taking delivery directly from the ship's rail but after some time of discharge near or at the wharf. This contrasts with a literal reading of the clause. Therefore, it was contemplated that the carrier would employ a subcontractor which explains the interrelationship between clauses 5 and 8. Clause 5 states that the carrier's responsibility ends as soon as the goods leave the ship's tackle. The reminder of the clause notes that the carrier still has some responsibilities after the goods are discharged. He cannot just dump the goods as this is commercially unreal and not contemplated by the bill of lading.[302] There is nothing in clause 8 which is inconsistent with the obligations as per clause 5. However, of importance is that clause 5 attributes responsibility to the carrier as a bailee and defines the period as "continuing after leaving the ship's tackle."[303]

The court posed the question what would happen if the carrier himself would stack the containers on the wharf; the answer is clearly that he still would be protected. Their Lordships therefore found that, if the carrier employs a stevedore, the situation would not change and hence the stevedore can take full advantage of the limitation clauses in the bill of lading.

The New York Star again explains how judges in England are aware of commercial realities which are never far away when interpreting terms in the bill of lading containing a Himalaya clause. Lord Wilberforce read the contract in the light of what normally happens:

> These provisions must be interpreted in the light of the practice that consignees rarely take delivery of goods at the ship's rail but will normally collect them after some period of storage on or near the wharf. The parties must therefore have contemplated that the carrier, if it did not store the goods itself, would employ

---

302   Ibid., 147.
303   Ibid.

some other person to do so.[304]

This case was decided after an appeal from the High Court of Australia[305] and in the Privy Council the decision was overturned. It is instructive to note how the Australian High Court viewed the Himalaya clause. Barwick CJ delivered the dissenting judgment. He succinctly stated his starting point by noting:

> ... questions as to how far, if at all, someone not a party to a contract, but for whose benefit it is made, can enforce the agreement made between others, do not arise. The decision in The Eurymedon (1975) AC 154 made the stevedore a party to the relevant parts of the bill of lading. It is, in my opinion, that feature of the decision which is so significant and important for the commercial community, particularly that section which is concerned with the transport of goods.[306]

He specifically observed:

> I would find it extremely difficult to fail to conclude in those circumstances that in the shipment the stevedore was responding to the terms of the bill of lading, accepting both its obligations and seeking the benefit of its restrictions.[307]

> Their Lordships' decision in The Eurymedon was of great moment in the commercial world and, if I may say so, an outstanding example of the ability of the law to render effective the practical expectations of those engaged in the transportation of goods. It is not a decision of its nature to be narrowly or pedantically confined. It established, as I have said, that the acceptance of the bill of lading by the consignor followed by the acts of the stevedore produced a binding contract to which consignor and stevedore were parties.[308]

---

304   Ibid., 147.
305   *Port Jackson Stevedoring Pty Ltd v Salmond & Spraggon (Aust) Pty Ltd*, (1977) 139 CLR 231.
306   Ibid., para 31.
307   Ibid., para 37.
308   Ibid., para 45.

He had no difficulty finding that a contract existed between all those who participated in the maritime venture based on the bill of lading. It is therefore not surprising that Barwick CJ, following the reasons given in *the Eurymedon*, allowed the appeal as did Sheppard J in the New South Wales Court of Appeal. Arguably, judicial decisions in England are clearly moving towards a consensus in relation to applying the Himalaya clauses. It is therefore difficult to understand that Stephen J in the Australian case found it important to note that:

> Anything approaching uniformity of the law affecting international trade is no doubt difficult of an attainment, but it may be that the path to it lays rather by route of international conventions and subsequent national legislation than by the adoption of any deliberate direction in the judicial interpretation of the parties' documents in particular cases.[309]

As history has shown, Stephen J was wrong in assuming that uniformity in the law can only be achieved through international conventions. In any event, changing the Privity Rule which is only applied in the common law, but not in civil law, will hardly find traction on this matter in any international body. Barwick CJ saw it correctly but in the end Stephen, Mason and Jacobs JJ rejected the stevedore's arguments and found against following the arguments put forward in the *The Eurymedon*. But as noted above, the Privy Council saw it differently and overrode the Australian decision.

5.2.5 *Raymond Burke Motors Ltd v The Mersey Docks and Harbour Co*[310]

This case demonstrates that a clause must be written carefully. Specifically, the risk which needs to be guarded against must be clearly identified and a corresponding clause needs to be written with the risk in mind. The Himalaya clause is no exception to

---

309   Ibid., para 14.
310   (1986) 1 Lloyd's Rep. 155.

this rule. This case also referred to all the seminal cases which were discussed above.

The facts were never disputed by the parties. The plaintiff bought ex-warehouse 60 motorcycles, hence, the plaintiff had title to sue. The seller acted as the plaintiff's agent to arrange the transport of the motorcycles to Canada. The defendants were the operators of the dock in Liverpool and agreed to provide the berth for ships owned by Manchester Liners Ltd and to provide service for the loading and unloading of containers. The sellers had arranged shipments with the English parties on several occasions and were aware of the Himalaya clause contained in the standard bill of lading conditions. The seller had acted as agent on previous occasions and there was a previous course of dealing between the plaintiffs and the defendant. The seller contacted Manchester Liners and asked them to arrange for the goods to be carried to the terminal and await shipment to Canada. The containers were stored in the container park and not on the quayside. While unloading a different vessel, one of the employees of the defendant negligently caused an accident in the container park and as a result damaged the motorcycles.

The question was whether the defendant can claim the benefits of the exclusion clause under the bill of lading. The defendant also relied on the terminal agreement with the owners, Manchester Liners Ltd. In brief, the agreement noted that Manchester liners Ltd are to include into their bills of lading a clause to ensure that the terminal operator is covered by the exemption clause, that is the relevant Himalaya clause. The clause in effect would have been sufficiently widely drafted to include the port operator. Clause 14 reads in its relevant part:

> No servant or agent (which includes an independent contractor) acting solely on behalf of the Carrier shall be under any personal liability whatsoever for any loss, damage or delay whatsoever whensoever and howsoever caused. Without prejudice to the generality of the forgoing, every term and exception herein

upon which the carrier is or would be entitled to rely shall extend to protect every such servant or agent. For the purposes of this clause the Carrier shall be deemed to be acting as agent on behalf of and trustee for the benefit of all persons who are or may be his servants or agents from time to time which persons shall to this extent be deemed parties hereto.[311]

Importantly. the conditions on the bill of lading were followed at the end (for the purpose of this discussion) with a statement confirming that the owners of the goods expressly agreed to be bound by the terms.

Leggatt J observed that the goods were damaged before they crossed the ship's rail and that no bill of lading was issued. The question therefore was whether "the damage occurred during the contract of carriage by sea, and also whether the sellers were party to the contract of carriage".[312] It was held that the carriage of goods by sea had not commenced, hence, no sea carriage document was in existence on which the stevedore could rely.

The court agreed that there was a bailment, but this occurred before the contract of carriage had started and:

In my judgment, there never was an act by the defendant referrable to the contract for carriage by sea such as would have constituted acceptance of an offer by the plaintiff. The result is that there was no concluded contract between the parties and the exception clause whatever its true construction could never have operated and never did operate in favour of the defendants.[313]

Manchester liners could also not be held liable because what occurred was not within their scope of responsibility and hence could not be liable under the bill of lading. In essence, the defendant could not rely for the protection under clause 14 and, hence, were held liable for the damage.

---

311   Ibid., 158.
312   Ibid.
313   Ibid., 162.

5.2.6 The Pioneer Container[314]

Goods were shipped from Taiwan to Hong Kong under a feeder bill. The vessel collided with another ship and sank. The plaintiffs commenced litigation in rem against the *Pioneer Container*, a sister ship of the sunken vessel, in Hong Kong. The carriage of goods was subcontracted, and each Bill of Lading contained the clause 4(1), namely:

> The carrier shall be entitled to sub-contract on any terms the whole or any part of the carriage, loading, unloading, storing, warehousing, handling and any and all duties whatsoever undertaken by the carrier in relation to the goods.[315]

As there was no contractual relationship between the plaintiffs and the shipowners the issue arose whether the shipowner can rely on the exclusive jurisdiction clause in the bill of lading (clause 26) which named Taiwan as the forum and whether the clause was binding on all the plaintiffs. The point was that some cargo owners were parties to the bill of lading, but others had no direct contract with the ship as they had a contract with another shipping line which trans-shipped the goods.

Lord Goff immediately looked at the central problem and started with commercial considerations:

> ... it [is] right to observe, at the outset, that in commercial terms it would be most inconvenient if these two groups of plaintiffs were not so bound. Here is a ship, upon which goods are loaded in a large number of containers; indeed, one container may contain goods belonging to a number of cargo owners. One incident may affect goods owned by several cargo owners, or even (as here) all the cargo owners with goods on board. Common sense and practical convenience combine to demand that all of these claims should be dealt with in one jurisdiction,

---

314   [1994] 2 A.C. 324.
315   Ibid., 334.

in accordance with one system of law.[316]

It is often the case especially when transhipment or subcontracting arises that commercial reality dictates that a common solution ought to be a prime objective. As Lord Goff noted: "if this cannot be achieved, there may be chaos."[317] He also pointed to the issue that English law still maintains, though with increasing criticism, the Privity of contract rule. The question was posed by Lord Goff: "How long these principles will continue to be maintained in all their strictness is now open to question."[318] In this case, again, there was no contractual relationship between the shipowners and certain cargo owners.

Their Lordships turned their attention to the issue of bailment and sub-bailment and of course whether the Himalaya clause which was part of the bill of lading protects all parties concerned in the supply chain. In relation of the Himalaya clause counsel for the plaintiff argued:

> the "Himalaya" clause gives sufficient effect to the commercial expectations of the parties, and that to allow a sub-bailee to take advantage of the terms of his own contract with the bailee was not only unnecessary but created a potential inconsistency between the two regimes.[319]

However, the court saw it differently as they pointed out that "the mere fact that such a clause is applicable cannot ... be effective to oust the sub-bailee's right to rely on the terms of the sub-bailment as against the owner of the goods."[320]

Lod Goff stated, in more detail:

> the incorporation of the relevant clause in the sub-bailment would be in accordance with the reasonable commercial

---

316   Ibid., 335.
317   Ibid.
318   Ibid., 335.
319   Ibid., 344.
320   Ibid., 344.

expectations of those who engage in this type of trade, and that such incorporation will generally lead to a conclusion which is eminently sensible in the context of the carriage of goods by sea, especially in a container ship, in so far as it is productive of an ordered and sensible resolution of disputes in a single jurisdiction, so avoiding wasted expenditure in legal costs and an undesirable disharmony of differing consequences where claims are resolved in different jurisdictions.[321]

It goes without saying that here is no inconsistency as the plaintiff can simply chose the terms which are most favourable to him. The conclusion is that the *Pioneer Container* established that two regimes are potentially applicable: first the Himalaya clause, a contractual issue and, secondly the bailment or sub-bailment and they are applicable in their own right without creating any inconsistencies. The court in effect agreed with the defendant that, "The doctrine of sub-bailment does not bind the bailor to a contract to which he was not a party. He is bound by reason of a separate relationship based on Privity of bailment."[322]

5.2.7 The Mahkutai[323]

The facts of this case are that the vessel was an on a time charter. It was later sub-chartered on a voyage charter by P. T. Rejeki Sentosa ("Sentosa") who contracted with P. T. Jabarwood ("the shippers") to transport wood from Indonesia to China. A clean bill of lading (Sentosa's form of bill) was issued providing that, "For further terms and conditions the clauses as stipulated in the B/L will apply."[324] The Bill of Lading as far as relevant contained the following clauses:

"4. Subcontracting.

---

321   Ibid., 347.
322   Ibid., 329.
323   [1996] A.C. 630.
324   Ibid., 656.

"(i) The carrier shall be entitled to subcontract on any terms the whole or any part of the carriage, loading, unloading, storing, warehousing, handling and any and all duties whatsoever undertaken by the carrier in relation to the goods, (ii) The merchant undertakes "that no claim or allegation shall be made against any servant, agent or subcontractor of the carrier, including but not limited to stevedores and terminal operators, which imposes or attempts to impose upon any of them or any vessel owned by any of them any liability whatsoever in connection with the goods and, if any such claim or allegation should nevertheless be made, to indemnify the carrier against all consequence thereof. Without prejudice to the foregoing, every such servant, agent and subcontractor shall have the benefit of all exceptions, limitations, provision, conditions and liberties herein benefiting the carrier as if such provisions were expressly made for their benefit, and, in entering into this contract, the carrier, to the extent of these provisions, does so not only on as [sic] own behalf, but also as agent and trustee for such servants, agents and subcontractors. The carrier shall be entitled to be paid by the merchant on demand any sum recovered or recoverable by such merchant from any such servant, agent or subcontractor of the carrier for any loss, damage, delay or otherwise, (iii) The expression 'subcontractor' in this clause shall include direct and indirect subcontractors and their respective servants and agents.
. .

19. Jurisdiction clause.

"The contract evidenced by the bill of lading shall be governed by the law of Indonesia and any dispute arising hereunder shall be determined by the Indonesian courts according to that law to the exclusion of the jurisdiction of the courts of any other country."[325]

After the vessel arrived at Shantou in China it was discovered that the timber was damaged by sea water. The vessel proceeded

---

325   Ibid., 656-657.

to Hong Kong where the owners of the timber sued for damages. The shipowners issued a summons seeking a stay of proceedings relying on clause 19 of the bill of lading. The court of appeal of Hong Kong in the end noted that the shipowners were not a party to the Bill of Lading which contained the Himalaya clause and hence the stay of proceedings was not upheld. The parties were granted leave to appeal to the Privy Council.

The Privy Council commented that the two principles, namely the desirability of recognition of modification to the strict doctrine of Privity of contract on one hand, and the accommodation of allowing certain terms of the contract to be made available to parties involved in the maritime adventure but are not parties to the contract have not been totally reconciled into a doctrine.[326] It therefore is "inevitable that technical points of contract and agency law will continue to be invoked".[327]

In the *Mahkutai* their Lordships turned to the application of the principles as elicited in the *Eurymedon*. Two questions needed to be answered. First whether the shipowners qualified as subcontractors within the meaning of the Himalaya clause as noted in clause 4 of the bill of lading and, secondly, whether the shipowners can take advantage of the exclusive jurisdiction clause 19 in the contract.[328] The exclusive jurisdiction clause was addressed with the assumption that the shipowners were subcontractors. Lord Goff analysed the impact of the Himalaya clause and stated (citations omitted):

> The two principles which the shipowners invoke are the product of developments in English law during the present century. During that period, opinion has fluctuated about the desirability of recognising some form of modification of, or exception to, the strict doctrine of Privity of contract to accommodate situations which arise in the context of carriage of goods by

---

326   Ibid., 658.
327   Ibid., 664.
328   Ibid., 665.

sea, in which it appears to be in accordance with commercial expectations that the benefit of certain terms of the contract of carriage should be made available to parties involved in the adventure who are not parties to the contract. These cases have been concerned primarily with stevedores claiming the benefit of exceptions and limitations in bills of lading, but also with shipowners claiming the protection of such terms contained in charterers' bills. At first there appears to have been a readiness on the part of judges to recognise such claims, especially in *Elder Dempster & Co. Ltd v. Paterson, Zochonis & Co Ltd,* concerned with the principle of bailment on terms. Opinion however hardened against them in the middle of the century as the pendulum swung back in the direction of orthodoxy in *Midland Silicones Ltd v Scruttons Ltd;* but in more recent years it has swung back again to recognition of their commercial desirability, notably in the two leading cases concerned with claims by stevedores to the protection of a Himalaya clause The *Eurymedon and The New York Star.*[329]

The question the court posed was whether the jurisdiction clause falls within the Himalaya clause which notes, among others, that subcontractors have the benefit of "all exceptions, limitations, provision, conditions and liberties herein benefiting the carrier as if such provisions were expressly made for their benefit."[330]

As most bills of lading incorporate The Hague Visby rules in which responsibility and liabilities for the benefit of the carrier are contained – primarily in article IV – the point is that subcontractors can also derive the same benefit if the Himalaya clause is drafted wide enough to do so. Three crucial words within the Himalaya clause were highlighted by the court namely *exceptions, limitations* and *provision.*

The first question was whether the jurisdiction clause is an

---

329   Ibid., 658.
330   Ibid.

exemption or a limitation. Their Lordships stated:

> Such a clause can be distinguished from terms such as exceptions and limitations in that it does not benefit only one party, but embodies a mutual agreement under which both parties agree with each other as to the relevant jurisdiction for the resolution of disputes. It is therefore a clause which creates mutual rights and obligations. Can such a clause be an exception, limitation, provision, condition or liberty benefiting the carrier within the meaning of the clause?[331]

The second question was whether the jurisdiction clause is a provision. The court noted that the jurisdiction clause is not a provision as it cannot be extended to include a mutual agreement which follows naturally from the observation above. This view is supported by looking at the function of the Himalaya clause. Their Lordships defined the function of the Himalaya clause to "prevent cargo owners from avoiding the effect of contractual defences available to the carrier (typically the exceptions and limitations in The Hague-Visby Rules) by suing in tort persons who perform the contractual services on the carrier's behalf."[332]

Importantly, the court distinguished this case with the decision in *The Pioneer Container*.[333] In that case the goods were subcontracted under a feeder bill of lading and the Himalaya clause contained the words "on any terms." The court noted that, "The present case is however concerned not with a question of enforceability of a term in a sub-bailment by the sub-bailee against the head bailor, but with the question whether a subcontractor is entitled to take the benefit of a term in the head contract."[334]

As far as the second point was concerned, namely whether the shipowners were able to take advantage of clause 19 (the

331   Ibid., 666.
332   Ibid.
333   [1994] 2 A.C. (74) 324.
334   The Mahkutai, (323) 667.

Himalaya clause) the court answered that in the affirmative but clearly noted that "those terms did not include the exclusive jurisdiction clause."[335] Of importance is the crucial point of the judgment by Lord Goff who observed:

> Though these solutions are now perceived to be generally effective for their purpose, their technical nature is all too apparent; and the time may well come when, in an appropriate case, it will fall to be considered whether the courts should take what may legitimately be perceived to be the final, and perhaps inevitable, step in this development, and recognize in these cases a fully-fledged exception to the doctrine of Privity of contract, thus escaping from all the technicalities with which the courts are now faced in English law. It is not far from their Lordships' minds that, if the English courts were minded to take that step, they would be following in the footsteps of the Supreme Court of Canada: See *London Drugs Ltd v Kuehne & Nagel International Ltd* and, in a different context, the High Court of Australia: See *Trident General Insurance Co. Ltd v McNiece Bros Pty Ltd*. Their Lordships have given consideration to the question whether they should face up to this question in the present appeal. However, they have come to the conclusion that it would not be appropriate for them to do so, first, because they have not heard argument specifically directed towards this fundamental question and, second because, as will become clear in due course, they are satisfied that the appeal must in any event be dismissed."[336]

In addition, Lord Goff observed:

> Furthermore, it is of some significance to observe how adventitious would have been the benefit of the exclusive jurisdiction clause to the shipowner in the present case. Such a clause generally represents a preference by the carrier for the jurisdiction where he carries on business. But the same cannot

---

335   Ibid., 668.
336   Ibid., 664 to 664.

necessarily be said of ... stevedores at the discharging port, who provide the classic example of independent contractors intended to be protected by a Himalaya clause. There is no reason to suppose that an exclusive jurisdiction clause selected to suit particular carriers would be likely to be of any benefit to such stevedores; it could only be conceivable be so in the coincidental circumstance that the discharging port happened to be in the country where the carrier carried on business.[337]

Lord Goff arguably advanced the public policy rationale when he stated that, "the bold step taken by the Privy Council in *The Eurymedon*, and later developed in The New York Star, has been widely welcomed."[338]

5.2.8 Canada Maritime Ltd v Oerlikon Aerospace Inc [339]

This is an appeal from the Commercial court. The facts are not too complicated. An army tank belonging to Her Majesty the Queen, in her right as sovereign of Canada, was on loan to Oerlikon, a company. It was to be transported from Canada to Turkey where it was to be exhibited. During trans-shipment in Valencia, Spain the tank was damaged while being moved by a lorry. The damages amounted to Canadian Dollars 3 million. The tank at the time of the accident was in the custody of Maritima Valencia (MV), the port authority. However, as the two defendants did not enter an appearance, the cargo owners obtained a default judgment. After three years the cargo owners attempted to enforce the judgment. The sub-contractors entered an appearance and applied to the court to set the judgments aside. The issue here is whether they have an arguable defence and to that end they invoked the Himalaya clause. It was fortunate for the sub-contractors that in the meantime *the Mahkutai* was decided after entry of the default judgments, but before the

---

337   Ibid., 667.
338   Ibid., 664.
339   [1998] Int. Com. L. R. 02/06.

sub-contractors applied to set them aside. The difficulty was that, if *Midland Silicones* was not overturned, they could not have ratified the contract within a reasonable time. The sub-contractors argued that:

> as *Himalaya* clauses in bills of lading might (in the opinion of the Privy Council as expressed in *The Mahkutai)* soon form a full exception to the doctrine of Privity of contract in English law (thus rendering ratification and other such technicalities unnecessary), they had a good prospect of establishing a defence to the claim.[340]

The court agreed with the above argument of the sub-contractors and overlooked *Midlands* because - as Hirst LJ put it - the Privity doctrine was "on the brink of collapse."[341]

Under the terms of the agreement contained in the bill of lading Canada Maritime Ltd agreed to carry the tank from Montreal to Turkey. The bill of lading at clause 4.2 contained the following Himalaya clause:

> The [plaintiffs] undertake that no claim or allegation shall be made against any person whomsoever by whom the Carriage or any part of the Carriage is performed or undertaken (other than the Carrier) which imposes or attempts to impose upon any such person, any vessel owned by any such person, any liability whatsoever in connection [with] the Goods or the Carriage of Goods, whether or not arising out of negligence on the part of such person and, if any such claim or allegation should nevertheless be made, to indemnify the Carrier against all consequences thereof. Without prejudice to the foregoing every such person shall have the benefit of every exemption, limitation, condition and liberty herein contained and of every right, exemption from liability, defence and immunity of whatsoever nature applicable to the Carrier as if such provisions were expressly for his

---

340   K. Barnett, "The validity of Himalaya clauses-Privity of contract on the brink of collapse?" *The International Journal of Shipping Law,* 178. 180.

341   *Canada Maritime* (n339) para 23.

benefit...; and in entering into this contract, the Carrier, to the extent of these provisions, does so not only on his own behalf but also as agent and trustee for such persons."[342]

Hirst LJ noted that in the Commercial court reference was made to the decision in *The Mahkutai* where it was established that as a "matter of law Himalaya clauses in a bill of lading are an exception to the doctrine of Privity of contract, and that therefore proof of ratification is unnecessary."[343] The court specially noted what Lord Goff had to say in relation to independent contractors enjoying the benefit of exemption and limitations contained in the Himalaya clause against the cargo owner. The explanation by Lord Goff was:

(1) the problem of consideration in these cases is regarded as having been solved on the basis that a bilateral agreement between the stevedors and the cargo owners, entered into through the agency of the shipowners, may, though itself unsupported by consideration, be rendered enforceable by consideration subsequently furnished by the stevedors in the performance of their duties as stevedors for the shipowners. (2) the problem of authority from the stevedors to the shipowners to contract on their behalf can, in the majority of cases, be solved by recourse to the principle of ratification; and (3) consignees of the cargo may be held to be bound by the principle in *Brandt v Liverpool, Brazil and River Plate Steam Navigation Co. Ltd*[344]

The court dismissed the arguments of the defendant that the judgment of *Midland Silicone* is still good law and must be followed. Hirst LJ stated that Tuckey J of the Commercial court was correct to come to the conclusion that, "*The Mahkutai* case shows that, in cases of carriage of goods by sea like the present, the doctrine of Privity of contract may well be tottering on the

---

342   Ibid., para 5.
343   Ibid., para 13.
344   Ibid., para 17.

brink of collapse."[345]

Hirst LJ concluded that:

> I consider that Maritima Valencia and Transportes Fuente do enjoy real prospects of success; and I also consider that this furnishes very strong grounds for setting Rix J's judgment aside, especially as his judgment was given prior to the decision in *the Mahkutai,* which furnishes Maritima Valencia and Transportes Fuente with a strongly arguable defence of which they should not in the interests of justice be lightly deprived.[346]

The court agreed that *The Mahkutai* case shows that, in cases of carriage of goods by sea like the present, the doctrine of Privity of contract may well have collapsed.[347] It must be noted that the decision in *Oerlikon* v. *Maritima Valenciana* was given on the basis of this prospective change in English law which had not yet occurred.[348]

As far as shipping contracts are concerned, the courts' predictions that this uncertainty will not continue were correct as further jurisprudence built on *the Mahkutai* refined their arguments. The Himalaya clause is now an exception to the doctrine of Privity of contract.

5.2.9 The Rigoletto[349]

The facts were that seven Lotus Esprit cars were destined to be shipped on the *Rigoletto*. Lotus prepared a standard shipping note to the road haulier. At the port, a representative from the stevedores - who were also appointed as cargo handlers by the Associated British Ports - received the cars. The cars were

---

345   Ibid., para 23.
346   Ibid., para 35.
347   Ibid., para 33.
348   Barnett, (340) 181.
349   [2000] 2 Lloyd's Rep. 532.

physically received by the stevedores and driven into a vehicle compound. One of the cars was stolen from the fenced and locked compound. The remaining cars were loaded onto the *Rigoletto* and a bill of lading was issued on behalf of the carrier on their standard form.

The court distinguished between four potential contractual relationships, first the one between Lotus and the stevedore, secondly the one between the stevedores and the Ports, thirdly the one between the stevedores and the shipowner and fourthly the one between Lotus and the shipowner. Lotus claimed against the stevedores and the Port in bailment and under the terms of the shipping note. The court in the end held that the stevedores (SCH) were liable to Lotus.

The court set out the relevant documents of the four possible contracts.

5.2.9.1 The SCH conditions

The conditions by which the stevedores accept goods were "construed as reversing the burden of proof in bailment so that [the stevedores] accepted liability if negligence was proven against them."[350] The court only found clause 18 of importance which stated:

> The user shall include in its Bill of Lading a provision that [the stevedores] its employees, agents and subcontractors shall have the benefit of any terms in such a Bill of Lading excluding or limiting the liability of the user in respect of cargo."[351]

User under clause 1(e) was defined to include shipper and shipowner.

5.2.9.2 The bill of Lading

---

350   Ibid., 535.
351   Ibid.

The bill of lading included the following terms which are relevant:

2. Responsibility.

The Hague Rules contained in the international convention for the unification of certain rules relating to bills of lading, dated Brussels the 25th August 1924 as enacted in the country of shipment shall apply to this Contract ...

The Carrier or his Agents shall not be liable for loss of or damage to the goods during the period before loading or after discharge howsoever such loss or damage arises ...

7. Loading, Discharging and Delivery

Carrier's Agent unless otherwise agreed. Landing, storing and delivery shall be for the Merchant's account. Loading and discharging may commence without previous notice . . . The Merchant or his Assign shall tender the goods when the vessel is ready to load and as fast as the vessel can receive ... The Merchant or his Assign shall take delivery of the goods and continue to receive the goods as fast as the vessel can deliver ... Otherwise the Carrier shall be at liberty to discharge the goods and any discharge to be deemed to be a true fulfilment of the contract . . . If the goods are not applied for within a reasonable time, the Carrier may sell the same privately or by auction.

16. Exemptions and immunities of all Servants and Agents of the Carrier

It is hereby expressly agreed that no servant or agent of the Carrier (including every independent Contractor from time to time employed by the Carrier) shall in any circumstances whatsoever be under any liability whatsoever to the Merchant for any loss, damage or delay arising or resulting directly or indirectly from any act, neglect or default on his part while acting in the course of or in connection with his employment and, but without prejudice to the generality of the foregoing provisions in this clause, every exemption, limitation, condition and liberty herein contained and every right, exemption from liability, defence and immunity of whatsoever nature acceptable to the Carrier or to which the Carrier is entitled hereunder shall also be available and shall extend to protect every such Servant or Agent of the Carrier acting as aforesaid and for the purpose of all the foregoing provisions of this clause the Carrier is or shall be deemed to be acting as Agent or Trustee on behalf of and for the benefit of all persons who are or might be his Servants or Agents from time to time (including independent Contractors as aforesaid) and all such persons shall to this extent be or be deemed to be parties to the contract evidenced by this Bill of Lading.

The Carrier shall be entitled to be paid by the Merchant on demand any sum recovered or recoverable by the Merchant or any other from such Servant or Agent of the Carrier for any such loss, damage or delay or otherwise.[352]

The terms and conditions of the other two contracts namely between SCH and the shipowner and between SCH and the Port Authorities were not relevant in the court's decision. Judge Hallgarten of the lower court had reasoned that:

First, that SCH were independent contractors acting as [the shipowners] agents for receipt   and pre-shipment storage of the cars. They were not, however, acting "merely as agents" as an employee does. Nor was their handling of the cars merely fleeting, as it often is in classic stevedoring duties. They were therefore bailees of the cars, and they received them on the terms of their conditions, and it was to their conditions that the shipping note referred in speaking of "published regulations and conditions", and not to any prospective bill of lading. Prima facie therefore SCH's liability to Lotus was governed by their conditions, under which the

---

352   Ibid., 535.

burden of proof in bailment was reversed so that they were only liable for negligence that had been proven against them and such negligence had been proven.[353]

Rix L.J of the Court of Appeal turned to the three issues argued in this appeal. First, he asked the question whether SCH were bailees. In response to the applicant his Lordships argued SCH were agents of the shipowner, but they were not their servants "nor is the agency of an independent contractor incompatible with bailment. Moreover, the fact that a person may owe duties in more than one direction does not mean that he cannot be a bailee."[354]

Because SCH signed the shipping note which states that Lotus is the exporter because Lotus prepared the note, and it was signed for Lotus. It contains a statement that "The company preparing this note" makes a declaration that the goods are properly described, and asks the receiving authority to receive the goods described for shipment subject to the latter's terms.[355] Lord Justice Rix accepted that the shipping note is a direct contract between the two parties.

The next question was whether the Himalaya clause was wide enough to protect SCH under a separate contract evidenced by the bill of lading.

Rix L.J. started with the assumption that the Himalaya clause provides SCH with a complete defence.[356] If it does so the question is whether the liability under the shipping note is replaced by the limitations contained under the bill of lading. Simply put: which contract takes precedence and can SCH choose which of the two contracts is more advantageous to them. The answer was that:

---

353   Ibid., 538.
354   Ibid., 539.
355   Ibid., 540.
356   Ibid., 541.

SCH had already chosen between the regimes when they signed the shipping note and elected to receive the cars on the terms of their own conditions. Whether or not that created a contract between them, or only a relationship of bailment or sub-bailment on terms, there was such direct contact between the two parties then, through the shipping note, as to eliminate the possibility that SCH did intend to rely, or could rely, as against Lotus, on the potential inconsistent contract which might otherwise have come into being through the Himalaya clause in [the shipowners] bill of lading.[357]

Rix L.J also noted that the dictum of Lord Goff in *The Pioneer Container* does not apply as Lord Goff made it clear that, *"Their Lordships are therefore satisfied that the mere fact that a "Himalaya" clause is applicable does not of itself defeat the shipowners' argument on this point."*[358] In this case SCH has already made the choice and hence has no ability to subsequently change its mind.

His Lordship before coming to a conclusive decision suggested that it would only be proper "to try to read the two contractual regimes together. Where there is inconsistency, it would be in accordance with principle to think that an acceptance of liability was intended to take effect over an exclusion of liability."[359] He concluded that:

at any rate where there is inconsistency, it seems to me that SCH's own conditions ought to be construed as intended to prevail. After all, such conditions have been specifically drafted by SCH as appropriate to their individual circumstances, as distinct from the alternative regime via the Himalaya clause, which applies indiscriminately to any agent or independent contractor employed by the carrier.

For all or any of these reasons, I think that even if the Himalaya

---

357   Ibid., 541.
358   *The Pioneer Container* (n74) 603.
359   Rigoletto, (n349) 542.

clause could otherwise apply to SCH and to the theft of the car so as to exclude all liability on their part, the assumption of liability for proven negligence to be found in SCH's own conditions would take precedence: and that is so whether SCH and Lotus were in direct contractual relations or whether their relationship was merely that of a bailment or sub-bailment on terms.[360]

Rix, L.J. declared:

Lord Reid's fourfold test for the successful invocation of a direct contract between shipper and stevedore via a Himalaya clause contained in a contract of carriage between shipper and carrier is set out in *Midland Silicones v. Scruttons* .... Forty years on, there now tends to be little difficulty in giving successful effect to that test.[361]

The court also made a further point namely that the bill of lading only contemplated protection for the carriage of goods. The bill of lading notes in cl 2 "the period before loading" for the purposes of cl. 2 should be taken to mean (and be limited to) "the period between the commencement of pre-loading operations (ie cargo checks and stowage arrangements on 30 August) and actual physical loading".[362] The question was when does it start? The court argued that at best it began when the cars were shifted from the lock-up to the wharf; a time after the car was stolen. In other words, the pre-loading arrangements stood on their own feet - that is - they are regulated by the contract between Lotus and SCH. In the end SCH was not protected by the Himalaya clause.

---

360   Ibid., 542.
361   Ibid., 542.
362   Ibid., 543.

5.2.10 Homburg Houtimport BV v Agrosin Ltd (The Starsin)[363]

The *Starsin* sailed from Belawan in Indonesia to Antwerp with a parcel of cargo of timber. Due to negligent stowage, the timber deteriorated. The owner claimed damages against the ship owners and demise charterers of the *Starsin*.

Lord Bingham put the issue simply as raising questions whether the shipowner is liable to the cargo owners under the bill of lading contracts and, if not, whether he is liable to any of the cargo owners to any (and if so, what) extent in tort.[364]

The first contentious issue was whether the bill of ladings was a shipowner's bill or charterer's bill. The issue was that the printed terms in the bill of lading did not correspond with the word chosen by the parties and were not written into the contract. The intention of the parties was given more weight than the printed words and the court found that the Bills were charterer's bills which, in essence, assumes that Continental Pacific Shipping (CPS) is the contractual carrier.[365]

Once the parties to the contract were identified, the second issue was whether the terms of the contract protected the shipowner against liability to the cargo owners. Clause 5 was the relevant clause in question which read in the relevant parts as follows (including the mistakes noted below by the court).

(1) It is hereby expressly agreed that no servant or agent of the carrier (including any person who performs work on behalf of the vessel on which the goods are carried or of any of the other vessels of the carrier, their cargo, their passengers or their baggage, including towage of and assistance and repairs to the vessels and including every independent contractor from time to time employed by the carrier) shall in any circumstances whatsoever be under any liability whatsoever to the shipper,

---

363   [2004] 1 AC 715.
364   Ibid., 734.
365   Ibid., For a closer examination of the reasons see 736 - 738.

for any loss, damage or delay of whatsoever kind arising or resulting directly or indirectly from any act neglect or default on his part while acting in the course of or in connection with his employment and,

(2) without prejudice to the generality of the provisions in this bill of lading, every exemption limitation, condition and liberty herein contained and every right exemption from liability, defence and immunity of whatsoever nature applicable to the carrier or to which the carrier is entitled hereunder shall also be available to and shall extend to protect every such servant or agent of the carrier is or shall be deemed to be acting on behalf of and for the benefit of all persons who are or might be his servants or agents (including any person who performs work on behalf of the vessel on which the goods are carried or of any of the other vessels of the carrier, their cargo, their passengers or their baggage, including towage of and assistance and repairs to the vessels and including every independent contractor from time to time employed by the carrier)

(3) and all such persons shall to this extent be deemed to be parties to the contract contained in or evidenced by this bill of lading

(4) The shipper shall indemnify the carrier against any claim by third parties against whom the carrier cannot rely on these conditions, in as far as the carrier's liability would be excepted if said parties over bound by these conditions.[366]

The court noted that the printing of this clause leaves something to be desired, as words and punctuations are missing forcing the court to insert words where they are obviously missing. The court agreed with the submissions of council that the words which were missing are those found in the Conline bill of lading form, on which clause 5 had been closely modelled.[367] The court proceeded to analyse each of the paragraphs of clause 5.

---

366   Ibid., 740.
367   Ibid., 741.

The clause in the first part on its face confers wide ranging immunity – which all members of the lower court agreed - that it was a covenant not to sue, enforceable by injunction.[368] Lord Bingham disagreed with the Court of Appeal and found that, "it is in my judgment impossible to spell a covenant not to sue out of the language of this clause."[369]

The second part of clause 5 filled the lacuna in *Adler* and followed the solutions as noted in *Midlands, the Eurymedon* and *the New York Star* as noted above.

The third part of clause 5 raised the question whether the shipowner was an independent contractor which was confirmed by the court.[370]

The next issue was whether the duties imposed by The Hague Rules were fulfilled, specifically article III rules 1 and 2 which notes that, "Subject to the provisions of article IV the carrier shall properly and carefully load, handle, stow, carry, keep, care for, and discharge the goods carried." In addition, article III rule 8 provides that:

> "Any clause, covenant, or agreement in a contract of carriage relieving the carrier or the ship from liability for loss or damage to, or in connection with, goods arising from negligence, fault, or failure in the duties and obligations provided in this article or lessening such liability otherwise than as provided in these Rules, shall be null and void and of no effect."

The cargo owners contended that the rule limits the protection to the carrier which includes also the servants, agents and independent contractors, otherwise article III rule 8 would have no relevance.[371] The counter argument was that the definition of carrier in the Hague Rules includes "the owner or the charterer

---

368 Ibid., 742.
369 Ibid.
370 Ibid., 743.
371 Ibid., 744.

who enters into a contract of carriage with a shipper" and that CPS and not the shipowner entered into a contract with the shipper hence the liability of the shipowner should not be excluded.[372]

Lord Bingham disagreed with the counter argument. He noted that,"The Himalaya clause itself, and the undoubted artificiality of the reasoning relied on to uphold it in [previous judgments] were a deft and commercially-inspired response to technical English rules of contract, particularly those governing Privity and consideration"[373]

As noted - as an example in the *Mahkutai* - the problem that there was no contract between carrier and stevedores was overcome "by holding, in effect, that a bilateral contract came into existence upon the performance by the stevedore."[374]

Having noted the crucial issue Lord Bingham observed that, "The present case however is factually different, because the act performed to bring any contract into existence between the shipowner and the cargo owners is the carrying of the goods."[375]

This difference gave rise to a legal difference and taking The Hague Rules into consideration the court noted that it is a contract of carriage and the shipowner enters into it with the shipper. Hence article III rule 8 of The Hague Rules do not protect the shipowner by the exemption clause 5 and the shipowner therefore did not become subject to the positive obligations laid on to the carrier by article III rules 1 and 2 of the Hague Rules.[376]

That said the issue therefore arises whether the cargo owners have a tort claim against the shipowner; this claim was also

---

372   Ibid., 744.
373   Ibid.
374   Ibid.
375   Ibid.
376   Ibid., 745.

dismissed.

Of interest is the dissenting judgment of Lord Steyn in relation to whether the shipowner was the carrier under the bill of lading. In Lord Steyn's view the issue was the inconsistency of provisions noted on the face of the bill and two clauses on the reverse side which contradict the provisions on the face of the bill. He solved the issue by applying the reasonable person versed in the shipping trade test and stated:

> In my view, he would give greater weight to words specially chosen, such as the words which appear above the signature, rather than standard form printed conditions. Moreover, I have no doubt that in any event he would, as between provisions on the face of the bill and those on the reverse side of the bill, give predominant effect to those on the face of the bill. Given the speed at which international trade is transacted, there is little time for examining the impact of barely legible printed conditions at the time of the issue of the bill of lading. In order to find out who the carrier is it makes business common sense for a shipper to turn to the face of the bill, and in particular to the signature box, rather than clauses at the bottom of column two of the reverse side of the bill.[377]

Lord Steyn relied also on the comments by Rix LJ who observed that, "commercial certainty and indeed honesty is promoted by giving greater effect to the front of the bill of lading."[378] He therefore concluded that it was a charterer's bill. In relation to the issue in tort he reached the same conclusion and allowed the appeal. The court in the end noted that the shipowner's appeal ought to be allowed because greater weight should attach to terms specially chosen by the parties than to standard printed conditions.[379]

---

377   Ibid., 747.
378   [2001] Lloyd's Rep 437, 451.
379   Homburg Houtimport BV v Agrosin Ltd, (n363) 716.

5.2.11 Whitesea Shipping and Trading Corp & Anor v El Paso Rio Clara Ltda & Ors.[380]

This is an interesting case as it not only involves a Himalaya clause but also an anti-suit injunction. The issue was that an exclusive jurisdiction clause was incorporated into one of the clauses in the bill of lading. The issue was that the vessel grounded in the Dominican Republic. There were in all nineteen defendants (cargo interests covered by three bills of lading) and two claimants namely the demise charterer and the owner of the vessel.

There was no damage to the cargo which was offloaded in the Bahamas but for the rest general average claims were made against the cargo owners. The defendants commenced proceedings in Brazil.

Each bill contained an English jurisdiction clause as well as that the bills must be governed by English law. The Bill of lading also contained the following clauses:

'1. DEFINITIONS

f. "Subcontractor" includes stevedores, longshoremen, lighters, terminal operators, warehousemen, truckers, agents, servants, any person, firm, corporation or other legal entity who performs services incidental to the goods and/or the carriage of the goods, including direct and indirect subcontractors and their servants and agents

3. SUBCONTRACTING a. The carrier shall be entitled to subcontract on any terms the whole or any part of the carriage, loading, unloading, storing, warehousing, handling and any and all duties whatsoever undertaken by the carrier in relation to the goods. b. [1] The merchant undertakes that no claims or allegations shall be made against any servant, agent, stevedore or subcontractor of the carrier which imposes or attempts to

---

380   [2009] 2 CLC 596.

impose upon any of them or any vessel owned or chartered by any of them any liability whatsoever in connection with the goods, [2] and if such claim or allegation should nevertheless be made, to indemnify the carrier against all consequences thereof. [3] Without prejudice to the foregoing, every servant, agent, stevedore and subcontractor shall have the benefit of all provisions herein benefiting the carrier as if such provisions were expressly for their benefit, and all limitations of and exonerations from liability provided to the carrier by law and by the terms hereof shall be available to them, and in entering into this contract the carrier, to the extent of those provisions, does so not only on its own behalf, but also as agent and trustee for such servants, agents, stevedores and subcontractors. c. The defences and limits of liability provided for in this bill of lading shall apply in any action whether the action is founded in contract or in tort.'[381]

Flaux J summarised the claimants' case as being straightforward namely that all the defendants are covered by the Himalaya clause and pursuant to clause 3b are bound in equity that they will not sue the third parties. Furthermore, the defendants cannot commence proceedings in Brazil as it is in breach of the English jurisdiction clause.

The insurer Defendants argued that clause 3b is in breach of article III Rule 8[382] of The Hague:

> The effect of entitling either the carrier under the bill of lading contract or the third party to enforce the covenant not to sue in the first part of clause 3b would be to confer blanket immunity upon the third party, which is contrary to Article III rule 8 of

---

381 Ibid., 601.
382 Article III states:'Any clause, covenant or agreement in a contract of carriage relieving the carrier or the ship from liability for loss or damage to or in connection with the goods, arising from negligence, fault, or failure in the duties and obligations provided in this section, or lessening such liability otherwise than as provided in this chapter, shall be null and void and of no effect.'

the Hague Rules to which the Himalaya contract is subject. Accordingly, the first part of clause 3b is null and void and of no effect.[383] The argument relies heavily on the decisions in *The Starsin*.[384]

The court compared the clauses contained in *The Starsin* and the present one and concluded that there were two principal distinctions between the clauses;

> the first part of [*the Starsin*] clause does not in terms set out an undertaking or covenant not to sue and that the present clause does not contain a 'deeming provision' such as is contained in the third part of [*The Starsin*] clause in that case.[385]

Flaux J referred back to Coleman J in *The Starsin* and referred to them at length. Of interest to this case is Coleman's views on the leading cases on Himalaya clauses namely:

(1) There is no sign in the leading cases on the Himalaya clause, *The Eurymedon, The New York Star*, and *The Makhutai*, each of them in the Privy Council, of any reliance on part 1 of the clause or of finding there a complete exemption of liability for the benefit of third parties. Mr Berry submits that that is not surprising in that at any rate the first two of those cases relied on the bills' Hague Rules one year time bar – and that a time bar is as good as a blanket exemption, so that there was no need to raise an additional point under part 1 of the clause. That may be so, but it does not explain why the additional point was not taken, if there to be taken, nor why in The New York Star [1981] 1 WLR 138 at 142E/F and again at 143E/F Lord Wilberforce explained the function of the Himalaya clause, which was present there in very similar (albeit not identical terms) to clause 5 here, as being, for instance, to extend "the benefit of defences and immunities conferred by the bill of lading upon the carrier to independent contractors employed

---

383   Ibid., 605.
384   [2004] 1 AC 715.
385   *Whitesea Shipping,* (n380) 606.

by the carrier"; nor why in The Makhutai, where again the clause was similar but not identical, and where the issue was whether an exclusive jurisdiction clause was available for the benefit of the shipowner, the shipowner did not simply apply to strike out the claim as a whole. There it was this time Lord Goff of Chieveley who described the function of the Himalaya clause ([1996] CLC 799; [1996] AC 650 at 809F; 666G) as, "to prevent cargo owners from avoiding the contractual defences available to the carrier (typically the exceptions and limitations in the Hague-Visby Rules) by suing in tort persons who perform the contractual services on the carrier's behalf."[386]

His conclusion was that, "In my judgment, [the reasoning of the House of Lords] as to why, if the first part of the clause is a covenant not to sue (as it undoubtedly is in the present case), it inures only to the benefit of the contractual carrier and not third parties, remains compelling."[387]

Another point which required a solution was whether clause 3b was a contract of carriage within the meaning of article III rule 8.[388] To find an answer it requires an investigation as to the functions which the relevant third parties were performing actually. There was no doubt that all the third parties performed duties incidental to the actual carriage of goods. Flaux noted:

> Once it is seen that none of the third parties undertook the sea carriage or was in fact the carrier within the meaning of The Hague Rules (unlike the owners in The Starsin), the conclusion that the enforcement of the covenant not to sue is not contrary to Article III rule 8 is clearly correct.[389]

In the end the court stated that, "I consider that the Claimants have shown a sufficient practical interest, which is more than merely academic, in obtaining an injunction to restrain the

---

386   Ibid., 607, Quoting Coleman J.
387   Ibid., 609.
388   Ibid.
389   Ibid., 615.

insurer Defendants from breaching the covenant not to sue. "[390]

5.3   Conclusion

There is nothing new in the endeavour by contractual parties to limit their liabilities through exemption clauses. Since the 19th century exemption clauses were subject to the strict Privity of contract principle. Only parties to a contract could rely on the protection of the clause. However, during the 20th century a slow change has taken place where the Privity rule has been modified to take account in maritime adventures of commercial expectation. The benefits of the terms in the contract were made available to all those who are involved in the carriage of goods but are not parties to the contract expressed either in the Bill of lading or charter party.

Two issues became prominent; first claiming protection under the contractual clause and, secondly, protection under the principle of bailment on terms. *Elder Dempster* dealt with the issue of bailment terms and concluded that the exceptions and limitations of liability stipulated in the bill of lading protected the stevedores. This decision was much maligned and criticised. *Midland Silicones* reverted back to the Privity rule. Furthermore Fullager J in *Wilson v Darling Island Stevedoring and Lighterage Co Ltd*[391] noted " [*Elder Dempster* exhibits] a curious and seemingly irresistible anxiety to save grossly negligent people from the normal consequences of their negligence."[392] *Elder Dempster* was either referred to or followed or, until 1985, subject to derogatory remarks such as Donaldson J in *Johnson Matthey & Co Ltd v Constantine Terminals Ltd.*[393] where he noted that *Elder Dempster* was "something of a judicial nightmare"[394]

---

390   Ibid., 618.
391   (1956) 95 CLR 43.
392   Ibid., para 7.1.
393   [1976] 2 Lloyd's Rep. 215.
394   Ibid., 219.

and Ackner LJ in *the Forum Craftsman*[395] that the decision was "heavily comatose, if not long-interred."[396]

These comments obviously proved to be wrong as without doubt *Elder Dempster* can be regarded as the "legal spring" in the development of the Himalaya clause. *Midland Silicones* as noted above showed how the Privity rule can be overcome. Of great significance were the decisions in *the Eurymedon* in 1975 and *the New York Star* in 1981 which established the realisation that commercial reality reveals that the Privity rule is outdated and does not correspond to business practices in the shipping industry.

The *Mahkutai* firmly established that the Privity rule is no longer applicable but fell short of establishing a fully fleshed exception to the Privity rule. It was not necessary as the court had not heard full arguments on this point. The real importance of the *Mahkutai* lies in the fact that Lord Goff took the opportunity to conduct a detailed review of the development of *Himalaya* clauses as outlined above (although this was not strictly necessary to the decision), and to express the following opinion on the methods used by the courts to that date to circumvent problems of Privity of contract:

> Though these solutions are now perceived to be generally effective for their purpose, their technical nature is all too apparent; and the time may well come when, in an appropriate case, it will fall to be considered whether the Courts should take what may legitimately be perceived to be the final, and perhaps inevitable, step in this development, and recognise in these cases a fully-fledged exception to the doctrine of Privity of contract, thus escaping from all the technicalities with which the Courts are now faced in English law."[397]

It is now left to courts to interpret the exemption clauses in

---

395   [1985] 1 Lloyd's Rep. 291.
396   Ibid., 295.
397   Barnett, (n340) 180.

order to elicit the exact meaning of, and to what extent non-contractual parties are protected by, the Himalaya clause. This has been confirmed in the latest significant case namely, *Homburg Houtimport BV v Agrosin Ltd.*[398]

However, a second issue has also been discussed in connection with the embedding of a circular indemnity clause within the Himalaya clause. The circular indemnity clause, that is to indemnify the carrier against all consequences of breaking its undertaking not to sue such third parties, has been upheld in *The Elbe Maru.*[399] It was further tested in *The Starsin, Homburg Houtimport BV v Agrosin Ltd* and recently in *Whitesea Shipping and Trading Corp & Anor v El Paso Rio Clara Ltda & Ors.* The argument has been that the covenant not to sue runs contrary to Article III rule 8. However, as noted in *Whitesea Shipping and Trading Corp & Anor v El Paso Rio Clara Ltda & Ors.* none of the third parties undertook the sea carriage or was in fact the carrier within the meaning of The Hague Rules.

In summary, despite many "contradictory things were said in the judgments; the result of the cases is very largely consistent and the result of nearly all the cases is right."[400] In many of the earlier cases, such as *Adler v Dickson* and *Wilson v Darling Island*, the exemption clause was not drafted correctly to achieve the argued and desired outcome. However, once the Himalaya clause was further developed and the Privity rule was found to be inapplicable, the courts clearly gave effect to the exemption clause especially in *The Eurymedon, the New York Star* and the *Pioneer Container*.

In addition, *The Contracts (Rights of the Third Parties) Act* 1999 specifically section 1(6) makes the drafting of contract terms easier. The section states:

1.(6) Where a term of a contract excludes or limits liability in

---

398   [2004] 1 AC 715.
399   [1978] 1 Lloyd's Rep 206.
400   Furmston and Tolhurst, (n1) 157.

relation to any matter references in this Act to the third party enforcing the term shall be construed as references to his availing himself of the exclusion or limitation.

The point is that the Act does not take away any of the common law qualifications to Privity, however, case law in England arguably has turned the tide in relation to protection of non-parties. In England, the Himalaya clause has now taken on the role of a tested and approved principle in drafting and applying exemption clauses.

6

AUSTRALASIAN JURISPRUDENCE ON THE HIMALAYA CLAUSE

6.1 Introduction

Australia being a common law country also subscribed to the Privity of contract principle. However, a similar if somewhat different development took place. In the end, the Himalaya clause as developed in England took root and is finally entrenched in the Australian legal landscape. This Chapter will trace the Australian development of the Himalaya clause. In addition, two New Zealand cases are added as both countries have the same legal heritage.

The Australian Jurisprudence is significant insofar as the Privity rule was maintained longer than in the English context. Furthermore, even jurisprudence which was decided after the *Mahkutai* still persisted in relying on earlier case law. Of interest is that the Australian decision of the *New York Star* has been noted as an English development because the Australian High Court decision was overturned on appeal to the Privy Council. The dissenting view has been noted in Chapter 5.

Of interest is the fact that *Midland Silicones* features in most of the Australian jurisprudence despite the fact that it preceded *Adler*. The four criteria as set out by Lord Reid[401] did not only

---

401   Midland, (n244) 474.

prove to be the essential argument in the introduction of the Himalaya clause in *Adler* but also in the Australian development of the Himalaya clause.

Glimpses of protecting third parties to a contract can be observed in *Water Trading Co Ltd. v Dalgety & Co Ltd.*[402] *and Gilbert Stokes & Kerr Pty Ltd v Dalgety & Co Ltd*[403] but these cases were subsequently overruled by the High Court, hence did not create any lasting precedent.

In the Australian context, a further point needs to be noted. Australia ratified The Hague-Visby rules with a significant difference. The enabling legislation, in s 11 of COGSA, states that:

> (1) All parties to:
>
> (a) a sea carriage document relating to the carriage of goods from any place in <u>Australia</u> to any place outside <u>Australia</u>;
>
> are taken to have intended to contract according to the laws in force at the place of shipment.

It follows that shipments originating in Australia are governed by Australian law and any clauses to the contrary are void as s 11 is a mandatory law.

6.2 Jurisprudence

6.2.1 *Wilson v. Darling Island Stevedoring* [404]

The High Court on appeal from the Supreme Court of New South Wales held that the stevedores were not a party to the contract evidenced by the bill of lading. Therefore, the stevedores had no

---

402   (1951) 52 S.R. (N.S.W.) 4.
403   (1948) 48 S.R. (NSW) 435.
404   (1956) HCA8.

protection from the tortuous act of its servants.[405] The decision of the Supreme Court was reversed by the High Court. Arguably, therefore, this case can be considered to be the watershed between decisions supporting the privity rule and the emergence of the Himalaya clause on the Australian legal landscape.

The facts were that the plaintiff imported textiles from France to be transported to Sydney. The goods were off-loaded and handed over to a stevedoring firm. An employee handled a crane negligently and ruptured a water pipe. The result was that the textiles were damaged beyond any use. Clause 1 – the relevant clause in the contract - provides that:

> ... the carrier has no responsibility whatsoever for the goods ... subsequent to the discharge from the vessel. Goods in the custody of the carrier or his agents or servants before loading and after discharge whether being forwarded to or from the vessel or whether awaiting shipment, landed or stored ... are in such custody at the sole risk of the owners of the goods and the carrier shall not be liable for loss or damage arising or resulting from any cause whatsoever. [406]

Two questions were asked, first is the defendant entitled to the benefit of any protection or immunities afforded under the bill of lading as set out in clause 1. Secondly, if so does the bill of lading afford the defendant a valid defence to the claim of the plaintiff?

The parties agreed that:

> ... In the event of question 1 being answered in the negative judgment should be entered for the plaintiff ... (2) in the event of question 1 being answered in the affirmative and question 2 in the negative judgement should be entered for the plaintiff; and (3) in the event of both questions being answered in the affirmative, judgment should be entered for the defendant.[407]

---

405   Ibid., 43.
406   Ibid.
407   Ibid., 54.

The court noted that the proceedings were entered with the sole purpose of testing the decision in *Water Trading Co Ltd. v Dalgety & Co Ltd.*[408] In *Water Trading Co and Gilbert Stokes & Kerr Pty Ltd v Dalgety & Co Ltd*[409] the court extended the doctrine of immunity to stevedores.[410] However, both cases were overruled in *Wilson.*

Williams J in his dissenting judgment referred to *Elder Dempster* in a lengthy discussion. He noted that *Elder Dempster* is an example where the Privity rule was not followed as the court argued that under certain circumstances a person not being a party to a contract might take advantage of clauses in the Bill of lading. His Honour concluded that:

> ... the contract prescribes the conditions upon which the goods are placed in the possession of the carrier in order that he may perform the contract of carriage, that it is obvious that in order that he may perform that contract the carrier must employ servants, agents or independent contractors to carry out part of his duties, and that the true intent of the contract is that all persons engaged by the carrier to performs it should participate in the performance on the same bases as the carrier himself.[411]

Arguably, as the views of Williams J have been influenced by the decision in *Elder Dempster* it appears to foreshadow the future development of the Himalaya clause. His Honour – relying mainly on clause 1 – argued that the contract would only be completely performed by the delivery of the goods or by the defendant taking a step which the parties had agreed. Therefore, clause 1 was still operative and the defendant was protected. He specifically stated:

> The principle on which the Elder Dempster case, sup., was decided may be anomalous, but it would be even more

---

408   (1951) 52 S.R. (N.S.W.) 4.
409   (1948) 48 S.R. (NSW) 435.
410   *Wilson* (n404) 45.
411   Ibid., 60.

anomalous to stop short at that point. The principle, whether it should be placed on implied contract or bailment terms, the latter probably being the preferable view, must surely be that the contract prescribes the condition upon which the goods are placed in the possession of the carrier in order that he may perform the contract of carriage, that it is obvious that in order to perform that contract the carrier must employ servants, agents or independent contractors to carry out part of his duties, and that the true intent of the contract is that all persons engaged by the carrier to perform it should participate in the performance on the same basis as the carrier himself. None of these persons is in possession or custody of the gods as a bald bailee. They are handling goods which are being carried on certain terms and conditions intended to govern the performance of the contract. Provided what they do is done in the course of performing that contract, they are not liable in tort if any damage that the goods sustain, although due to their negligence, is damage which is immune from liability under the terms of the contract.[412]

Kitto J proposed that the key concept in this case was consent and not contract. He noted:

the absence of Privity of contract between A and C would be irrelevant. It is all a question of consent or no consent. What must be decided is whether it is the right conclusion from all the facts, including the presence of such exempting provisions as may be expressed or implied in any relevant agreements, whoever may be the parties to them, that the plaintiff consented to the defendant being absolved from the duty of care which is alleged as the foundation of the action.[413]

Fullagar J stated the majority judgment by indication that the defendant is prima facie liable in damages to the plaintiff.[414] A plain reading of clause 1 suggests that the defendant is not a

---

412   Ibid.
413   Ibid., 82-83.
414   Ibid., 66.

party to the contract and hence cannot take advantage of the exemption clause referring back to *Tweddle v Atkinson*.[415] His Honour referred briefly to *Adler v Dickson* where the view was expressed that, in some cases, there is the possibility that with little difficulty the inference can be made that a third party can take advantage of an exemption clause. Moving on to *Elder Dempster* his Honour noted:

> A conceivable ground of the decision in the *Elder Dempster Case* is that the master of the ship, although for many purposes the servant of the owners, took possession of the goods not on behalf of the owners but on behalf of the charterers. On this view, the owners would not be responsible for the negligent stowing and they would have no need to rely on the exception clause in the bill of lading.[416]

Fullager J agreed with the views of Lord Summer and noted that the *ratio decidendi* in *Elder Dempster* is:

> ... in the circumstances of this case the obligations to be inferred from the reception of the cargo for carriage to the United Kingdom amount to a bailment upon terms, which include the exceptions and limitations of liability stipulated in the known and contemplated form of bill of lading.[417]

Referring back to what Denning L.J. had to say in *Adler v Dickson* Fullager J agreed namely that a distinction needs to be drawn; if A stipulates with B that he will not be liable for the actions of his servants or agents, his servants and agents are not protected, but if A stipulates with B that neither he nor his servants or agents are not liable his servants and agents are protected.[418] It is interesting to note that his Honour commented on the burgeoning development of the Himalaya clause. First, he correctly stated that here is a conspicuous lack of unanimity

---

415   (1861) 1 B. & S. 393.
416   *Wilson v. Darling Island Stevedoring*, (n404) 68.
417   Ibid., 69.
418   Ibid., 70.

as to what the real principle in *Elder Dempster* really is. He agreed that the principle has been extended to give the stevedores exemptions from liability by virtue of the bill of lading to which the stevedore is not a party and this is a development of the common law which is out of character and the opposite one would feel to be justified. [419] He continued to comment that:

> ... we seem to discern .... a curious, and seemingly irresistible, anxiety to save grossly negligent people from the normal consequences of their negligence – an anxiety which refuses to be baulked even by so well-established a general doctrine as that of *Tweeedle v Atkinson.*[420]

Fullager J, however, agreed with the views expressed by Jenkins L.J in *Adler v Dickson* that nobody yet has succeeded in satisfactorily formulating any new Principles. He noted:

> In my opinion, what the *Elder Dempster Case* decided, and all that it decided, is that in such cases, the master having signed the bill of lading, the proper inference is that the shipowner, when he receives the goods into his possession, receives them on the terms of the bill of lading. The same inference might perhaps be drawn in some cases even if the charterer himself signed the bill of lading, but it is unnecessary to consider any such question.[421]

He in effect suggested that *Elder Dempster* has nothing whatsoever to do with the current case and stated:

> The stevedore is a complete stranger to the contract of carriage, and it is no concern of his whether there is a bill of lading or not, or, if there is, what are its terms. He is engaged by the shipowner and by nobody else, and the terms on which he handles the goods are to be found in his contract with the shipowner and nowhere else. The shipowner has no authority whatever to bind

---

419   Ibid.
420   Ibid., 71.
421   Ibid., 78.

the shipper or consignee of cargo by contract with the stevedore, and there is, in my opinion, no principle of law—deducible from the Elder Dempster Case or from any other case—which compels the inference of any contract between the shipper or consignee and the stevedore. If the stevedore negligently soaks cargo with water and ruins it, I can find neither rule of law nor contract to save him from the normal consequences of his tort.[422]

Kitto J and Taylor J in substance made similar arguments in allowing the appeal.

The conclusion which can be drawn is – given the time where *Adler v Dickson* has just been decided – that the effects of change have been noted by the High Court. However, the majority rejected the ratio in *Elder Dempster* and gave the exemption clause its natural meaning by drawing also on *Adler v Dickson*. Arguably, this case is a watershed in the development of exemption clauses in Australia. The High Court in effect was divided three ways in the analysis of the facts and specially Williams J argued in a way which was later proven as the correct analysis. Arguably. the ghost of the Privity rule was still in command but only just.

However, something needs to be said in relation to *Water Trading Co Ltd. v Dalgety & Co Ltd*[423] which was overruled. The facts of the two cases are substantially the same. The issue was the application of the principle as stated in *Elder Dempster*. The court concluded that:

> until delivery of the goods to the consignee, the contract evidenced by the bill of lading remained in force; and (2) that, until such delivery, the stevedoring contractor was, either as agent or bailee, entitled to the same protection under the bill of lading as was given to the shipping company, its servants and agents for the purpose of carrying out the contract.[424]

---

422   Ibid., 79.
423   (1951) 52 S.R. (N.S.W.) 4.
424   Ibid., 4.

Clause 3 was in the following terms:

> The responsibility of the carrier shall commence only when the tackle of the carrier's ship is hooked on to the cargo for loading and cease absolutely when such tackle is unhooked in the process of discharging. Goods in the custody of the carrier or his servants before loading and after discharge whether being forwarded to or from the ship or whether awaiting shipment, landed, or stored, or put in to hulk or craft belonging to the carrier or not, or pending transhipment at any stage of the whole transport are in such custody at the sole risk of the shipper and the carrier shall not be liable for loss or damage arising or resulting from any cause whatsoever.[425]

The difference between the two cases could arguably be the definition in clause 1(b) which notes that "shipper" included the "consignee."[426] However Street C.J. stated that:

> The contract to deliver was still on foot, being carried out at this stage by the defendant engaged by the shipping company for the purpose of performing that portion of the contract which required the goods to be delivered to the consignee or its order. To suggest that the consignee was expected to take delivery on the wharf as the tackle was unhooked is absurd ... It was obviously contemplated by the parties that the goods have to be removed and stored for a period before being delivered, and during that period the contract was still on foot and bound the parties with the same efficacy as it did when the goods were on the ship at sea.[427]

Owens J dismissed the argument of the defence that the stevedore was not an agent of the carrier and hence was not entitled to the benefits of the exemption. He noted "I am by no means convinced that, even if the defendant was not an "agent." of the carrier within the definition clause, it would necessarily follow

---

425   Ibid., 5.
426   Ibid.
427   Ibid., 6 – 7.

that, at the relevant time, there was, to use Lord Sumner's words (1): "any such bald bailment with unrestricted liability, or such tortuous handling entirely independent of contract, as would be necessary to support" the plaintiff's claim."[428] He held that the goods were not delivered "according to the exigency of the bills of lading by being placed in the hands of the landing agents, and it may be admitted that bills of lading cannot be said to be spent or exhausted until the goods covered by them are placed under the absolute dominion and control of the consignees."[429]

Herron J was of the same opinion and noted: "Whatever may be the precise legal ground on which the immunity of the agent can be supported, I base my decision here on the broad proposition stated by Viscount Cave in the *Elder Dempster* case."[430] Viewing the decisions through the rear vision mirror it is clear that as noted elsewhere *Elder Dempster* was confusing and left courts to find a ratio which was different. However, whatever has been said Elder *Dempster* still was important and changed the perception of dealing with a contractually unconnected third party and clearly the Privity doctrine was challenged by a commercially sound look at exemption clauses.

6.2.2 BHP v Hapag-Lloyd Aktiengesellschaft[431]

The facts are that BHP, as the shipper and consignee, contracted with the carrier to transport a grinding machine from Hamburg to Newcastle, New South Wales. This involved carriage by sea and land. In Sydney, a transport company, agents of the carrier, transported the machine to Newcastle. It was damaged on route as a result of negligence but not amounting to recklessness.

The term "Carriage" is of importance. It was defined in

---

428   Ibid., 9.
429   Ibid., 11.
430   Ibid., 15.
431   [1980] 2 NSWLR 572.

condition 1.as meaning "the whole of the operations and services undertaken by the carrier in respect of the goods". Clause 4 defined the right of sub-contracting and the relevant indemnity.

> (1) The Carrier shall be entitled to sub-contract on any terms the whole or any part of the Carriage.

> (2) The Merchant undertakes that no claim or allegation shall be made against any person whomsoever by whom the Carriage or any part of the Carriage is performed or undertaken (other than the Carrier) which imposes or attempts to impose upon any such person or any vessel owned by any such person any liability whatsoever in connection with the Goods whether or not arising out of negligence on the part of such person and if any such claim or allegation should nevertheless be made to indemnify the Carrier against all consequences thereof. Without prejudice to the foregoing every such person shall have the benefit of all provisions herein benefiting the Carrier and if such provisions were expressly for his benefit; and in entering into this contract, the Carrier, to the extent of these provisions, does so not only on his own behalf but also as agent and trustee for such persons."

> Clause 5,

> "Carrier's Responsibility", in so far as it dealt with combined transport, provided that, in a case where loss or damage to the cargo did not result from an act or omission of the carrier done with intent to cause damage wilfully or recklessly, compensation for loss or damage "shall in no circumstances whatsoever and howsoever arising exceed $US 2.50 per kilo of the gross weight of the goods lost or damaged".[432]

Yeldham J consulted many cases in regard to the authority of the court to grant injunctions and noted that the court did have a discretion to exercise that right specifically when dealing with a negative covenant. The court noted that this case is a commercial contract entered into by large commercial corporations, hence, it was argued that:

---

432   Ibid., 575-6.

> Plainly, as the plaintiff would know, rates of carriage and other commercial considerations between the carrier and companies such as the second defendants would be affected and influenced by the latter's knowledge of the presence in the bill of lading of a clause which purported to protect them from liability to consignors or consignees of cargo.[433] ... I see no reason why the plaintiff should not be held to its contractual undertaking, and every reason why it should comply with it. Commercial considerations involving each party to this action render it just that an undertaking not to claim, as set out in cl 4(2) of the bill of lading, should, prima facie, be enforced.[434]

Yeldham J referred to *The Elbe Maru* in his decision to grant the application.

6.2.3 Sydney Cooke Ltd v Hapag-Lloyd Aktiengesellschaft[435]

This case again was presided over by Yeldham J. The facts are sufficiently identical to *Broken Hill Proprietary Co Ltd v Hapag-Lloyd Aktiengesellschaft*. This case involved a printing machine which was damaged by stevedores. Not surprising the same clauses as in the *BHP* case also applied here.

Again, not surprisingly Yeldman J came to the same conclusion and he stated:

> In my opinion, the orders sought by the first defendant should be made for reasons similar to those which I expressed in my earlier decision to which I have adverted. No discretionary defences, other than the one to which I earlier referred, were raised. I order that the plaintiff's action against the second defendant be permanently stayed.[436]

In essence, a consistent jurisprudence is being created taking

---

433   Ibid., 583.
434   Ibid.
435   [1980] 2 NSWLR 587.
436   Ibid., 596.

note of the Himalaya clauses as propounded in English law.

6.2.4 Godina v. Patrick Operations Pty Ltd [437]

The stevedores had been the carrier's agent for ten years. In this instance, they had negligently allowed the plaintiffs' goods to be damaged. The New South Wales Supreme Court relied on the *New York Star* and applied the Himalaya Clause against the plaintiff, despite the fact that there was a paucity of evidence on the relationship between the carriers and the stevedores. The Bill of Lading contained the following clauses:

Clause 4(2)

The Merchant undertakes that no claim or allegation shall be made against any servant, agent or subcontractor of the Carrier which imposes or attempts to impose upon any of them or any vessel owned by any of them any liability whatsoever in connection with the Goods, and, if any such claim or allegation should nevertheless be made, to indemnify the Carrier against all consequences thereof. Without prejudice to the foregoing, every such servant, agent and sub-contractor shall have the benefit of all provisions were expressly for their benefit; and, in entering into this contract, the carrier, to the extent of those provisions, does so not only on its own behalf but also as agent and trustee for such servants, agents and sub-contractors.[438]

Clause 5(c)(2)(b)

… all liability whatsoever of the carrier shall in any event cease unless suit is brought within eleven months after delivery of Goods or the date when the Goods should have been delivered.[439]

Hutley J noted that the proceeding would fail if the stevedore cannot avail himself of the clause. The appellant argued that the delivery of the carrier was when the goods were unloaded hence

---

437   [1984] 1 Lloyd's Rep. 333.
438   Ibid., 334.
439   Ibid.

the exemption clause ends at that point as well. However, Hutley J followed the decision in the *New York Star* and noted that, "it is quite clear that mere delivery to the wharf does not mean that this contract is exhausted and the immunities with it. It is only if there has been delivery to the consignee that this happens"[440] The court in essence felt that the Himalaya clause is already an established law and hence an established system of doing business in which the carrier have authorised the stevedores to obtain immunity on their behalf.[441]

Hutley J specifically noted:

> As a matter of commercial practice, we are here concerned with an established system of doing business in which it can be taken, unless, I would have thought, the contrary is shown, both carriers and stevedores have fitted themselves in a manner by which an attempt will be made to confer immunity upon the stevedores in the bill of lading, and it can be taken that stevedores have authorized the carriers to endeavour to obtain immunity on their behalf.[442]

Furthermore, the presentation of the Bill of Lading which contained the exemption clauses to the stevedores who were expected to act upon its presentation was in the opinion of the court a ratification of the clauses by the consignee.[443]

6.2.5 *Darlington Futures Ltd v Delco Australia Proprietary Limited* [444]

This case is of importance in relation to exemption clauses, despite the fact that is does not relate to a shipping contract. The facts relate to a broker client relationship where the broker

---

440   Ibid., 335.
441   Ibid.
442   Ibid., 355.
443   Ibid., 336.
444   [1986] 161 C.L.R, 500.

entered into un-authorised dealings resulting in losses for the client. The crucial question was "whether cl. 6 and 7 protect the appellant from the consequences of what otherwise would be breaches of contract."[445] The two clauses in question stated:

6. ... The Client ..,. acknowledges that the Agent will not be responsible for any loss should the Client follow any of the Agent's trading recommendations or suggestions, nor for any loss, in the case of Discretionary Accounts, arising from trading by the Agent on behalf of the Client. The Client finally acknowledges that the Agent will not be responsible for any loss arising in any way out of any trading activity undertaken on behalf of the Client whether pursuant to this Agreement or not ...

7.... c) Any liability on the Agent's part or on the part of its servants or agents for damages for or in respect of any claim arising out of or in connection with the relationship established by this agreement or any conduct under it or any orders or instructions given to the Agent by the Client, other than any liability which is totally excluded by paragraphs (a) and (h) hereof, shall not in any event (and whether or not such liability results from or involves negligence) exceed one hundred dollars.[446]

The court examined case law on the issue of interpretation of exception clauses including Port *Jackson Stevedoring Pty. Ltd. v. Salmond & Spraggon (Aust.) Pty. Ltd.* The conclusion was that:

These decisions clearly establish that the interpretation of an exclusion clause is to be determined by construing the clause according to its natural and ordinary meaning, read in the light of the contract as a whole, thereby giving due weight to the context in which the clause appears including the nature and object of the contract, and, where appropriate, construing the clause contra proferentem in case of ambiguity ... the same

---

445   Ibid., 507.
446   Ibid., 500-501.

principle applies to the construction of limitation clauses.[447]

The court in the end read clause 7 as limiting the liability of the brokerage firm considering the important words "claims arising out of or in connexion with the relationship established by the agreement." [448] This is so as even an unauthorised transaction has a connection to the relationship and hence "a limitation clause may be so severe in its operation as to make its effect virtually indistinguishable from that of an exclusion clause."[449] Despite the fact that this case is not dealing with a Himalaya clause it nevertheless is instructive as it gives guidance as to the interpretation of exemption clauses and the Himalaya clauses are in effect nothing more than an exemption clause.

6.2.6   *Nissho Iwai Australia Ltd v Malaysian International Shipping Corporation, Berhad*[450]

Three years later a further case within the discussion of exemption clauses was decided where a stevedore was involved. The decision was reached without referring directly to Himalaya clauses. The facts are simple. "A goods container was stolen shortly after it had been discharged from a ship and placed in a stack at a terminal in Sydney. The container had been placed in the stack by a stevedoring firm engaged by the carrier."[451] The court referred to *Darlington Futures Ltd* in interpreting the relevant exemption clause. The relevant parts of clause 8 stated:

8(2) Under no circumstances shall the Carrier be liable or responsible in any capacity for or in respect of

(a) Any loss or damage to or in connection with Goods which arises or is due to any occurrence before such goods are received by

---

447   Ibid., 510.
448   Ibid., 511.
449   Ibid., 510.
450   (1989) 167 CLR 219.
451   Ibid., 219.

or on behalf of the Carrier at the place of receipt or after such Goods have been delivered or made available by or on behalf of the Carrier at the place of delivery.

(d) any loss or damage to or in connection with Goods arising or resulting at any time from fire not caused by the actual fault or Privity of the Carrier, ... or any cause or event which the Carrier could not avoid or the consequences of which the Carrier could not prevent by the exercise of reasonable diligence.

3.The Carrier shall not under any circumstances be liable or responsible in any capacity for or in respect of any non-delivery or misdelivery of Goods, delay, or loss or damage of any kind which arises out of or in connection with the carriage covered by this Bill of Lading or anything done or not done by the Carrier or any Carrier's employee to or in respect of Goods ...[452]

The carriage was also covered under The Hague-Visby Rules and the court noted that clause 8(2) of the contract in effect is identical to article Art. IV, par. 2(b)-(q) of the Hague Rules.[453] In interpreting clause 8 the court took note of *Darlington Futures Ltd. v. Delco Australia Pry. Ltd* by stating that a clause must be construed according to its natural and ordinary meaning.

The court, analysing clause 8, concluded:

The conditions upon which cl. 8(2)(d) operates are causal events which have the common characteristic that ordinarily they will occur without any fault on the part of the carrier. The event which gives rise to the operation of d. 8(2)(a) will also usually occur without any fault on the part of the carrier. Similarly, the events which give rise to the operation of cl. 8(2)(b) and (c) will often occur in circumstances where there has been no fault on the part of the carrier. The loss and damage in respect of which cl. 8(2) gives exemption, therefore, depend on events against the consequences of which a carrier might reasonably be expected to seek protection notwithstanding that those events

---

452   Ibid., 220.
453   Ibid., 226.

might cause the non-delivery of goods accepted by the carrier for transportation or forwarding to the place of delivery.[454]

The court consequently read the clauses in context and argued that the wording "loss or damage to or in connection with Goods" in clause 8(2)(d) should be read "as covering "loss caused by loss of goods""[455] The obvious conclusion in interpreting cl. 8(2) is that it exempted the carrier from loss or damage resulting from non-delivery of the goods.

The court in an obiter noted that the decision was based on clause 8(2)(d) and it was unnecessary to look also at clause 8(2)(a).

6.2.7 Glebe Island Terminals Pty Ltd v Continental Seagram Pry Ltd [456]

In this case the court did not refer to the seminal British cases at all except the *New York Star* but not the appeal which was heard in the Privy Council. This case is symptomatic of the Australian jurisprudence.

The facts are simple. Goods were stolen from the terminal in broad daylight before the consignee could take delivery. It was found that the employees of the terminal operator were involved in the theft of 830 cases of Scottish Whisky. The relevant clauses read as follows:

> Cl 4. ... The carrier shall not in any circumstances whatsoever be liable for any loss of or damage to the goods howsoever caused occurring ... after they were discharged at the oceans vessel's rail at the port of discharge...
>
> Cl 8. (3) The exemptions limitations terms and conditions in this bill of lading shall apply whether or not loss or damage

---

454   Ibid., 227-228.
455   Ibid., 229.
456   (1993) 40 NSWLR 206.

is caused by negligence or actions constituting fundamental breach of contract."

By cl 3(2), a Himalaya clause in the traditional sense noted that the exemptions were extended to any "servant, agent or sub-contractor of the carrier" by whom the carriage or any part of it was undertaken.[457]

Clause 4 alone would not have protected the terminal operator specifically in view of the obligations also contained in the Bill of lading that the carriage would be subject to the provisions of the carrier's applicable tariff which were deemed to be incorporated. Clause 5.3.2.1 of the tariff provided, as far as relevant:

> The Container/Goods will be released if the Bill of Lading and/or delivery/sub-delivery order is accompanied by a copy of the relevant Customs Entry endorsed by the Australian Customs Authority showing full description of the Goods.[458]

Allowing the delivery which took place without a presentation of a Bill of lading was prima facie a breach of cl 5.3.2.1 and a conversion for which the carrier and the terminal operator were legally responsible.[459] However taking cl 8(3) and 3(2) into consideration both the carrier and subcontractors are protected from breaching cl 5.3.2.1.

Handley JA carefully noted:

> [Cl 5.3.2.1] would impose no effective legal obligation on the carrier and would not form part of the contract or at best would be an illusory promise. This result and the corresponding immunities of the carrier and its subcontractors are so startling that it is necessary to examine the legal reasoning leading to such results with the greatest care.[460]

---

457   Ibid., 207.
458   Ibid., 210.
459   Ibid.
460   Ibid.

The starting point was considered to be *Darlington Futures Ltd v Delco Australia Pty Ltd*[461] and *Nissho Iwai Australia Ltd v Malaysian International Shipping Corporation, Berhad* .[462] The court in essence relied on *Darlington Futures*. Interestingly this case did not refer to any of the leading English cases relying instead on domestic construction of exemption clauses. Arguably therefore the court did not view a Himalaya clause as requiring different interpretation than any other exemption clause whether contained in a shipping case or any other actual issues such as futures trading or parking issues.

The court quoting *Darlington Futures* noted that:

> the interpretation of an exclusion clause is to be determined ... according to its natural and ordinary meaning, read in the light of the contract as a whole, thereby giving due weight to the context in which the clause appears including the nature and object of the contract, and where appropriate, construing the clause *contra proferentem* in case of ambiguity.[463]

The court in *Nissho* referring to *Darlington Futures* dealing with a similar issue of non-delivery stated that the interpretation and hence meaning of the clause "ultimately depends on its language, read in context, and not on any *a priori* notion that the non-delivery of goods was not intended to be protected."[464] The court at this stage noted that jurisprudence in relation to interpretation of exemption clauses in general need to be consulted. In effect the court treated the Himalaya clause as part of the general law of exemption clauses and not in a class of its own. The court looked at *Sydney City Council v West*[465] where a parking ticket stated: "The Council does not accept any responsibility for the loss (of) or damage to any vehicle ...

---

461   (1986) 161 CLR 500.
462   (1989) 167 CLR 219.
463   *Darlington Futures Ltd.* (n444) 510.
464   *Nissho Iwai Australia Ltd.* (n450) 227.
465   (1965) 114 CLR 481.

however such loss, damage ... may arise or be caused."[466] The ticket also noted that the ticket needs to be presented on leaving.

A thief drove the vehicle out of the parking lot without presenting the ticket. The court found that the clause did not protect the City council by stating that "in the absence of express words or necessary intendment it would be going too far to construe the clause as excusing loss by miss-delivery or delivery to an unauthorised person."[467] This statement of construction was supported by Lord Denning in the decision of the Privy Council in *Sze Hai Tong Bank Ltd v Rambler Cycle Co Ltd*.[468]

> There is therefore an implied limitation on the clause which cuts down the extreme width of it: and as a matter of construction their Lordships decline to attribute to it the unreasonable effect contended for. ... If such an extreme width were given to the exemption clause it would run counter to the main object and intent of the contract. ... It would defeat this object entirely if a shipping company was at liberty, at its own will and pleasure, to deliver the goods ... to someone not entitled at all, without being liable for the consequences. The clause must therefore be limited and modified to the extent necessary to enable effect to be given to the main object and intent of the contract.[469]

The court after consulting several other judgements firmly returned to the view as expressed in *Darlington Futures* namely:

> construing the (exclusion) clause according to its natural and ordinary meaning, read in the light of the contract as a whole, thereby giving due weight to the context in which the clause appears including the nature and object of the contract, and, where appropriate, construing the clause *contra proferentem* in case of ambiguity.[470]

Sheller JA in his judgement noted, after considering the

---

466   *Glebe Island Terminals Pty Ltd.* (n456) 211.
467   *Sydney City Council* (n465) 490.
468   [1959] AC 576.
469   Ibid., 586-587.
470   *Darlington Futures Ltd.* (n444) 510.

exemption clauses and relying on *Darlington Futures* that:

> The determination of whether or not a carrier or bailee is dealing
> with the goods in a way that can be regarded as in intended
> performance of his contractual obligation or in a way that is
> quite alien to his contract, and of whether, having concluded
> that the latter is the appropriate categorisation, even so the
> language of the exemption clause, read naturally, will extend to
> it, may present great difficulty.[471]

The point Sheller JA was making is that the words in the relevant
clause must convey a particular event or intended performance.
If the intended performance includes the actual claim as in this
case, a delivery to a thief, the question is whether the words used
in the Himalaya clause includes the actual event. He contrasted
Sydney City Council with *Nissho.* In *Nissho,* the court stated that
clause 8(2) was wide enough to protect the subcontractor:

> It is difficult to understand, therefore, why the parties would
> have intended that the carrier's exemption from liability
> should be confined to partial loss of or damage to goods ... In
> the circumstances of this case, the main object of the contract
> provides no ground for concluding that non-delivery of the
> goods was outside the protection of cl 8(2).[472]

In *Sydney Council*, the point was made that the clause contained
an important part namely that;

> [it is] implied from this provision which was pleaded, in the
> statement of claim, as an undertaking that "the said motor car
> could not and would not be obtained or removed from the
> parking station without presentation of the parking check at
> the office and the obtaining in exchange therefore of a delivery
> ticket.[473]

Sheller JA – taking the above judgements into consideration
posed three questions:

---

471   *Glebe Island Terminals* (n456) 232.
472   *Nissho Iwai Australia Ltd.* (n450) 223.
473   *Sydney City Council* (n453) 653.

1. Did the bill of lading with the incorporated tariff expressly or by implication impose upon the carrier a duty only to deliver in exchange for the bill of lading?

2. Was there a delivery of the containers and if so was it unauthorised in the sense that a person for whom the carrier, or Glebe Island, or both, were responsible permitted the goods to be handed over to a person who did not produce a bill of lading?

3. If the answer to these questions is yes, and accordingly there was a breach of the special undertaking, can the exemption be construed as extending to a breach of this special undertaking?[474]

As far as question 1 is concerned the important point is whether the goods have been delivered or not. It is well established that, if a carrier delivers goods without a bill of lading which is negotiable, he must suffer the consequences. Simply put, "To do so deliberately is prima facie conversion of the goods. To do so negligently is a breach of contract."[475] In the absence of an exemption clause the court would need to conclude that Continental is authorised to sue for conversion. Sheller JA concluded that:

> ... the actions of the employee or employees of Glebe Island were in fundamental breach of the contract evidenced by the bill of lading. The terms of cl 8(3) are plain. Notwithstanding the loss was so caused, the exemption clauses, and particularly cl 4, apply. That being so, in my opinion, Continental's claim against ABC is defeated.[476]

Continental did also attempt to sue Glebe Island and the question is whether Glebe Island can take advantage of the exemption clause.

As noted above in point 2 the issue was at what time the goods

---

474   *Glebe Island Terminals Pty Ltd.* (n456) 237.
475   Ibid., 238.
476   Ibid., 240.

were delivered. The court stated that the goods were stolen before they could be delivered pursuant to the clauses in the Bill of Lading.

> In my opinion, on no basis could it be said that before the time the containers were stolen they had been, pursuant to the contract of carriage, delivered to Continental. Until that point of time, the obligation of ABC to deliver remained unperformed and the carriage on foot. It is unreal to suggest that Glebe Island was employed other than to perform or undertake part of "the carriage" which is defined as meaning "the whole of the operations and services undertaken by the carrier in respect of the goods". In my opinion Glebe Island was clearly entitled to rely upon the exemption clauses and accordingly the claim of Continental against it also failed.[477]

In the end, the court came to the conclusion that "The terminal operator was entitled by operation of cl 3(2) to rely on the exemption clauses as it was sub-contracted to undertake part of the carriage, which at the time of the theft was still on foot as the obligation to deliver to the consignee remained unperformed".[478]

6.2.8 Chapman Marine Pty Ltd v Wilhelmsen Lines A/S.[479]

The facts are that the plaintiff (Chapman) bought a cruiser from Wellcraft International in Texas. The cruiser had to be shipped to Sydney and was to be delivered by the seller to the first defendant, the carrier (Wilhelmsen). When the cruiser arrived in Sydney – in a state which amounted to a constructive total loss – the claimant sued the carrier as well as the stevedore (second defendant, Conaust Ltd).

The carriage was regulated by the Carriage of Goods by Sea Act 1936 of the United States of America ("COGSA"). The

---

477   Ibid., 241.
478   Ibid., 207.
479   [1999] FCA 178.

carrier relied on the limitation provision within COGSA. There was also a dispute as to the position of the cruiser. The shipper argued that the cruiser should have been stowed below deck whereas the carrier argued that the bill of lading contained an express provision permitting stowage of a "yacht" on deck.

The stevedore also argued that they can rely on the limitation clause as the bill of lading contained a Himalaya clause which reads in the relevant parts as follows:

> "6(c) ... every such person by whom the whole or any part of this contract is performed or undertaken, including but not limited to underlying carriers, stevedores, terminal operators, subcontractors and independent contractors shall have the benefit of every exemption, limitation, condition and liberty herein contained and of every right exemption from liability, defence and immunity of whatsoever nature applicable to [Wilhelmsen]..."[480]

Furthermore, the carrier sought to restrain the shipper from suing the stevedores as the bill of lading contained the following circular indemnity clause:

> "6(b) ... no claim or allegation shall be made against any person other than [Wilhelmsen] (whomsoever by whom the Carriage or any part of the Carriage was performed or undertaken) which claim imposes or attempts to impose upon any such person... any liability whatsoever in connection with the goods or the Carriage of the Goods, whether or not arising out of negligence on the part of such person."[481]

Alternatively, Wilhelmsen relied on the following provision:

> "6 (e) The Merchant further undertakes that no claim or allegation in respect of Goods shall be made against [Wilhelmsen] by any person other than in accordance with the terms and conditions of this bill of lading which imposes or attempts to impose

---

480   Ibid., para 28.
481   Ibid., 29.

upon [Wilhelmsen] any liability whatsoever in connection with the Goods or the carrying of Goods... and if any such claim or allegation should nevertheless be made to indemnify [Wilhelmsen] against all consequences thereof."[482]

Emmett J considered that the carrier was in breach of s3(2) of COGSA that it would "properly and carefully load, handle, stow, carry, keep, care for and discharge the goods carried". The employee of the carrier warned the stevedores that they needed to be careful in relation to unloading of containers near the cruiser. However, the fact that the cruiser was damaged by the stevedores' negligence is proven. It follows that:

> Conaust was also under an obligation to Wilhelmsen to take care in those operations. I consider that the striking of the Cruiser was a breach of duty by Conaust. As a consequence, Chapman suffered loss and damage. As an additional consequence, Wilhelmsen suffered loss in the form of its liability to Chapman. Accordingly, subject to the limitation provisions and the Himalaya clause, both Conaust and Wilhelmsen would be liable for the loss suffered by Chapman. Subject to any question of contributory negligence, Conaust would be liable to indemnify Wilhelmsen in respect of Wilhelmsen's liability to Chapman.[483]

In essence, the sum of damages which can be claimed is subject to the interpretation of the Himalaya clause. There are two issues which needed to be resolved. If the stevedores are persons who undertake the whole or any part of the contract they would be protected by the Himalaya clause as noted in *Port Jackson Stevedoring Pty Ltd v Salmond & Spraggon (Australia) Pty Ltd*.[484] The stevedore obviously was not undertaking the whole of the carriage.

If the stevedore only performs a part of the carriage, the shipper is in breach of its undertaking contained in clause 6(b) of the

---

482   Ibid., para 29.
483   Ibid., para 33.
484   (1978) 139 CLR 231.

Bill of Lading in making and prosecuting its claim against the stevedores. Further, in that case, the shipper would also be in breach of its undertaking given in clause 6(e) that no person would make a claim or allegation which imposes or attempts to impose upon the carrier any liability in connection with the carrying of the Cruiser.[485]

The shipper also argued that the terms contained in the Himalaya clause were in breach of s3(8) of COGSA which reads as follows:

> "Any clause, covenant, or agreement in a contract of carriage relieving the carrier or the ship from liability for loss or damage to or in connection with the goods, arising from negligence, fault, or failure in the duties and obligations provided in this section, or lessening such liability otherwise than as provided in this chapter, shall be null and void and of no effect. A benefit of insurance in favour of the carrier, or similar clause, shall be deemed to be a clause relieving the carrier from liability. 46 US Code Appendix 1303."[486]

However, Emmett J ruled that this issue was resolved in *Sidney Cooke Ltd v Hapag-Lloyd Aktiengesellschaft*[487] where Yeldham J had decided that the subcontractor was not a carrier for the purpose of COGSA. He furthermore ruled that a grant of stay was warranted by relying on *Broken Hill Proprietary Co Ltd v Hapag-Lloyd Aktiengesellschaft.*[488] In order to prevent a circuit of action pursuant to clause 6(e) the court relied on *The Elbe Maru.*

Emmet J significantly commented that:

> It is commercially unrealistic to expect that, in the international carriage of goods by sea, a carrier will itself perform all of the activities concerned with the carriage. It could not be suggested that a consignor or merchant would enter into a contract of

---

485   *Chapman Marine Pty Ltd. (n479)* para 50.
486   Ibid., para 62.
487   [1980] 2 NSWLR 587 at 594B - 595C.
488   [1980] 2 NSWLR 572 at 578G, 581G and 583F-G.

carriage with such an expectation. Rather, the scheme of cl6 of the Bill of Lading is clearly to ensure that all subcontractors are treated as being under the single umbrella of the carrier. Its commercial object is clear, and in my view, should be given effect.[489]

The result is that the claim was stayed, and that the shipper can only claim $US500 pursuant to package limitations.

6.2.9 Toll (FGCT) Pty Limited v Alphapharm Pty Limited [490]

This case is not directly relevant to shipping contracts, however, it sheds light on the relationship between agent and principal. Clause 6 was the relevant clause which reads:

> Clause 6
>
> Notwithstanding any other clause of this Contract . . . under no circumstances shall the Carrier be responsible to the Customer for any injurious act or default of the Carrier, nor, in any event, shall the Carrier be held responsible for any loss, injury or damage suffered by the Customer either in respect of: (a) the theft, misdelivery, delay in delivery, loss, damage or destruction, by whatever cause, of any goods being carried or stored on behalf of the Customer by the Carrier at any time (and regardless of whether there has been any deviation from any agreed or customary route of carriage or place of storage) . . . ; (b) any consequential loss of profit, revenue, business, contracts or anticipated savings; or (c) any other indirect consequential or special loss, injury or damage of any nature and whether in contract, tort (including without limitation, negligence or breach of statutory duty) or otherwise. In this clause . . . 'Customer' includes the Customer's Associates.[491]

---

489   *Chapman Marine Pty Ltd.* (n479) para 67.
490   [2004] 219 CLR 167.
491   Ibid., 174.

The court looked for assistance to similar issues as found in shipping contracts, namely in Himalaya clauses. The important passage in relation to the application of the Himalaya clause reads as follows:

> The use of the concept of agency as a method of overcoming the requirements of Privity in a commercial context such as the present was suggested by Lord Reid in *Midland Silicones Ltd v Scruttons Ltd*, and taken up in *New Zealand Shipping Co Ltd v A M Satterthwaite & Co Ltd*, and *Port Jackson Stevedoring Pty Ltd v Salmond & Spraggon (Australia) Pty Ltd* . .. In the case of a stevedore seeking the benefit of a Himalaya clause, courts have been ready to conclude that the carrier was acting with the stevedore's authority.[492]

The court found that the respondent, Alphapharm Pty Ltd. was bound by clause 6 and hence the appellant was exempt from liability against Alphapharm's claim under clause 6.

6.2.10 Nudrill Pty Ltd v LaRosa [No 3][493]

Keen DCJ delivered the judgment in a case which revolved around bailment and, of course, whether third parties are protected by exemption clauses by implication of terms. The court noted that this issue was dealt with in *Scruttons Ltd v Midland Silicones Ltd*[494] but stated that, "There have been inroads into the strict confines of the protection laid down in *Midland Silicones*" specifically in the *Eurymedon*.[495] The court did not explore more recent decisions and simply noted that, "By reason of the finding that I make in this matter it is not necessary for me to descend into those arguments but to adopt so far as it is necessary the criteria laid down in *Midland Silicones*."[496]

---

492   Ibid., 193.
493   [2011] WADC 178.
494   [1962] AC 446.
495   *Nudrill Pty Ltd.* [No 3] (n 493) para 132.
496   Ibid., para 136.

6.3 New Zealand Judgments

For the sake of comprehensiveness, two New Zealand judgments are added to the Australian developments. Despite the fact that all exports have to be carried by sea most contracts dealing with New Zealand shipping are not governed by New Zealand law and hence a shortage of New Zealand judgements is evident. However, one early judgement is interesting as it was handed down in 1975 before the Himalaya clause was fully developed but was already noted in seminal judgments. The second judgment was decided after the Himalaya clauses were well established in England.

6.3.1 *Herrick v. Leonard and Dingley Ltd and Another* (third parties)[497]

The plaintiff sued the stevedore for negligently damaging his motor car while unloading it from the vessel. The plaintiff concluded a contract with the charterer of the ship. An automobile carriage contract was drawn up but never signed by the plaintiff. The contract on the reverse side contained clauses exempting the carrier from all liabilities for loss or damage to the motorcar including negligence from loading to unloading. (which included the carrier as well as the charterer).

In addition, the carrier made the same terms and conditions for itself on behalf of those who might be his servants or agents.

The first issue - the court resolved - was the fact that the plaintiff, though in possession of a copy of the contract of carriage never signed it. The court held that despite the fact the contract was not signed it nevertheless was impliedly adopted.

Of importance is the legal relationship between the stevedore and the plaintiff. It was factually proven that the stevedore was

---

497   (1975) 2 NZLR 566.

negligent. The contractual terms as relevant to this case were:

> 7.The carrier shall be exempt from all liability for loss of or damage to the car of whatsoever nature of form whatsoever cause arising including negligence which may occur at any time from the period of loading until (and including) the unloading of the car.

> 9. The carrier is not liable for loss of or damage to lose parts of equipment or personal property left in the vehicle. The carrier is to have the right to move the vehicle at the owner's risk and expense whenever it becomes necessary.

> 13. The carrier in making these terms and conditions does so for itself and on behalf of those who may be his agents and servants from time to time and all such persons shall be deemed to be parties to the contract in respect of all the exemptions from liability contained herein.[498]

McMullin J correctly noted that the stevedore cannot rely on clause 7 or 9 as he is not a party to the contractual clauses only the carrier and the charterer are bound to these terms. The defendant relied then on clause 13 and the court asked the question whether the stevedore was an agent or servant pursuant to clause 13. The court relied on *Midland Silicones Ltd v Scruttons Ltd* where two propositions were advanced, first the Privity rule applies and secondly that the principal argument was that the stevedore should have the benefit of the immunity despite the fact that he is not a party to the contract. McMullin J stated that, "Lord Reid held it to be firmly established that a stranger to a contract could not, in a question with either of the contracting parties, take advantage of the provisions of the contract."[499] The court also refereed to *Dunlop Pneumatic, Elder Dempster* and *Wilson v Darling Island Stevedoring and Lighterage.*

The court moved the discussion onto the newest case (in 1975) namely *The Eurymedon* noting that:

---

498   Ibid., 571.
499   Ibid., 573.

> [Council for the defendant] has asked me to treat New *Zealand Shipping company Ltd v A. M Satterthwaite & Co.* Ltd as being an acceptance by the majority of the Judicial Committee of the minority judgment of Lord Denning in *Midland Silicones v Scruttons Ltd.* If I were to do this, then it seems to me that it would be saying that the four propositions enunciated by Lord Reid were no longer to be regarded as definitive of the exceptions to the general rule principle that a contract between two parties cannot be sued on by a third person. There appears to be nothing in the opinions delivered in [The Eurymedon] which would suggest that Lord Reid's four propositions are less valid today.[500]

Lord Reid's propositions were not featuring prominently in *The Eurymedon*. Arguably, therefore, referring to the decision in *The Eurymedon* would have been more appropriate as it was the (then) current thought of the Privy Council. This is specifically so as the Privy Council overturned the original decision. In the end, the court noted that there is nothing in the Automobile contract suggesting that the stevedore is able to rely on the terms. In effect, the contract is "completely silent on the position of the stevedore."[501] They found for the plaintiff.

The interesting point in this case is the perception of the court in analysing the three seminal cases preceding this one. It needs to be remembered that, at that time, the Highest Court in the New Zealand Hierarchy was still the Privy Council in England and hence the quoted cases were treated as precedent. It is only speculative to ask why McMullin J did not take more notice of the important passage in the discussion in *The Eurymedon* which was decided before this case was argued. The passage notes:

> In so concluding I must not be taken to be doubting that a suitably drawn instrument could bring a consignor and a stevedore into a relationship of obligation and meet Lord Reid's five conditions

---

500   Ibid., 574.
501   Ibid., 575.

in such a way that a stevedore could claim the benefit of an exemption clause even against a consignee. In this connection, I note that the clause instantly in question appeared in bills of lading before the Midland Silicones case and was not drawn in the light of that case. Alternatively, no doubt, exemption could in practice be secured by a suitably drawn indemnity clause. Finally, there seems no reason to question that, as Turner P. thought, a bill of lading could, if appropriately drafted, contain an offer giving rise to a unilateral contract with a stevedore.[502]

It is true to say that the exemption clause was not written in a manner which made it easy for the court to accept that an unconnected third party is covered by the clause. If the court would have looked at clause 9 where the carrier has the right to move the vehicle "whenever it becomes necessary" it can be suggested that the carrier has done exactly that. It contracted the stevedore to do so on his behalf. This arguably could enliven clause 13. The fact that an independent contractor is not mentioned in clause 13 is correct and indeed the stevedore is an independent contractor but at the same time it can be implied that the plaintiff was aware - and it makes commercial sense – that the car needs to be moved from the deck of the vessel to shore and that the carrier needs to contract that task out. Arguably - and the court has taken the view – that the stevedore is not a servant nor an agent of the carrier hence he is not explicitly included in clause 13. It is argued that both arguments in relation to the point of the stevedore in clause 13 are strained.

6.3.2 Air New Zealand Ltd v The Ship "Contship America" [503]

Containers of goods were washed overboard while in transit from Europe to New Zealand. The plaintiff argued that the defendants were bailees and or alternatively acted negligently. The court

---

502   New Zealand Shipping v Satterthwaite Ltd [1974] *International Commercial Law Review*, 02/25, para 68. http://www.nadr.co.uk/articles/published/ CommercialLawReports/Eurymedon%201974.pdf.

503   [1992] 1 NZLR, 425.

relied on the leading English and Australian cases in relation to Himalaya clauses. The issue was whether the arbitration clause binding the shipowner was valid.

Greig J. noted the principle as expressed by Lord Wilberforce in *New Zealand Shipping Co Ltd* as being a general proposition that a contract between two parties cannot be sued upon by a person even though the contract is expressed to be for his benefit. [504] He went on to state:

> There is however, the possibility in any particular case that a stranger may have the benefit of exemptions and limitations and presumably other provisions in a contract if that is to give effect to the clear intentions of a commercial document. The way in which that can be done is in accordance with the requisites set out by Lord Reid in his speech in *Midland Silicones* which was expressly approved by the majority in the *New Zealand Shipping case* and applied to the stevedores there.[505]

The court examined the four pre-requisites of Lord Reid and came to the conclusion that a carrier is defined exclusively and does not extend to a shipowner and furthermore s 20 does not suggest that the carrier was acting as agent on behalf of anybody else.[506] Furthermore s 21 which is similar to a Himalaya clause again does not name the shipowner as falling under the protection and, hence, the benefits are not extended beyond the parties to the contract. Simply put the court found that:

> There was no particular exception in a contract for carriage by sea, available for all persons including stevedores and other independent contractors, from the fundamental rule that third parties are not entitled to the benefit of a contract. [507]

The claim of the defendant therefore failed. [508]

---

504   Ibid., 433.
505   Ibid., 433.
506   Ibid., 433.
507   Ibid., 425.
508   Ibid., 434.

It appears that New Zealand courts were not as willing as the English courts to depart definitively from the Privity principle. Lord Reid's' pre-requisites have been mentioned in later judgments but in a "sanitised form" in order to assist in the development of the Himalaya clause. This has not happened in the later New Zealand case.

6.4 Conclusion

As a general comment, it can be observed that Australian courts were less willing to embrace the change from the Privity rule to the Himalaya clause in the interpretation of exemption clauses. However, the problem was partially resolved in the revision in the Australian Carriage of Goods by Sea Act 1991. The relevant change was embedded in Article 4bis(2) which states:

> ARTICLE 4 bis
>
> **2.** If such an action is brought against a servant or agent of the carrier (such servant or agent not being an independent contractor), such servant or agent shall be entitled to avail himself of the defences and limits of liability which the carrier is entitled to invoke under this Convention.

A limitation on the protection has been placed in Article 4bis(4)

> **4.** Nevertheless, a servant or agent of the carrier shall not be entitled to avail himself of the provisions of this Article, if it is proved that the damage resulted from an act or omission of the servant or agent done with intent to cause damage or recklessly and with knowledge that damage would probably result.[509]

In effect, the Himalaya clause is still of importance as far as any independent contractors are concerned as well as servants or agents as Article 4(4) restricts their cover under COGSA.

What can be said is that the Australian case law indicates that

---

509   http://www5.austlii.edu.au/au/legis/cth/consol_act/cogbsa1991196/sch1a.html.

the judiciary did not refer extensively to English jurisprudence. Arguably the judiciary was aware that the Australian decision in *Port Jackson Stevedoring Pty Ltd v Salmond & Spraggon (Australia) Pty Ltd* (The New York Star) was overturned on appeal in England in 1981. Arguably, the reversal did not appear to greatly influence the Australian courts. In essence, the courts did take note of the demise of the Privity rule but as far as the application of the Himalaya clause was concerned, they attempted to find their own solutions to the application and interpretation of exemption clauses.

7

UNITED STATES JURISPRUDENCE ON THE HIMALAYA CLAUSE

7.1 Introduction

The United States development is not dissimilar to the English one with the exception that the initial changes to the Privity rule were introduced earlier than in England. Arguably, therefore, at least the earlier developments in the United States were independent of those generated in England, but in the end both converged and the Himalaya clause is now applied in the same way in both countries. In this Chapter, selected cases are analysed in order to follow the development of the Himalaya clause in the United States.

In order to understand the United States development, pre-1959 jurisprudence needs to be considered. As early as 1859 in *Lawrence v. Fox* [510] the court did not follow *Tweddle v. Atkinson*[511] as the court found that contractual terms can benefit a third party despite the lack of consideration. The crucial point is that a clear intention that a third party can benefit from the contract has to be clearly expressed.

---

510   (1859) 20 N.Y. 268 (N.Y. C.A.).
511   (1861) 1 B. & S. 393, 121 E.R. 762.

184

Early American judgments extended bill of lading exceptions even where the bill of lading clauses in question were far from specific. Thus, in *National Federation of Coffee Growers of Columbia v. Isbrandtsen Co*[512] the limitation period was extended to the defendant without much analysis. The court accepted that the plaintiff was an agent of the carrier relying on *Collins & Co. v. Panama R. Co.* [513]

A.M. Collins & Co. v. Panama Railroad Co[514] - a seminal case – should be briefly mentioned as it was the accepted law before it was overruled by *Herd & Co. v. Krawill Machinery Corp.*

The facts were that the stevedore damaged goods during unloading and claimed the carrier's limitation pursuant to The Hague-Visby rules. The bill of lading did not include a Himalaya clause and the court noted that the stevedore was not a party to the contract contained in the bill of lading.[515] Interestingly, the court held that the bill of lading governed every step of the maritime adventure including the unloading and in addition it did not matter whether the carrier or a third party undertook the unloading.[516] The stevedore was successful in claiming protection under The Hague Rules section 4(5) because the court showed deference to the agency theory and hence Railroad Co. was the "alter ego" of the carrier. Several courts followed *Collins* during the mid-fifties until the *Krawill* decision overruled it only for the pendulum to swing back again.

In addition to the jurisprudence and unlike anywhere else the question of party intention had been noted in the Restatement (Second) of 1981. These statements are not binding on courts but are treated as guidelines and judicial opinions on a subject matter.

---

512   17 Misc.2d 113, 185 N.Y.S.2d 392.
513   5 Cir., 197 F.2d 839.
514   197 F.2d 893 (5th Cir.), cert. denied, 344 U.S. 875 (1952).
515   Ibid., 895.
516   Ibid., 896-97.

The *Restatement (Second) Contracts 1981* in s 302 (not part of the UCC) states:

(1) Unless otherwise agreed between promisor and promisee, a beneficiary of a promise is an intended beneficiary if recognition of a right to performance in the benefitiary is appropriate to effectuate the intention of the parties and either

(a) the performance of the promise will satisfy an obligation of the promisee to pay, money to the beneficiary; or

(b) the circumstances indicate that the promisee intends to give the beneficiary the benefit of the promised performance.

(2) An incidental beneficiary is a beneficiary who is not an intended beneficiary

The jurisprudence post 1959 is analysed using the available court reports which on occasions are not very extensive.

A change in dealing with exemption clauses came in 1959 with the decision of the Federal Court in *Herd & Co. v. Krawill Machinery Corp*. The facts in *Wilson v Darling Island Stevedoring and Lighterage Co Ltd.* are very similar with the US case under discussion.

This case proved to be the pivotal point in the United States in the development of the Himalaya clause.

7.2   Jurisprudence

7.2.1 Herd & Co. v. Krawill Machinery Corp [517]

The petitioner in this case was an independent stevedoring company who was orally engaged by the carrier to load the cargo on board of the vessel. Through their negligence they dropped a machine and caused extensive damage. They denied

---

517   359 U.S. 297, 79 S.Ct. 766 (1959).

the allegations of negligence and also contended that they were covered by the terms in the bill of lading and the limitations of liability provisions in the Carriage of Goods by Sea Act limiting the liability to $500.

The relevant exemption clause in ss30 and 37 in the bill of lading provided as far as pertinent:

s30.

In consideration of a choice of freight rates having been offered to the shipper by the Carrier, it is agreed that in case of loss of, or damage to * * * goods of an actual value exceeding $500 * * * per package * * * the value of such goods, shall be deemed to be $500 per package * * * and the Carrier's liability, if any, shall be determined on the basis of a value of $500 per package * * * unless the nature of such goods and a value higher than $500 per package * * * shall have been declared in writing by the shipper upon delivery to the Carrier and noted on the face hereof and unless payment of the extra freight charge incident thereto shall have been made or promised * * *, in which case such declared value, or the actual value if less, shall be the basis for computing damages and any partial loss or damage shall be adjusted pro rata. * * *'

s37.

This bill of lading shall have effect subject to the Carriage of Goods by Sea Act of the U.S.A. and the Carrier the ship shall be entitled to all of the rights and immunities set forth in said Act.'[518]

The court held that the stevedores were not protected neither by the Carriage of Goods by Sea Act nor the clause in the bill of lading.

The stevedores first argued that both the provisions of the bill of lading and the Carriage of Goods by Sea Act should be construed to limit its liability a well as that of the carrier. Secondly. if

---

518   Ibid., 768.

only the carrier is protected, it is also protected by the majority decision in *A. M. Collins & Co. v. Panama R. Co.* [519]

As to the first contention the court looked first at the relevant provisions of the Carriage of Goods by Sea Act specifically ss 1300 – 1315. The court found that the Act "says that 'neither the carrier nor the ship' shall be liable for more than $500 per package. s 1304(5). It makes no reference whatever to stevedores or agents."[520]

The court commented in detail on the text of The Hague rules as they were adopted in COGSA.

> The debates and Committee Reports in the Senate and the House upon the bill that became the Carriage of Goods by Sea Act like wise do not mention stevedores or agents. There is, thus, nothing in the language, the legislative history or environment of the act that expressly or impliedly indicates any intention of Congress to regulate stevedores or other agent of a carrier, or to limit the amount of their liability for damages caused by their negligence. [521]

The next step was to examine the limiting provisions in the bill of lading. The court came to the same conclusion when looking at the exemption clause in the bill of lading.

As to the second contention the court turned its attention to the majority decision in the *Collins* case. The premise of that court was that:

> all agents of the carrier who perform any part of the work undertaken by the carrier in the contract of carriage, evidenced by the bill of lading, are, by reason of that fact alone, protected by the provisions of the contract limiting the liability of the carrier, though such agents are not parties to nor express beneficiaries of the contract.[522]

---

519   197 F.2d 893.
520   *Herd & Co.* (n 517) 769.
521   Ibid., 883.
522   Ibid., 770.

In addition, in *Collins* the view was further expressed that:

> A stevedore so unloading, in every practical sense, does so by virtue of the bill of lading and, though not strictly speaking a party thereto, is, while liable as an agent for its own negligence, at the same time entitled to claim the limitation of liability provided by the bill of lading to the furtherance of the terms of which its operations are directed.[523]

The court in *Herd* disagreed with that conclusion and noted that "an agent is responsible for his own act, to the full extent of the injury (caused thereby)."[524] The court specifically rejected the notion that simply because the agent is performing some part of the work undertaken usually by the carrier he is protected to same extent as is the carrier. Of importance is also the Supreme Court's statement that "contracts purporting to grant immunity from, or limitation of, liability must be strictly construed and limited to intended beneficiaries."[525]

The court consulted not only U.S. jurisprudence but also referred to *Elder, Dempster* and Australian jurisprudence, namely *Wilson v. Darling Island Stevedoring & Lighterage Co., Ltd.* Whitaker J commenting on *Elder Dempster* noted:

> A careful reading of the several lengthy opinions of their lordships in that case discloses that the question whether a provision in the bill of lading limiting the liability of the carrier likewise limits the liability of its negligent agent, though the agent is neither a party to nor an express beneficiary of the bill of lading, was not involved in or decided by that case. Nor has any English case ever held that a bill of lading that expressly limits the liability of only the carrier nevertheless applies to and limits the liability of its negligent agent. It is important to note that this case turns on what the bill of lading says and not on any doctrine of Privity which the United States does not have.[526]

---

523   *A.M. Collins & Co v Panama R. Co* 197 F.2d, 896.
524   *Herd & Co.* (n517) 770.
525   Ibid., 771.
526   Ibid., 772.

In relation to *Wilson v. Darling Island Stevedoring & Lighterage Co., Ltd.* the court noted that the High Court of Australia after extensively reviewing *Elder Dempster* found that the case, unlike two other New South Wales cases – was rightly decided.[527]

7.2.2 Taisho Marine & Fire Ins. Co Ltd v Vessel Gladiolus[528]

It took in effect sixteen years before the next seminal case was decided. The facts again are not complicated. Taisho, an insurance company sued the freight company for losses as they caused damage to the goods on the inland route. The goods were delivered from Japan to Los Angeles on the vessel Gladiolus. The carrier included a Himalaya clause into the bill of lading which provided in the relevant parts:

> [A]ll servants, agents and independent contractors (including in particular, but not by way of limitation, any stevedores) used or employed by the Carrier for the purpose of or in connection with the performance of any of the Carrier's obligations under this Bill of Lading, shall, in consideration of their agreeing to be so used or employed, have the benefit of all rights, defenses, exceptions from or limitations of liability and immunities of whatsoever nature referred to or incorporated herein applicable to the Carrier as to which the Carrier is entitled hereunder....[529]

At issue was the one-year statute of limitation as set by s 3(6) of the Carriage of Goods by Sea Act ("COGSA"), 46 U.S.C. § 1303(6) (1982), and expressly incorporated into Taisho's bill of lading. If the freight company falls within this clause, they are protected by the limitation period otherwise they are obliged to cover the losses. The district court as well as the circuit court agreed that the freight company was protected.

The court stated that a Himalaya clause should be strictly

---

527   Ibid., 772.
528   762 F2nd 1364 (1985).
529   Ibid., 1366.

construed and limited to intended beneficiaries relying on *Robert C. Herd & Co. v. Krawill Machinery Corp.,*[530] Furthermore, when a party is not specifically mentioned in the Himalaya clause, "the party should, at a minimum, be included in a well-defined class of readily identifiable persons to which COGSA benefits are extended under the terms of the clause."[531] The court noted that in *Toyomenka, Inc. v. S.S. Tosaharu Maru,* [532] a stevedore hired an independent contractor to guard the cargo on the pier. The clause only applied to:

> all servants, agents and independent contractors (including in particular, but not by way of limitation, any stevedores) used or employed by the Carrier for the purpose of or in connection with the performance of any of the Carrier's obligations under this Bill of Lading...."[533]

The clause was inapplicable to the independent contractor as he was hired by the stevedore rather than by the carrier. The same arguments apply in this case as the freight company - performing a non-maritime function - was hired by the consignee and hence was not a party to the Himalaya clause as the carrier's obligations had ended after discharging the goods. The proper test whether a party can benefit from a Himalaya clause is to consider "the nature of the services performed compared to the carrier's responsibility under the carriage contract.'"[534]

7.2.3 Institute of London Underwriters v Sea-Land Services Inc [535]

A yacht was damaged while being unloaded from a cargo ship. The question was whether the carrier and the stevedore were protected by the limitation per package pursuant to the Carriage of Goods by Sea Act of $500. Goodwin C.J first noted that a

---

530   359 U.S. 297, 305, 79 S.Ct. 766, 771, 3 L.Ed.2d 820 (1959).
531   Ibid., 1367.
532   523 F.2d 518 (2d Cir.1975).
533   *Taisho Marine* (n528) 521 n. 7.
534   Ibid., 1367.
535   881 F.2d 761, (1989).

question to which a definitive answer in this circuit has not been given must be answered, namely:

> In a contract for foreign carriage that incorporates the Carriage of Goods by Sea Act (COGSA ... but to which COGSA does not apply *ex proprio vigore*, what is the effect of otherwise valid contract terms inconsistent with COGSA? We hold that in such a contract, COGSA has the effect of a contractual term only, and inconsistent terms may therefore be given force.[536]

As the yacht was carried on deck COGSA did not apply as s1301(c) states 'goods' [excludes] ... cargo which by the contract of carriage is stated as being carried on deck and is so carried."[537] However, the clause paramount of the bill of lading stated that, "The defences and limitations of said Act shall apply to goods whether carried on or under deck."[538] The court held that "terms inconsistent with COGSA, but which are otherwise valid contract terms, may be given force where COGSA is incorporated into a contract for foreign carriage to which it would not apply *ex proprio vigore*."[539] The court turned its attention to the Himalaya clause which reads (emphasis added):

> If it shall be adjudged that *any person other than the owner or demise charterer* (including the master, time charterer, agents, *stevedores*, lashers, watchmen and other *independent contractors*) is the carrier or bailee of the goods, or is otherwise liable in contract or in tort, all rights, exemptions, and limitations of liability ... shall be available to such other persons.[540]

The court found that the clause was not ambiguous and relied on *Taisho Marine & Fire Ins. Co Ltd v Vessel Gladiolus* and extended the limitation of liability under COGSA to the stevedores.

---

536   Ibid., 763.
537   Ibid., 764.
538   Ibid.
539   Ibid., 766.
540   Ibid., 767.

7.2.4 Caterpillar Overseas S.A. v Marine Transport Inc [541]

The shipper sued a trucking company for damage to the cargo, namely a tractor. The incident took place while the goods were transferred overland by a trucker employed by the carrier from the port of delivery to another port in the same vicinity. The defendants were the terminal operators, the carrier and the trucking company.

The facts were as follows. The plaintiffs engaged Lusk Shipping Company as its agent and freight forwarder. However, the carrier encountered a problem as its original vessel was not available and a substitute vessel was ready to take the cargo but in the adjacent port. Such transfers were not unusual. The carrier was responsible to arrange for the transfer and hence employed the defendant as an independent contractor. Farrell supplied the flat rack container and chassis. The driver did question whether this arrangement was safe and having been told it was safe he proceeded with the transport. Due to delivery of the wrong flat rack and chassis the tractor slid off the truck and was damaged.

In the court's opinion the presumed bill of lading never intended to apply to activities connected with the transportation by an independent trucker over public highways from one port to another. It follows, therefore, that neither the carrier nor the trucking company are protected. The court noted that:

> Marine was hired and paid for by Farrell to transport the flat rack for NIT. Farrell did not select the route of travel and did not control Marine's driver. Negligence of Marine was a proximate cause of the accident and damages. Neither the shipper nor the freight forwarder had notice that Farrell would contract with Marine to haul the goods to NIT, or how it would be loaded. [542]

The court decided that the terminal operator was free of negligence but not the carrier (Farrell) nor the trucking company

---

541   900 F.2d. 714 (4th Cir. 1990).
542   Ibid., 718.

(Marine Transport Inc). The carrier was protected by the package limitation provision under COGSA but not the trucking company. The court also refused to include loss of profit into the actual damages awarded to the plaintiff.

In essence, this case was decided on the facts and the Himalaya clause merely gave protection to the carrier in relation to the package limitation under COGSA.

7.2.5 Lucky Goldstar v. S. S. California Mercury [543]

A shipper sought to recover damages to goods caused by a rail carrier while the goods were in transit. Before the shipment left Korea on its way to Seattle two bills of lading were issued. The first was issued by Haniel to Lucky's office in Korea as the shipper and the New Jersey office as the consignee. The second bill was issued by Uni-International Co as the shipper on behalf of Lucky and Haniel's New York office as the consignee. While transported by the second rail-company (Conrail) the goods were damaged. The argument was that Conrail, the rail operator, was not entitled to the package limitation clause because the bill of lading clauses only applies during marine transport.

The first question was whether the COGSA protection extends directly to Conrail. The court noted that s1301(d) of COGSA only applies to "carriers" and "ships". As Conrail was neither the shipper nor the carrier it cannot be directly entitled to the COGSA protection.[544]

The second question was whether Conrail was protected under the bills of lading, specifically clause 5 which states:

> The carrier shall be entitled to sub-contract on any terms the whole or any part of the handling, storage or carriage of the Goods ... [E]very such servant, agent and subcontractor shall

---

543   750 F. Supp 141, 1991.
544   Ibid., 144.

have the benefit of all provisions herein for the benefit of the
Carrier as if such provisions were expressly for their benefit. [545]

The court quoted *Krawill* as noting the required standard when
reviewing bills of lading as being:

> contracts purporting to grant immunity from, or limitation of,
> liability must be strictly construed and limited to intended ben-
> eficiaries, for they 'are not to be applied to alter familiar rules
> visiting liability upon a tortfeasor for the consequences of his
> negligence, unless the clarity of the language used expresses
> such to be the understanding of the contracting parties.[546]

The court found that the language in clause 5 was not sufficiently
clear to protect Conrail as in international shipping we are
"dealing in a field where recognition of technical precision of
language has been the benchmark."[547] The court further noted
that "the absence of the phrase 'inland carriers' in clause 5 is
particularly significant considering the fact that the term is used
elsewhere in the bill of lading."[548] That court, hence, dismissed
Conrail's claim for protection either under COGSA or the
Himalaya clause.

7.2.6 *Mikingberg v Baltic S.S. Co* [549]

Goods were shipped from Russia to the United States. While in
the custody of the stevedores the goods were handed wrongly to
a thief. The plaintiff was asked to wait while the investigation
was on foot before lodging a claim. Due to this reason, the one-
year limitation period pursuant to COGSA expired but did not
influence the court in their decision of the next issue.

The second point was whether the stevedore was an agent of

---

545   Ibid.
546   *Herd & Co.* (n517) 771.
547   *Lucky Goldstar* (n543) 145.
548   Ibid.
549   988 F.2d 327, 1993.

the carrier – and hence can claim the protection under COGSA - within the meaning of the Himalaya clause which states.

> Every exemption, limitation, condition and liberty herein contained and every right, exemption from liability, defence and immunity of whatsoever nature applicable to the Carrier or to which the Carrier is entitled hereunder shall also be available and shall extend to protect ... [every] servant or agent of the Carrier (including every independent contractor) ... employed by the Carrier.[550]

The court noted that unless there is a contractual relationship between the carrier and the stevedores - and not just the fact that the stevedores handled cargo shipped by the carrier - the stevedore cannot be protected by COGSA. The court declined to "extend COGSA protections through the Himalaya Clause to indefinite and unforeseeable defendants who may have only an attenuated connection to the carriage of goods by sea."[551]

7.2.7 Mori Seiki USA Inc v M.V. Alligator Triumph[552]

The facts are simple: a lathe was damaged while unloading but before it was released from the port. The plaintiff sued the carrier, the ship, the charterer, the seaport operator and the stevedore firm which unloaded and subsequently damaged the lathe. The court held that the carrier's bill of lading extended the $500 protection to all participants in the maritime venture. The reasons were given as follows:

The bill of lading notes in the relevant parts:

> [W]ith respect to loss or damage occurring during the period from the time when the Goods arrived at the sea terminal at the port of loading to the time when they left the sea terminal at the port of discharge ... [the carrier shall be responsible for such loss

---

550   Ibid., 332.
551   Ibid., 333.
552   990 F.2d 444 (1993).

> or damage] to the extent prescribed by the applicable Hague
> Rules Legislation....[553]

The plain reading suggests that the limitation period only extends to the time while the goods are in port that is until they are released. Hence, the Hague rules are applicable, and the damage is limited to $500.

Of importance in this case is whether the limitation of damages extends to all participants especially to the stevedore. The exemption clause reads in the relevant parts:

> The Carrier shall be entitled to sub-contract on any terms the whole or any part of the handling, storage or carriage of the Goods and any and all duties whatsoever undertaken by the Carrier in relation to the Goods.... [E]very such servant, agent and subcontractor shall have the benefit of all provisions herein for the benefit of the Carrier as if such provisions were expressly for their benefit....[554]

The plaintiff suggested that the Terminal operator was not covered under the Himalaya clause as they were a subcontractor of the seaport operator. The court referred to their decision in *Taisho Marine*:

> Whether an entity is an intended beneficiary of a Himalaya Clause depends upon the contractual relation between the party seeking protection and the ocean carrier, as well as the nature of the services performed compared to the carrier's responsibilities under the carriage contract.[555]

The lower court resolved the issue by arguing that the seaport operator was an agent for Mitsui the carrier when hiring the stevedores. The reliance of the Federal Court was placed on the *Restatement (Second) of Agency* which has been adopted in maritime law as an accurate statement of applicable general agency principles: "Agency is the fiduciary relation which results

---

553   Ibid., 446.
554   Ibid., 450.
555   Ibid.

from the manifestation of consent by one person to another that the other shall act on his behalf and subject to his control, and consent by the other so to act."[556] The conclusion was as stated above that the stevedores were included in the $500 package liability limitation.

7.2.8 Insurance Company of North America v M/V Savannah[557]

A stevedore while moving crates containing parts of an electric motor damaged it in transit to the warehouse. The insurance company paid the owner $605,000 and is now suing the stevedores for damages. The question was whether the stevedores were covered by the limitation provisions in The Hague-Visby rules. The Himalaya clause stated in the pertinent parts that:

> if it shall be adjudged that any other is the Carrier, all defences, including all limitations of and exonerations from liability, provided to the Carrier by law or by this Bill of Lading shall be available to such other.

> All defences under this Bill of Lading shall inure also to the benefit of the Carrier's agents, servants and employees and of any independent contractor, including stevedores, performing any of the Carrier's obligations with respect to the goods or acting as bailee of the goods.

The court referred to *Mikinberg* noting that there must be a contractual relationship between the carrier and the stevedore for the Himalaya clause to apply. The plaintiff argued that the language of the bill of lading only extends to defences of the stevedore who were performing any of the carrier's obligations. In this regard, the court decided that the bill of lading does extend to the stevedore.

556   Restatement (Second) of Agency § 1(1) (1958.
557   Westlaw 1998 A.M.C. 1029, United States District Court, Southern District of New York, December 4, 1997. 94 Civ. 8846.

In the end, the court correctly noted:

> While it is true that ambiguities must be construed against the carrier, the bill of lading in the present case is not ambiguous. Bills of lading, like all contracts, must be enforced by the courts in order to protect the rights of carriers and shippers to contract freely and according to their preferences. The terms agreed upon by Ivaran and General Electric are not to be set aside based on ambiguities manufactured by plaintiff.[558]

The court limited the liability of the stevedores to $500 per package.

7.2.9 Akiyama Corp. of America v. M.V. Hanjin Marseilles [559]

The terminal operator and stevedore maintained that they were protected by the limitation of liability provided by Carriage of Goods by the Sea Act (COGSA). The shipper appealed. COGSA in its relevant part states:

> Neither the carrier nor the ship shall in any event be or become liable for any loss or damage to or in connection with the transportation of goods in an amount exceeding $500 per package.'[560]

In addition, the Himalaya clause was also included into the bill of lading stating:

> ... [e]very servant, agent and sub-contractor TTT and the agents of each shall have the benefit of all provisions herein for the benefit of the Carrier as if the provisions were expressly for their benefit; and in entering into this contract of carriage, the Carrier does so not only on his own behalf but also as agent for all such servants, agents and subcontractors to the fullest extent permitted by the law applicable to Himalaya Clauses.[561]

---

558 Ibid., 1035.
559 162 F.3d 571 (9th Cir. 1998).
560 § 1304(5).
561 *Akiyama Corp. of America* (n559) 573.

The court noted – by referring to *Mori Seiki USA, Inc. v. M.V. Alligator Triumph,* that the shipper is given an opportunity to opt out of the limitation by declaring an excess value at a higher rate which he has not done.[562] Fitzgerald DJ observed that – in order to be protected under a Himalaya clause – the beneficiary must be clearly identifiable or at a minimum must be included into a well-defined class of readily identifiable persons. The definition of "``Subcontractor" includes terminal operators and stevedores, and the Himalaya Clause specifically extends the bill of lading benefits to subcontractors."[563] The appellants' argument that Privity of contract is required was rejected. The court applied – what was considered to be the proper test expressed in *Taisho Marine* which is ``the nature of the services performed compared to the carrier's responsibility under the carriage contract."[564] In line with the established principles that a Himalaya clause must be read in light of the understanding of the contractual parties a line by line reading differentiating the use of lower case ``s" and upper case ``S" obfuscates the plain reading and clear intent of the bill of lading and Himalaya Clause.[565] For this reason the arguments of the plaintiff were rejected.

7.2.10 *Komori America Corporation v Howland Hook Container Terminal Inc.*[566]

The Bill of lading covered services until the delivery of cargo was made. The consignee's custom broker asked Terminal to load the cargo onto a truck. Howland billed the consignee for its services. namely a fee for ocean carriage, a separate bill for Destination delivery and a separate fee for Container Freight Station Receiving charges.[567]

---

562   Ibid., 573.
563   Ibid.
564   Ibid., 574.
565   Ibid.
566   Westlaw, 1998 A.M.C. 289 also 97-Civ. 7243.
567   Ibid., 2895.

American Wold Cargo (AWC) acted as customs agent for Komori and arranged for Howland to load the containers unto a truck and the goods were to be sent by the plaintiff. The defendant dropped the cargo while loading and caused considerable damage. The point of contention was whether the bill of lading stops applying before or after Howland loaded the cargo onto the truck and whether Howland acted as a servant, agent or subcontractor of the carrier.[568] Howland argued that they were covered by the carrier's package limitation contained in the bill of lading.

The court posed two questions; first "whether the bill of lading governs the loading of the crates onto the truck at all. This question depends upon when "delivery "occurred, because the bill of lading states that Mitsui's obligations continue until "delivery. "[569]

The second question was whether Howland can seek protection under the bill of lading.

> Thus, even if the bill of lading governs because delivery had not yet occurred when the crates were dropped, Howland Hook may only claim its protection if Howland Hook was acting as Mitsui's servant, agent, or subcontractor when it dropped the crates.[570]

The conduct of the parties was crucial in determining the two questions specifically as Komori entered into a separate contract with Howland to load the cargo onto the truck. However, Howland had a contract with the carrier to unload containers from its ship and strip the cargo from those containers. The court noted that "Komori paid a separate fee for "delivery "and another for "Container Freight Station ". That stands in marked contrast to its payment of money directly to Howland for the loading of the truck.[571] The conclusion is that Howland did not act as a servant, agent, or subcontractor of the carrier when it

---

568   Ibid., 2896.
569   Ibid., 2897.
570   Ibid.
571   Ibid., 2898.

loaded the truck. It is obvious that clauses in the bill of lading ceased to apply.

The court proceeded to explain the differences of Container Freight Station (CFS) and pier-to-pier from house-to-house shipments.

The process commences when the shipper hands the cargo to a CFS, where that cargo is loaded into containers at the port of loading, a process known as "stuffing. "At the destination port the container is unloaded and brought to another CFS, where the cargo is removed from the container, a process known as "stripping. "A bill of lading containing a CFS term next to the port of loading or destination means that the carrier stuffs or conversely strips the cargo. This task usually is contracted out to a stevedoring firm.[572]

The designation "pier-to-pier" also means that the carrier stuffs and strips the shipper's cargo into and from containers and on the other hand the term "house-to-house" means that the shipper stuffs its cargo into containers itself, the carrier picks up the entire container and ships it all the way to the consignee, who in turn strips the cargo from the container.[573]

The conclusion is that depending on the terms different parties are tasked to perform the stuffing or stripping. However, loading onto a truck is not part of the carrier's duty. The court also distinguished between handling and loading the goods onto the truck as well as who actually charges the shipper for the task.

Because Howland charged an extra amount of money for loading the cargo onto the truck it went beyond the requirement under the CFS term and "hence the liability limitations contained in the bill of lading and in the defendant's tariff have no application in this case."[574]

---

572   Ibid., 2898-99.
573   Ibid., 2899.
574   Ibid., 2901.

The decision whether there was a breach of contract or bailment duties and the measure of damages had to be decided later.

7.2.11 Acciai Speciali Terni USA, Inc, v M/V Berane [575]

The plaintiff engaged the carrier to transport steel sheets from Italy to Baltimore. The sheets of steel were damaged by the offloading stevedore Transcom. Clause 3, the forum selection clause provided that any disputes arising under the bill of lading must be decided in the country where the carrier has his principal place of business. Clause 18, the Himalaya clause provided:

> It is hereby expressly agreed that no servant or agent of the Carrier (including every independent contractor from time to time employed by the Carrier) shall in any circumstances whatsoever be under any liability whatsoever to the [consignee and owner of the cargo] for any loss, damage or delay arising or resulting directly or indirectly from any act, neglect or default on his part while acting in the course of or in connection with his employment and, but without prejudice to the generality of the foregoing provisions in this clause, every exemption, limitation, condition and liberty herein contained and every right, exemption from liability, defence and immunity of whatsoever nature applicable to the Carrier or to which the Carrier is entitled hereunder shall also be available and shall extend to protect every such servant or agent of the Carrier acting as aforesaid and for the purpose of all the foregoing provisions of this clause the Carrier is or shall be deemed to be acting as agent or trustee on behalf of and for the benefit of all persons who are or might be his servants or agents from time to time (including independent contractors) and all such persons shall to this extent be or be deemed to be parties to the contract evidenced by this Bill of Lading.[576]

The court noted that forum selection clauses and the choice

---

575   United States District Court, D. Maryland, Northern Division. 181 F.Supp.2d 458 (D.Md. 2002).
576   Ibid., 461.

of law provisions are basically valid unless the party resisting the enforcement would be "unreasonable under the circumstances."[577] As the plaintiff has not shown any cause to indicate that "enforcement would be unreasonable; the Court finds the choice of forum and law clauses valid and enforceable against AST."[578]

The next issue was whether the stevedore - Transcom - is entitled to rely on the Himalaya clause. As noted above the Himalaya clause extends to "every right, exemption from liability, defence and immunity" to the carriers' servants, agents, and independent contractors "while acting in the course of or in connection with [their] employment."

Smalkin J.C, referred to *Robert C. Herd & Co. v. Krawill Mach. Corp.*, where it was stated that such clauses "must be strictly construed and limited to intended beneficiaries."[579] The court also noted that the word stevedore in itself is sufficient to recognise the intended beneficiary.

As the Himalaya clause applies to all defences the forum selection clause is as good a defence as any other might be. [580] The court also noted that:

> a third-party beneficiary is bound by the terms and conditions of the contract it invokes. The beneficiary "cannot accept the benefits and avoid the burdens or limitations" of the contract. Therefore, Transcom, as a "Himalayan," third-party beneficiary of the bills of lading, is bound by the forum selection clauses it now asserts as a defence in this Court. It cannot take advantage of the clauses here but then object to jurisdiction in the appropriate court(s).[581]

The court therefore dismissed the motion of Transcom Terminals Ltd.

---

577   Ibid., 462.
578   Ibid., 464.
579   *Robert C. Herd & Co.* (n517).
580   *Acciai Speciali Terni USA, Inc,* (n575) 464.
581   Ibid., 465.

7.2.12 Steel Coils, Inc. v. M/V Lake Marion[582]

This case is not so much a question as to the interpretation and application of a Himalaya clause but whether COGSA applies to carriers and managers acting in tort.

The cause of the damage to the steel coils was that seawater entered the hold due to leaking hatches as well as a crack was found in Hold No. 1. The defendant pleaded protection under COGSA. The lower court awarded damages "against the vessel, its owner, Lake Marion, Inc., its manager, Bay Ocean Management, Inc., collectively the "vessel interests," and the time charterer, Western Bulk Carriers K/S Oslo.

Of interest is how the manager of the vessel Bay Ocean was liable. They did hire the master and crew of the vessel. The action was *in rem* against the vessel and *in personam* against the other defendants. The main defence was that the limitation clause of COGSA applies and that Bay Ocean Management should also be able to take advantage of the COGSA limitation.

The issue can be best divided into two parts. First is COGSA applicable and secondly – if COGSA applies – is the management group able to claim protection under COGSA.

COGSA will apply if the defendant exercised:

> due diligence TTT to make the ship seaworthy, and to secure that the ship is properly manned, equipped, and supplied, and to make the holds ... and all other parts of the ship in which goods are carried fit and safe for their reception, carriage, and preservation.[583]

All reports available to the court indicated that the maintenance of the ship was poor and hence saltwater was allowed to enter the hatches. Because the duty to make a sip seaworthy is non-delegable the limiting clauses in COGSA cannot apply. The

---

582   331 F.3d 422 (5th Cir. 2003).
583   46 U.S.C.App. § 1304.

defendant as a second argument contended that section 1304(2) of COGSA is applicable which reads: "n]either the carrier nor the ship shall be responsible for loss or damage arising or resulting from ... [p]erils, dangers, and accidents of the sea or other navigable waters." They argued that the storm which was encountered by the vessel constituted a "peril of the sea". This argument was rejected because the weather conditions were no different than expected in winter and no damage to the vessel was sustained.

In addition, it was argued that the crack in the hull was a latent defect and could not have been discovered by due diligence. However, the court rejected that argument as well as the crack was pre-existing and was merely an extension of a prior defect.

The claim against the managing agent Bay Ocean was based on the fact that they hired the crew and were responsible to make the ship seaworthy: that is, they were negligent of testing hatches and failing to take precautions against the crack in the hull. The lower court held the manager liable under tort and hence not covered by COGSA limitations. The court decided that the term "carrier" includes "the owner or the charterer who enters into a contract of carriage with a shipper. We have held that as long as an entity is a party to the contract of carriage, it is a carrier." Following the decision in *Herd* where a negligent stevedore was unable to claim limitations under COGSA, hence, the same principle applies in this case.[584] Finding no error in the lower court's decision the judgment was affirmed.

7.2.13 Norfolk Southern Railway Company v James N. Kirby Pty. Ltd[585]

This case is of importance as it dealt with a train wreck caused by a derailment under maritime law. The facts are that an Australian

---

584   Ibid., para 10.
585   543 U.S. 14, 125 S.Ct. 385 (2004).

cargo owner sued the railroad for damages sustained to goods when the railroad derailed. The railroad responded that they are covered by the Himalaya clause in the bill of lading which was issued by the carrier. The court noted[586] that the transport of goods "from a port in Australia to inland city in the United States, and between intermediary and shipper for end-to-end transportation of these same goods, were in nature of "maritime contracts." The cargo owner was bound to the clauses contained in the bill of lading.

The Supreme Court reversed the decision of the Eleventh Circuit which relied heavily on *Herd v Krawill* but disagreed with the Eleventh Circuit court that *Herd* stood for a strict approach. In effect, the *Eleventh Circuit* held that the Railway could not claim protection under the first bill as they were not in Privity with the Freight Forwarder and secondly the court stated that the Freight Forwarder was not an agent of Kirby and hence could not bind Kirby to the second bill of lading. Until the dispute reached the Supreme Court the parties were under an assumption that federal law would apply. The Supreme Court did not sidestep the issue and classified multimodal bill of lading as maritime contracts and, hence, emphasised the importance of applying a uniform standard for their interpretation of shipping contracts and their enforcement. Consequently, federal law applies.

The court noted that Kirby hired a freight forwarding company (ICC) to arrange for the end-to-end transport. ICC was a contracting carrier and did not act as agent for Kirby. They undertook the responsibility throughout the journey and Kirby was designated as shipper. The through bill of lading noted that the journey started in Sydney; the goods were off-loaded in Savannah and then transported by rail to Huntsville. The ICC bill of lading limited the liability under the US Carriage of Goods by Sea Act (COGSA) for the seas leg but put in a higher amount for the land leg.

---

586   Ibid.

Kirby did not take the opportunity to declare the true value instead opting for the contractual limitation liability set out in COGSA:

> Neither the carrier nor the ship shall in any event be or become liable for any loss or damage to or in connection with the transportation of goods in an amount exceeding $500 per package lawful money of the United States ... unless the nature and value of such goods have been declared by the shipper before shipment and inserted in the bill of lading.[587]

The ICC Himalaya clause furthermore stated:

> These conditions [for limitations on liability] apply whenever claims relating to the performance of the contract evidenced by this [bill of lading] are made against any servant, agent or other person (including any independent contractor) whose services have been used in order to perform the contract.[588]

ICC being a non-vessel owning carrier engaged Hamburg-Sud for the sea leg and Norfolk Southern Railway Company as the land carrier.

The carrier (Hamburg Sud) also issued a bill of lading declaring itself as the carrier and ICC as the shipper. The Himalaya clause was similar to one issued by ICC, namely the benefit of the limitation clause extends to "all agents ... (including inland) carriers ... and all independent contractors whatsoever."

The first question the court resolved was whether the issue was one of maritime law or not. The court decided that, "[T]he trend in modern admiralty case law ... is to focus the jurisdictional inquiry upon whether the nature of the transaction was maritime."[589] This was so despite the inclusion of the land legs but because the conceptual rather than spatial approach does not alter the essentially maritime nature of the contracts especially considering that the "international transportation industry

---

587   Ibid., 391.
588   Ibid.
589   Ibid., 393.

"clearly has moved into a new era—the age of multi-modalism, door-to-door transport based on efficient use of all available modes of transportation by air, water, and land."[590] The court arguably famously wrote that "the shore is now an artificial place to draw a line."'[591] This was the response to the oral argument of the respondent asking the court not "to doctrinally extend the Jenson [sic] line to a place where it has never before existed."[592]

This contention was rather controversial as it extends the Himalaya clause from the sea leg to the land leg which is not really related to admiralty jurisdiction. The prevailing view that "jurisdiction arises only when the subject-matter of the contract is 'purely' or 'wholly' maritime in nature"[593] is not valid anymore.

Turning to the merits the court observed that the language in the first Himalaya clause makes it clear that the limitation extends to "*any* servant, agent or other person (including any independent contractor)."[594] The word "*any*" has an expansive meaning and hence the language "corresponds to the fact that various modes of transportation would be involved in performing the contract."[595] The conclusion was that the railroad was an intended beneficiary of the Himalaya clause.

The court turned its attention to the second bill of lading, the Hamburg Sud one. The question was whether the forwarding agent acted as Kirby's agent which was answered in the negative by the court. However, relying on *Great Northern R. Co. v. O'Connor*[596] the court described the relationship as "only

---

590   Ibid.
591   Ibid., 394.
592   Oral Argument transcript, 3, 11. 17-20, *available at* http://www. supremecourtus.gov/oraLarguments/argument-transcripts/02-1028.pdf. at at 35,11. 15-17.
593   *Hartford Fire Ins. Co. v. Orient Overseas Container Lines (UK) Ltd.*, 230 E3d 549, 555, 2001 AMC 25, 30 (2d Cir. 2000).
594   Ibid., 397.
595   Ibid.
596   232 U.S. 508, 34 S.Ct. 380, 58 L.Ed. 703 (1914).

[requiring] treating ICC as Kirby's agent for a single, limited purpose: when ICC contracts with subsequent carriers for limitation on liability ... we hold that intermediaries, entrusted with goods, are "agents" only in their ability to contract for liability limitations with carriers downstream."[597] The court acknowledged that there was resistance in the shipping industry and it was therefore a close call but the belief was expressed that the court's decision tracks industry practice.[598] The court noted three reasons to come to their decision.

First in intercontinental ocean shipping, carriers may not know if they are dealing with an intermediary or the cargo owner. To find out would be too difficult specifically considering the fact that goods change hands in intermodal transports.

Secondly "a rule prompting downstream carriers to distinguish between cargo owners and intermediary shippers might interfere with statutory and decisional law promoting non-discrimination in common carriage."[599]

Thirdly –referring back to *Great Northern* – the decision produces an equitable result as Kirby can sue the Freight Forwarder for the loss exceeding the liability limitation. The court justified the decision by stating:

> It seems logical that ICC − the only party that definitely knew about and was party to both of the bills of lading at issue here − should bear responsibility for any gap between the liability limitations in the bills.[600]

Norfolk however can enjoy the benefits of not only the Hamburg Sud liability limitation but also the one between the Freight Forwarder and the carrier and the decision does no more than provide a legal backdrop against which future bills of lading

---

597   *Norfolk Southern Railway Company (n585)* 399.
598   Ibid.
599   Ibid.
600   Ibid., 400.

will be negotiated.[601]

In effect, the court followed what has been argued in *Herd*:

> *Herd* stands for the proposition that there is no special rule for
> Himalaya clauses. Contracts of carriage of goods must be con-
> strued like any other contracts: by their terms consistent with
> the intent of the parties. *'Any independent contractor' means
> 'one or some indiscriminately of whatever kind'.* There is no
> justification in importing a requirement that it means an inde-
> pendent contractor in direct privacy with the carrier who has
> issued the bill of lading.[602]

Not surrisingly the Supreme Court noted that, if the parties
decided to extend the liability limitations broadly, the
interpretation of the clause should also be broad and not narrow.
In addition, the court emphasised the need for uniformity in
admiralty jurisdiction.[603] The Supreme Court simply did not
follow the Eleven Circuit court which distinguished between a
'subcontractor' and a 'sub-subcontractor.' [604]

7.2.14 Mazda Motors of America, Inc. v M/V Cougar ACE [605]

This is an interesting case *in rem*[606] where the question was
whether the vessel was an "agent, servant or Sub-Contractor"
of the carrier under the plain meaning of the Himalaya Clause
in the bill of lading. If so, the vessel could invoke the forum
selection clause.[607]

---

601   Ibid.
602   C. Nicoll, "Himalaya clauses and sub-bailment on terms, A default rule set by
       the US Supreme Court"., *Shipping and Trade Law*, Vol 5, No 7, (2005), 1, 2.
603   Ibid., 385, 396.
604   Nicoll, (n602) 2.
605   565 f.3D 573 (2009).
606   An *in rem* action recognises the vessel as a separate legal entity which can
       be sued. A vessel, therefore, which is sometimes the only asset when the
       owner cannot be reached, can be arrested in a harbour and it is prevented from
       leaving.
607   *Mazda Motors of America, Inc. v M/V Cougar ACE* .

A shipment of automobiles was damaged, but Mazda did only name the vessel as the defendant and not the carrier nor owner of the vessel. The point is that the jurisdiction clause in the Bill of lading named Japan whereas Mazda filed in Oregon. They contended that the forum clause only applied to *in personam* suits and not *in rem* and, hence, only the carriers are bound by it. The court rejected the argument and found that the vessel could benefit under the Himalaya clause[608]

The Himalaya clause states:

> The Merchant undertakes that no claim or allegation shall be made against any servant, agent or Sub-Contractor of the Carrier which imposes or attempts to impose upon any of them, or upon any vessel owned or operated by any of them, any liability whatsoever in connection with the Goods, and, if any such claim or allegation should nevertheless be made, to indemnify the Carrier against all consequences thereof. Without prejudice to the foregoing, every such servant, agent and Sub-Contractor shall have the benefit of all provisions herein benefiting the Carrier as if such provisions were expressly for their benefit; and in entering into this contract, the Carrier, to the extent of those provisions, does so not only on its own behalf, but also as agent and trustee for such servants, agents and Sub-Contractors.[609]

The bill of lading also defined each of the terms and the definition of 'subcontractor' was crucial in deciding the issue.

> Sub-Contractor" includes owners and operators of Vessels and space providers on Vessels (other than the Carrier), stevedores, terminal and group age operators, any independent contractor directly or indirectly employed by the Carrier in performance of the Carriage, their respective servants and agents, and *anyone assisting the performance of the Carriage.*[610] (emphasis added).

The first observation the court made was that the Himalaya clause is a contract like any other and general interpretative

---

608   Ibid., 574.
609   Ibid., 577.
610   Ibid.

principles apply. The problem with the Himalaya clause is the sentence which forbids "claims against any "servant, agent or Sub-Contractor" that would impose liability on them "or upon any *vessel* owned or operated by any of them."[611]

However, under COGSA such a disclaimer is null and void and of no effect but does not reduce or nullify liabilities upon a vessel. The second sentence is unaffected insofar as the exemptions are still valid. Hence, the court noted that in the second sentence the exemption clause also benefits sub-contractors which are defined as *anyone assisting the performance of the Carriage.*[612] .

The court decided – as *anyone* has an expansive plain meaning – that the vessel "is a Sub-Contractor because it plainly assisted the performance of the Carriage; as the carrying vessel, it was indispensable to that performance."[613] Hence, *"anyone assisting the performance of the Carriage'* included the vessel.[614] The court also dismissed Mazda's contention that Himalaya clauses are used only "to extend a carrier's defences and liability limitations to certain *third parties* performing services on its behalf." [615] However, Mazda agreed that, "the vessel ratified the bills of lading by transporting the cargo, which made the vessel a *first party* to those bills of lading."[616] There is a logical difficulty of a party – in this case the vessel's statues "as both a first and third party to the bills of lading."[617]

The court resolved the problem by stating that: "that merely transporting the cargo made the vessel a party to the bills of lading."[618]

---

611   Ibid., 578.
612   Ibid.
613   Ibid.
614   Ibid., 580.
615   Ibid.
616   Ibid.
617   Ibid.
618   Ibid.

The result is that the vessel can become a party to the bill of lading and, hence, because factually "sailing with the cargo, the vessel ratified the bills of lading, thereby allowing her to assert the contractual defences therein.[619] The fact is that this is the first case where the Himalaya clause covered a vessel in an action *in rem*. It has been argued that:

> The *Kirby* decision may have made it inevitable that a vessel would one day achieve this culmination of personification, but the *Mazda Motors* court went to unnecessary lengths to find that the vessel was a Himalaya beneficiary.[620]

The effect is that US courts favour a broad construction of Himalaya clause and as a result make it harder for cargo owners to succeed leaving them to simply rely on insurance.

7.2.15 Sompo Japan Insurance of America and Another v Norfolk Southern Railway Co. [621]

An action was commenced against the railway as goods were damaged due to a derailment (identical circumstances as found in *Kirby* discussed above). It was a multimodal contract where the Himalaya clause was embedded in the bill of lading. In effect "Their entire international journey was governed by through bills of lading - essentially, contracts - issued by ocean carriers to the cargo owners or their intermediaries."[622] The issue was whether the ocean carrier is the sole entity which is responsible of the carriage of goods and all others including rail carriage are included in the exemption clause.

The exoneration clause in the bill provided that:

> It is understood and agreed that, other than the Carrier, no Per-

---

619   G. Gurley, "the ninth Circuit Breaches Life into a vessel as a Himalaya Beneficiary." 34 Tulane Maritime Law Journal 2099-2020, 619.

620   Ibid., 629.

621   (2014) 907 LMLN 3.

622   Ibid., 168.

> son, firm or corporation or other legal entity whatsoever (Including the Master, officers and crew of the vessel, agents, Underlying Carriers, Sub–Contractors and/or any other independent contractors whatsoever utilized in the Carriage) is, or shall be deemed to be, liable with respect to the Goods as Carrier, bailee or otherwise.[623]

The bill's definition of an "Underlying Carrier" is:

> the party on whose behalf this Bill is issued, as well as the Vessel and/or her Owner, demise charterer (if bound hereby), the time charterer and an[y] substituted or *Underlying Carrier* whether any of them is acting as a Carrier or bailee.[624]

The bill's definition of an "Underlying Carrier" included "rail... or other carrier utilised by the Carrier for any parts of the transportation [of] the shipment covered by the Bill".

The parties did agree that the Railway was included in the definition of "underlying carrier." The problem as noted by the court was that:

> Because "Underlying Carriers" are included within the bill's definition of "Carrier," the Railroads are also "Carriers" per the definition of that term. As a result, although the Exoneration Clause purports to state that *only* "the Carrier" shall be liable, and that no one else—including any Underlying Carrier—shall be, because of the inclusive definition of the term "Carrier," the Exoneration Clause simultaneously states that the Railroads *can* be held liable and that they *cannot* be.[625]

The claimant argued that the *contra proferentum* rule should apply. However, the court disagreed because the maxim only applies where the contract is ambiguous and not "where it is *susceptible of two reasonable and practical interpretations.*"[626] In this case it is not ambiguous as only one entity, namely

---

623   Ibid., 170.
624   Ibid., 178.
625   Ibid., 179.
626   Ibid., 179.

the carrier issued all bills of lading, hence, he was the only underlying carrier. In addition, the court relied on *J. Aron & Co. v. The Askvin*[627] and noted that, "Our interpretation is also supported by the rule of construction that a specific contract provision should prevail over a general one."[628] The court also noted that *Kirby,*[629] a case decided 10 years ago, controls this case.[630]

In the end, the US Court of Appeals (Second Circuit) rejected this argument and held that the only reasonable interpretation of the exoneration clause, pursuant to the Himalaya clause, was that YM, the carrier who issued the bill of lading, should alone be liable to the cargo owners and subrogated insurers.[631]

7.3 Conclusion

By virtue of *Herd v. Krawill* Himalaya clauses were first adopted in the United States courts and subsequent jurisprudence built on it. However, the courts have developed three basic conditions which must be present.

First, a contractual relationship must exist between the contracting party and anyone who seeks to be protected by the Himalaya clause.[632]   The courts also found it necessary that the party seeking protection under the clause must perform part of the contract which is included in the Himalaya clause.[633] Furthermore, an independent contractor must perform an

---

627   267 F.2d 276, 277 (2d Cir.1959).

628   *Sompo Japan Insurance of America and Another (n621)* 179.

629   *Norfolk Southern Railway Company (585)* 385.

630   Ibid., i85.

631   http://www.hfw.com/downloads/HFW-Logistics-Bulletin-June-2015.pdf.

632   As an example, see *Mori Seiki USA, Inc. v. M.V. Alligator Triumph* 990 F.2d 444 at 448-450.

633   As an example, see *Tashio Marine & Fire Ins. Co. v. The Vessel Gladiolus* 762 F.2d 1364 at 1367.

operation which can be termed to be of a maritime nature.[634]

Secondly, the Himalaya clause must be drafted in such a way that it becomes clear who is protected,[635] or at least the party must be able to be identified clearly. Courts have adopted a more flexible approach in the description of a protected third party. In the past, the word "bailee" was not considered to be precise enough,[636] however this is not the case anymore.[637] A clause indicating a well-defined class of beneficiaries such as stevedores or terminal operators is now acceptable. In *Certain Underwriters at Lloyds'v. Barber Blue Sea Line* the court stated:

> When a party seeking protection under a Himalaya Clause is not specifically mentioned therein, the party should, at a minimum, be included in a well-defined class of readily identifiable persons to which COGSA benefits are extended under the terms of the clause.[638]

However, as soon as inland carriers are employed, involving a door to door contract, the term to protect the inland carriage must be clear and unambiguous.[639]

Thirdly, the benefit must be clearly stated such as the package limitation or the one year delay for suit but only if the benefit is not automatically granted via COGSA.[640] If the COGSA limitation or any package limitation is part of the contractual clause, the shipper or the consignee must have been given an opportunity to increase the value of the goods.[641] Treitel furthermore argues

---

634 As an example, see *Caterpillar Overseas, S.A. v. Marine Transports, Inc.* 900 F.2d 714 at 724, 1991.

635 See *Herd & Co. v. Krawill Machinery Corp* 359 U.S. 297 at p. 305.For an example, where a party was not clearly mentioned can be found, seen *Steel Coils, Inc. v. M/V Lake Marion* 2002 AMC 1680 at 1699.

636 See *De Laval Turbine Co. v. West India Industries* 502 F.2d 259, 1974.

637 See *LaSalle Machine Tool v. Maker Terminals* 611 F.2d 56 at p. 60, 1978 AMC 1374 at p. 1380 (4 Cir. 1979).

638 675 F.2d 266 at 270.

639 *Classic Fashions, Inc. v. Narrieras N.P.R., Inc.* 68 F.Supp.2d. 1312 (S.D. Fla. 1999).

640 See *Croft & Scully v. M/V Skulptor* 508 F. Supp. 670 at. 673, 1981.

641 See *Mori Seiki USA, Inc. v. M.V. Alligator Triumph* 990 F.2d 444, 451.

that the United States position is somewhat different as it does only rely on Lord Reid's first requirement but is similar to the English approach under the Contract (Right of Third Parties) Act 1999.[642] Most importantly as noted in *Sompo*, the Himalaya clause must be drafted carefully with the expected coverage of risk and associated entities in mind. *Sompo* as well as *Kirby* express a new judicial creativity in extending the Himalaya clause firmly unto land carriage despite the fact that rail and land do have their own conventions. Three rules emerged, namely:

> First, the land segments of multimodal transports fall under admiralty jurisdiction unless the ocean segment is "insubstantial" (the "Jurisdiction Rule") Second, Himalaya clauses, properly drafted, extend downstream to all subcarriers, because the contemplation of various modes of transport means that the parties must have anticipated that a land carrier's services would be necessary in performing the contract (the "Beneficiary Rule"). Third, Himalaya clauses extend upstream to the shipper (not party to a subcarrier's bill of lading) only as far as limitations of liability are concerned.[643]

However, Nicoll argues that the Supreme Court in *Kirby*, for pragmatic reasons perhaps, set a default rule which is out of step with English law but arguably is more attractive than the English view as it responded to the reality of multimodal transports. Nicoll argues that:

> Under English law the sub-bailee would need to show that there was consent on the part of the goods owner to the sub-bailment on term; while under the US 'default rule' consent would be assumed in the absence of rebutting evidence.[644]

In sum, the United States approach basically only relies on the existence of a clause conferring rights and immunities to a third

---

642   Treitel, F.M.B. Reynolds, Thomas Gilbert Carver, 474.
643   A. M. Costabel, Himalaya Strain?-A Forensic Examination of *Norfolk Southern Railway Co. v James N Kirby, Pty Ltd* and *Doe v Celebrity Cruises, Inc.*, 29 Tul. Mar. L.J. 2004-2005, 217, 218.
644   Nicoll, (n602) 3.

party in a contractual clause. The exception to an enforcement of a valid Himalaya clause may occur if the clause is 'contrary to public policy under state law.[645]

---

645   Thomas J Schoenbaum, *Admiralty and Maritime Law*, 3rd ed. (St. Paul, Minn.: West Group, 2001), 533.

8

HIMALAYA CLAUSE JURISPRUDENCE IN HONG KONG, SINGAPORE AND SOUTH AFRICA

8.   Introduction

This Chapter examines the application of the Himalaya Clause in former colonies of the United Kingdom. Especially, this Chapter looks at the development and application of the Himalaya clause in Hong Kong, Singapore, and in South Africa which has a mixed legal system. It will be shown that in South Africa the courts, in applying Himalaya clauses, tended to lean more towards the common law approach but with an eye on civil law procedures. Hong Kong and Singapore are important commercial centres with considerable shipping traffic. With P R China's endeavour to connect to Europe by construction of the new Silk Road (Belt and Road), the harbours along this Road have increased their significance and experience considerable shipping traffic. They are also key centres for dispute settlement, specifically for the resolution of disputes by arbitration. However, seminal shipping jurisprudence appears to be lacking in these countries. This Chapter deals successively with Hong Kong, Singapore and South Africa.

8.1 Hong Kong

In the Hong Kong jurisdiction, there is one case that stands out for discussion: *Bewise Motors Co. Ltd. v. Hoi Kong Container Services Ltd.*[646]Four cars were sold to a company in P R China and the seller entered into a contract with a freight forwarder (F). F then contracted with a container depot operator to put the cars in containers and then load them aboard a ship. F was never in possession of the cars and the seller delivered them at F's instructions directly to the container depot operator. The contractual relationships extended from the Seller to F and from F to the depot operator on an agency basis. The cars were stolen from the depot due to negligence, but not wilful negligence. The seller sought to recover the value of the cars from the depot operator under bailment or sub-bailment.

Ching PJ noted that the clauses in both contracts consist of identical worded Himalaya clauses. Clause 15 reads:

> Extension of terms.
>
> Each and every servant, agent or sub-contractor of the company shall have the benefit of these terms .... In entering into any contract pursuant to these terms, the company does so not only on its own behalf but as agent and trustee for such servants, agents or sub-contractors.[647]

Furthermore, the relevant clause in the contract between the plaintiff and the freight forwarder, clause 4(b)(ii), so far as relevant, reads:

> The customer expressly authorises the company to do such acts and enter into such contracts on behalf of the customer so as to bind the customer by such acts in all respects .... The customer agrees that the company is not obliged to consult the customer before the company enters into any such contracts or does any such acts. The company is not obliged to advise the customer

---

646   [1998] 2 HK.I.RD. 645.
647   Ibid., 655.

of the terms and conditions of such contracts or details of such acts unless specifically requested by the customer in writing. [648]

The dispute arose because there were differences in the degree of exemptions between the two sets of terms. The freight forwarder included the term 'wilful neglect or default' whereas the phrase in the defendant's terms read: 'theft unless by employees of the company, its agents, servants or sub-contractors.'[649] The court digressed for a moment as it found it necessary to reinforce the duties of a bailee irrespective as to the wording difference as shown in this case. The court stated:

> In reading the judgments ... it is important to bear in mind that the bailee was found not to have been negligent in any way. The question before the Court was whether the bailee was nevertheless liable for the theft by its servant. It was held that it was on a vicarious basis, a bailee remaining liable for its responsibilities when it delegates in that way. Subject to any modifying terms, the duty of a bailee is to take reasonable care of the article bailed to it. It follows logically that if a bailee negligently allows the article to be stolen it is liable whether the theft is committed by a stranger or by a servant or agent whether entrusted with the article or otherwise.[650]

The defendant based his arguments on the existence of the Himalaya clause appearing in each of the contracts. Ching P.J was of the opinion that two of the conditions set out by Lord Reid were fulfilled bar the third one which reads: "the carrier has authority from the stevedore to do that, or perhaps later ratification by the stevedore would suffice" This is so as the evidence did not show that the defendant had authorised the freight forwarder to contract on its behalf and the freight forwarder was never in possession of the cars, hence no sub-bailment took place. However, Ching P.J observed:

---

648   Ibid., 655.
649   Ibid., 655-656.
650   Ibid., 657.

> There is, instead a more basic point raised by Mr Ma which we would address. Both the "Himalaya" clause and the so-called doctrine of sub-bailment are mechanisms designed to extend the benefit of the terms between the original parties to the sub-contractor or sub-bailee. Neither, however, are mechanisms which can supervene over the actual terms of a sub-contract or a sub-bailment. So, in logic, where a sub-contractor or a sub-bailee expressly declines to enter into a transaction except upon his own terms alone there can be no room for the incorporation of the terms of the contractor or bailee, still less ratification of those terms after the event. No reported decision produced to us dealt with such a question.[651]

The court turned to the terms upon which the defendant contracted with the freight forwarder or the terms upon which it accepted the cars into its bailment or sub-bailment. From the evidence, it was clear that the freight forwarder had authority to contract so as to bind the plaintiff to whatever terms these might have been.[652] Taking this fact into consideration and understanding that freight forwarders do not have container facilities it is obvious that the plaintiff must have known that the freight forwarder would sub-contract the containerisation and carriage to other subcontractors. This was evident in clause 4(b)(ii) of the freight forwarders terms and conditions. The logical conclusion is:

> If the plaintiff, knowing of and assenting to the defendant's terms, had dealt directly with the defendant there can be no doubt that the defendant's terms would have applied either in contract or in bailment. It makes no commercial sense or logic to say that the position, so far as bailment is concerned, must be different simply because an intermediary was used.[653]

Essentially, the court applied facts based on commercial reality without losing sight of the relevant law in interpreting and applying the exception clauses. Hence, the court noted:

---

651   Ibid., 658.
652   Ibid., 659.
653   Ibid., 660.

The interpretation of the clause is not without difficulty. In the final analysis, the choice is between the two constructions discussed. The second of them involves straining the language whereas the first reads easily and naturally however extreme the result. It means that the defendant is not to be liable for theft save for the exceptions set out in part (1)(iii) but that is not as startling as it might seem at first, for cl.13 of the defendant's terms warns that it will not affect insurance on any goods except upon express instructions so in effect advising the customer to obtain its own cover if desired. It follows that, negligent and in default as the defendant was, the defendant is exempted from liability for theft. In addition, ordinary language cannot permit the words "unless it is conclusively proved ..." to qualify only the word "theft" but not the other words in part (1)(iii). Finally, if those other words were so qualified it would make a nonsense of their inclusion since part (1)(iii) would then provide that the defendant would not be liable for any loss or damage due to theft unless it was due to the proven neglect or default of the defendant or its employees and then go on again to provide that the defendant would be liable for theft by employees of the defendant, its agents, servants or sub-contractors if it was a loss due to the proven neglect or default of the defendant or its employees. That cannot be the right construction.[654]

The court dismissed the appeal.

8.2 Singapore

In Singapore, a discussion of the Himalaya clause requires consideration of a case, which does not deal with shipping, but with air transport: *Yusen Air & Sea Service (S) Pty Ltd v Changi International Airport Services Pty Ltd.*[655] As it is an air transport case, the Warsaw Convention is applicable. However, the airway bill contained a Himalaya clause and, therefore, it merits its inclusion in this treatment of the application of the Himalaya clause.

---

654   Ibid., 661-62.
655   [1999] 3 SLR (R) 95.

The facts are that that the appellant, a freight forwarder, was engaged to deliver a cargo of integrated circuits. CIAS was a cargo handling agent of KLM. The weight of the cargo was consistently stated as being 19 kg in all documents. However, the delivered cargo was noted to weigh only 9kg. The documents were not corrected and, in addition, the cargo was lost.

Lai Kew Chai J delivered the judgment and the first point was to answer the question whether the cargo of integrated circuits weighting 19 kg was delivered to CIAS. The court agreed with Yusen that the Warsaw Convention, specifically Article 11 notes that the airway bill is *prima facie* evidence of the contract and hence 19 kg was the applicable weight. However, on the balance of probabilities the court concluded that only 9 kg were delivered. The trial judge found that the actual cargo was never delivered and hence CIAS never became the bailee of the goods. However, as CIAS had misplaced the parcel they are liable for the loss

The next main issue was whether CIAS is entitled to rely on the limitation clause within the airway bill. Clause 7 states as follows:

> Any exclusion or limitation of liability applicable to the carrier shall apply to and be for the benefit of carrier's agents, servants and representatives and any person whose aircraft is used by the carrier for carriage and its agents, servants and representatives. For purpose of this provision carrier acts herein as agent for all such persons.[656]

The court, in its discussion, relied on the *dicta* of Lord Reid in *Scruttons Ltd* and the judgments in *The Eurymedon* and *The Makutai* as well as *The New York Star*. Lai Kew Chai J expressed the view that similar policy considerations apply also in an air cargo scenario.[657]

656　Ibid., para 32.
657　Ibid., para 36.

Returning to the facts he noted that the first and second requirements laid down by Lord Reid had been satisfied. The court also found that CIAS had impliedly authorised KLM to contract within the meaning of clause 7 in the light of commercial practices.[658]

The court, furthermore, in light of Article 22 of the Warsaw Convention, found that CIAS is entitled to limit their liability to Yusen.

8.3 South Africa

8.3.1 A mixed legal system

South African law is a combination of different legal systems. Due to its historical past it is influenced by the civilian tradition. Early Dutch settlers brought with them Roman-Dutch law, which is itself a blend of indigenous Dutch customary law and Roman law. Later, during the British colonial period, common law was introduced.[659] Hence, South Africa has a mixed legal system.

South Africa, like many other countries, implemented a Carriage of Goods by Sea Act in 1986 after ratifying The Hague-Visby Rules. After 1986, Article V of the Rules extended the statutory right of the shipper and carrier to servants and agents but not to independent contractors, such as stevedores. It is not unexpected that the South African court system, in its own right, adopted the Himalaya clause. Not surprisingly, unlike the English legal system, South African courts have also attempted to rely on the principle of *stipulatio alteri*. This rule enables South African lawyers to be more comfortable with the Himalaya clause. The civil law influence is never far away, as even a suggestion that

---

658   Ibid., para 45.
659   http://www.southafrica.info/about/democracy/judiciary.htm#
Veaqk7sViUk#ixzz3kZ8IKj86

226

the shipper makes the contractual offer of carriage to a class of potential acceptors does not stretch the doctrine beyond its limits.[660]

Case law is significant and explains that South Africa very comfortably managed to blend the common law with the civil laws in relation to the interpretation and application of Himalaya clauses. The first significant case was adjudicated in 1989, three years after *The New York Star.*

8.3.2 Jurisprudence

8.3.2.1 *Santam Insurance Co Ltd v. SA Stevedores Ltd.*[661]

The facts again are simple. Engines belonging to Toyota ware discharged from the vessel Sanko Vega by servants of the defendant. Due to their negligence, one case was dropped and the engines were damaged. The question was whether the independent contractor was able to take advantage of the one-year limitation period and the limitation per package provisions pursuant to the applicable Hague-Visby Rules.

Wilson J understood that the ratio of the Himalaya clause was the relevant issue, namely whether an unconnected party to a contract can still rely on the exemption clause. He proceeded to analyse the relevant English jurisprudence in detail beginning with *Elder Dempster* and progressing via *Adler* to *Scruttons Ltd* and eventually arriving at *The New York Star*. He furthermore consulted Australian, Unites States and Canadian cases. [662]

Reverting to the present case, Wilson J looked at Clause 4 of the bill of lading which stated:

---

660 John Hare, *Shipping Law & Admiralty Jurisdiction in South Africa* (1999) Juta & Co Ltd., 403. The Author specifically quotes Powles LMCQ August 1979 at 336 and see the dissenting judgment of Viscount Dilhorne in *the Eurymedon.*
661 [1989] 1 All SA 196 (D).
662 See 196-205.

(LIABILITY OF STEVEDORES AND OTHERS)

Without prejudice to any provision hereof, it is hereby expressly agreed that all servants, agents and independent contractors
including in particular but not by way of limitation stevedores
used or employed by the carrier for the purpose of or in conjunction with the performance of any of the Carrier's obligations under this Bill of Lading shall in consideration of their agreeing to
be so used or employed have the benefit of all rights, defences,
exceptions from or limitation from liability and immunities for
whatsoever nature and referred to incorporated herein applicable to the Carrier or to which the carrier is entitled hereunder so
that in no circumstances shall any such servants, agents or any
independent contractor be under any liability greater than that
of the Carrier hereunder. It is hereby further expressly agreed
that for the purposes of the foregoing provision the Carrier is or
shall be deemed to be acting as agent or trustee on behalf and for
the benefit of all persons who are or might be its servants, agents
and independent contractors from time to time for the purpose
of or in connections with the performance of any of the Carrier's
obligations under this Bill of Lading and that all such persons
shall to this extent be or be deemed to be parties to the contract
contained in or evidenced by this Bill of Lading.

Evidence was produced that Sanko Shipping working directly
with Toyota Japan was aware of the Himalaya clauses in the
1984 and 1983 Bills of Lading.

It was also agreed that this was a test case as to the efficacy of
a Himalaya clause in a Bill of Lading in terms of Roman-Dutch
law.[663] However, the evidence in effect pointed to the fact that
the parties were aware of the clauses and Wilson J noted:

Thus, in reading of the contract itself it appears that the carrier
was acting on behalf of the stevedores and that Clause 4 was
an acceptable "Himalaya clause" conferring protection on and
exemption to the Defendant. I have however, in addition, in deciding what the intention of the parties to the agreement was,

---

663   Ibid., 207.

had regard to the agreement in its contextual setting.[664]

Wilson J also observed that Sanko inserted clause 4 into the contract and that the defendant satisfied the first three requirements enunciated by Lord Reid in *Scruttons Ltd* and is therefore entitled to the protection and limitations as set out in clause 4.[665]

8.3.2.2 *Bouygues Offshore and Another v Owner of the MT Tigr and another*[666]

This case deals with a towage contract where a clause was inserted exempting the Charterer of the tug from any liability for loss or damage sustained by the tow. The first applicant was the owner of a barge which had been grounded on the Cape Town coastline while being towed by a tug owned by the first respondent and chartered by the second respondent. The applicant sued the two respondents for damages as well as for repayment of the towage price it had already paid. The problem was that the tug - due to problems with the engines - could only operate at 60% capacity. It was considered to do repairs before the towage took place in Point Noire in the Congo. As it turned out, it could not be done and hence repairs were to be undertaken in Cape Town after the towage had been performed.

The towage contract contained a clause exempting the second respondent from liability for any loss or damage sustained by the tow, whether caused though breach of contract, negligence or any fault in addition to a Himalaya clause extending the exemption to the first respondent.

The applicant's case was that it had validly rescinded the contract by reason of a fraudulent misrepresentation concerning the tug's towing capacity.[667] The tug was not seaworthy, therefore, not

---

664   Ibid., 207.
665   Ibid., 208.
666   1995, (4) SA 49 (C).
667   Ibid.,50.

ready to perform the tow. It resulted that – due to a severe storm – the tug could not keep the tow away from the coast line and hence contributed to the grounding.

The court held that there was misrepresentation as to the capacity of the tug and that the applicant was entitled to rescind the contract. Importantly, because the misrepresentation was made by the first respondent, the applicant can rescind the contract between it and the first respondent and, hence, the first respondent could not rely on the Himalaya Clause.[668] Farlam J specifically noted:

> … the whole history of the Himalaya clause made it clear that the mischief which it has been designed to combat was the exposure of the servant, agent or subcontractor of a carrier or other such party to liability from which the carrier himself was exempted: it had not been intended (nor could the other contracting party, such as the shipper, reasonably have anticipated that there was an intention) to create an exemption which would enure for the benefit of the servant, agent or subcontractor even where the carrier's exemption was lost, for example, through rescission.[669]

The court subsequently allowed the claims of the applicant against the second respondent which was the charterer.

8.3.2.3 Owners of Cargo Formerly laden on Board of MV "Mas Tiga" v Confreight Cargo Management Centre Pty Ltd. [670]

The facts are rather complicated. Air-conditioning units of the plaintiff were damaged whilst being stored at the defendant's premises. Two Bills of lading were involved each containing a Himalaya clause.

Allied Sea Freight Line (ASL) issued a bill of lading, and so did the Cargo Management Centre (CMC). The plaintiff contracted

---

668   Ibid., 54.
669   Ibid., 54.
670   [2001] JPL 8954 (D).

with Italfreight acting as agent of ASL to carry the cargo from Hong Kong to Johannesburg under the ASL bill of lading. ASL then contracted the carriage from Hong Kong to Durban to the Malaysian International Shipping Corporation (MISC) on the terms of the MISC bill of lading.[671] MISC was the carrier to Aprile China Ltd, (an agent of ASL) the Aprile Group's Hong Kong based company was the shipper. Italfreight was named as the consignee.

Both bills of lading contained a clause entitling them to subcontract on any terms the whole or any part of the carriage as well as a Himalaya clause.

Bridge Shipping Ltd. as agent of MISC contracted with the defendant to store the goods pending transport to Johannesburg on terms of the contract between ASL and the plaintiff. The goods were damaged while in possession of the defendant due to negligence of his employees. At the time, the damage occurred the plaintiff was the owner of the air conditioners. The defendant admitted liability but contended that he was protected under the time bar in one or both of the bills of lading.

The central question was whether the defendant can establish the existence of a contractual relationship between him and the plaintiff.

Theron J noted that the Himalaya clause had its origin in *Adler* and that the Privity rule gave way to commercial reality in *Scruttons Ltd*. However, he distinguished this case by noting that the defendant was twice removed from a party to the contract.[672] He furthermore referred to *Santam Insurance Company* which introduced the Himalaya clause as part of South African law. He then proceeded to lay out the contractual chain as follows:

> The plaintiff contracted with ASL on an ASL bill of lading.

---

671   Ibid., 3.
672   Ibid., 1.

ASL in turn contracted with MISC on the MISC bill of lading.

MISC in turn contracted with the defendant according to the defendant's general trading terms.[673]

The defence contended that there are five grounds upon which the defendant can rely on the time bar on either the ASL or MISC bills of lading.

ASL acted as agent for the plaintiff

Defendant authorised MISC to contract for its protection

MISC ratified ASL's action

MISC acted as agent for ASL

Stipulatio alteri[674]

The court addressed each of the contentions in turn.

8.3.2.4.1 ASL acted as agent for the plaintiff

The court dismissed this argument. The starting point was the fact that the plaintiff contracted with Italfreight acting as agent of ASL to carry the cargo to Johannesburg on the terms of the ASL bill of lading. ASL was the carrier and, hence, liable from the time the cargo was taken into its charge until it was delivered in Johannesburg. ASL was entitled to sub-contract and did so by engaging MISC to carry the cargo from Hong Kong to Durban under the MISC terms. Theron J noted:

> In my view, the right of ASL to sub-contract for the performance of its obligations as carrier under the ASL bill of lading issued but it did not constitute any authority to ASL to act as agent for the plaintiff and hereby to bind the plaintiff as principal or otherwise as a party to the sub-contract. ... The plaintiff was certainly not a person "to whom a bill of lading was issued by MISC "which is the manner in which the authority contained

---

673   Ibid., 7.
674   Ibid., 7.

in clause 13.2.1 of the defendant's standard trading condition identifies the person with whom MISC was authorised to contract as agent for the defendant. ... The plaintiff's contractual relationship was with ASL and not with ASL's sub-contractors. There is accordingly no proper basis for the defendant's contention that the defendant can rely on the MISC bill of lading time-bar and Himalaya clause.[675]

8.3.2.3.2 Defendant authorised MISC to contract for its protection

The court also dismissed this argument as it is inconsistent with the terms of the authority granted to MISC and cannot be sustained:

There is no evidence whatsoever to suggest that MISC, whatever the terms of the authority furnished to it by the defendant, authorises or ratified ASL's act in purporting to contract as agent or trustee for persons such as MISC and the defendant.[676]

8.3.2.4.2 MISC acted as agent for ASL

The defence argued that the trading terms of MISC were wide enough to include ASL contracting with the plaintiff for the defendant's protection. The court dismissed this claim by arguing:

In my view, this contention can also not be sustained. Clause 4 of the MISC bill of lading provides that "the carrier shall be entitled to sub-contract on any terms the whole or any part of the carriage. "Accordingly, MISC, in contracting with the defendant to store the containers, was not acting on anybody's behalf, but its own.[677]

---

675   Ibid., 10-9.
676   Ibid., 13.
677   Ibid., 14.

8.3.2.3.4. *Stipulatio alteri*

The defence argued that the time-bar and the Himalaya clause in the ASL bill of lading constitute a *Stipulatio alteri*. The question was whether the defendant accepted the benefits of the *Stipulatio* which had to conform to the usual requirements of the acceptance of an offer, in particular that acceptance must be communicated to the offeror. Furthermore, the plaintiff knew that the goods would be stored by the defendant. The court noted:

> The argument that such knowledge, however gained, constitutes communication of the implied acceptance of the benefit extended by the ASL bill of lading, is fallacious. The plaintiff may well have acquired such knowledge only after the cargo had been damaged.[678]

Consequently, the court held that the defendant cannot rely on any of the Himalaya clauses as he was twice removed from any party to the contract.

8.3.2.4 *Tebe Trading Pty Ltd v Mediterranean Shipping Company (Pty) Ltd* [679]

The appellant entered into an agreement with the respondent to ship a consignment of litchis to the Middle East. He entered into the contract on the representation that the fruit would arrive within 14 days at its destination. It arrived more than a month late and could not be sold, hence, the appellant sued for breach of contract or alternatively breach of a duty of care. The respondent contended that there is no valid contract between the grower and the appellant and that ownership had not passed, and the risk remains with the grower. The lower court ruled that the essential elements of agreement as to price had not been established and that the appellant lacked jurisdiction.

---

678   Ibid., 14.
679   [2006] JOL 16093 (D).

On appeal Levinsohn J isolated six issues which needed to be resolved:

> Does the plaintiff have *locus standi* to sue, whether in contract or in delict?
>
> In concluding a contract with the plaintiff, did the defendant contract as principal or agent for Mediterranean Shipping Company SA of Geneva?
>
> If a contract was concluded between the plaintiff and the defendant, principal to principal:
>
> What were the terms of the contract? This includes whether or not the provisions of The Hague-Visby rules apply to the contract.
>
> Did the defendant breach the contract?
>
> Did the defendant owe a duty of care to advise the plaintiff if:
>
> The estimated date of departure of the MV "MSC Spain" on voyage from Durban to Jebel Ali was delayed; and
>
> The route of the vessel from Durban to Jebel Ali was changed?
>
> If such a duty of care did exist, did the defendant breach that duty with fault so as to incur liability to the plaintiff?
>
> Can the defendant rely on the Himalaya clause in the bills of lading, as pleaded; if so
>
> Is the defendant excused of all liability that it might otherwise have been found to have to the plaintiff?
>
> If not excused of all liability, can the defendant rely on the provisions of The Hague-Visby Rules as pleaded?[680]

It is convenient to examine the most important parts of this case under the headings as proposed by Levinsohn J.

---

680   Ibid., 2-3.

8.3.2.4.1 Does the plaintiff have *locus standi* to sue, whether in contract or in delict?

The court referred back to the facts as presented in the lower court. The lower court merely decided that the plaintiff had no standing and, therefore, any other issues were not deliberated upon. The salient facts were as follows. The vessel did not depart on 6 December and the plaintiff amended its booking. The containers would now be carried from Jebel Ali to Dammam in Saudi Arabia. The vessel duly sailed to the outer anchorage on December 13. On the same date, the vessel was instructed to re-enter the Durban and 171 containers were discharged and the vessel sailed to Maputo on December 15. The planners in Geneva decided that the vessel ought to take goods on board from another vessel which was towed into the harbour of Maputo. The vessel eventually arrived at Jebel Ali on 10 January 2002. Transhipment then took place and the containers finally arrived at Dammam on 14 January 2002. The lower court decided that the plaintiff had no standing as there was no contract between it and the supplier of the goods. The issue was that the essential element as to price was not established. The cross examination in the lower court essentially established that the grower was not paid any price nor was a price determined. The plaintiff would have sold the litchis at the best price in the Middle East, that is the price is only fixed once the market determines it at the place of sale. In essence, a base price is determined - that is - the grower indicates what price he would expect, in this case R35. The final price is only determined once the goods are sold. The plaintiff then would deduct costs and a profit mark up. If the market is favourable the grower gets more than R35 or conversely if the market is down, less than this amount. The plaintiff in this case – given the adverse situation – paid the grower R35. The court determined that the price was not expressly stated but determinable hence a contract existed. [681]

---

681   Ibid., 9-13.

8.3.2.4.1 In concluding a contract with the plaintiff, did the defendant contract as principal or agent for Mediterranean Shipping Company SA of Geneva?

Evidence was presented indicating that the shipping line sent a booking confirmation stating in para 2: Bills of Lading must be presented to MSC at least four (4) days prior sailing date. MSC require four (4) copies.

It was also established that MSC is the agent of MSC Geneva and it was established that the defendant does not operate any ships. Under the agreement the defendant was authorised to sign on behalf of the principals and/or master bills of lading and all other shipping documents as required. The court noted that there is clear authority in English law that the contract of carriage is concluded prior to the issuing of a bill of lading and it is contemplated that the bill of lading includes terms which are contemplated by the contract.[682] The court held that in this case the contract was formed by the forwarding agent and MSC Geneva and, hence, the plaintiff failed to prove that he has a contract with the defendant. The court found in favour of the defendant.

In the light of the finding in question 2 question 3 became obsolete.

8.3.2.4.2 Did the defendant owe a duty of care to advise the plaintiff in relation to time and route change?

The court noted that the defendant solicited the business of the plaintiff on the clear understanding that the ship would depart on or about 7 December and that there would be a short transit time to the port of destination.

The clear question that arises is whether the defendant in its

---

682   Ibid., 16-17.

capacity as an agent ought to have informed the plaintiff that the transit time would be significantly extended so that the plaintiff could then decide whether it elected to remove the containers from the vessel and make other arrangements for the disposal of the litchis.[683] The court noted that the defendant was not given the relevant information on 14 December and that there was an overwhelming probability that the defendant must have known of the re-routing of the ship and that it would take significantly longer to arrive at its intended destination.

This conclusion led the court to ask the next question, namely whether there was a duty to inform. The conduct in question is only unlawful "if there was a duty to act to avoid harm to the plaintiff."[684] The court stated:

> I am of the opinion that the defendant knew on 14 December 2001 that there would be an extended transit time. It failed to inform the plaintiff thereof in circumstances where it had a duty to do so and would have foreseen that a failure to do so would result in harm to the plaintiff. It was therefore negligent. The fourth and fifths question are answered in favour of the plaintiff.[685]

8.3.2.4.3 Can the defendant rely on the Himalaya clause in the bills of lading, as pleaded?

The defendant relied on clause 18 which in the relevant parts notes:

> "Liability of servants and sub-contractors" It is hereby expressly agreed that no servant or agent of the Carrier, including any independent sub-contractor employed by the Carrier in any circumstance whatsoever be under any liability whatsoever to the Merchant for any loss or damage or delay of whatsoever kind

---

683 Ibid., 20.
684 *McCann v Goodall Group Operations (Pty) Ltd* 1995 (2) SA 718 (C) at 722.
685 Tebe Trading, (n679) 29.

> arising or resulting directly or indirectly from any act neglect or
> default on his part while acting in the course of, or in connection
> with his employment ... [686]

The bill of lading was assigned by the defendant as agent of the carrier. The court noted the fact that Himalaya clauses are part of South African law referring to *Santam Insurance Co.*[687] As the court already found the defendant negligent the question was whether the negligence occurred "while acting in the course of, or in connection with his employment."[688]

Levinsohn J - after consulting the agency contract between the defendant and MSC Geneva – argued:

> The basis upon which the Himalaya Clause has been held, in shipping law in general, to constitute an effective stipulation in favour of parties other than the carrier, is one of commercial efficacy as is clearly indicated in the judgments to which I have referred. Wide wording in a clause containing such stipulations must be construed narrowly to achieve this object within the context of the contract of carriage and not beyond it. Thus, in the clause in question, where the expression "while acting in the course of ... his employment" is used, it must be understood to confine the particular "course of employment" to the acts which are required to assist in the performance of the contract of carriage. It could, in my view, hardly be contended by the defendant that if, in the course of marketing the services of MSC SA Geneva, the defendant somewhat negligently caused the plaintiff to suffer loss, the defendant could invoke the Himalaya stipulation in the bill of lading as a defence. This is because the bill of lading covers a specific contract of carriage and stipulations in it which limit liability are necessarily confined to stipulations concerning that specific contract. In my view, the words "in connection with," although objectively capable of a wide construction, must, for the purpose of ascertaining their meaning in the Himalaya Clause, be restrictively construed to

---

686   Ibid., 30-31.
687   Ibid., 32.
688   Clause 18 see 30-31.

limit their application to the contract of carriage. The conduct which I have found to be negligent in this case was an omission to give a customer of the carrier information which would, in all probability, have resulted in that customer cancelling his contract with the defendant's principal.[689]

The court found that the plaintiff was successful on issues 1,4,5 and 6 identified above and ruled in favour of the plaintiff. Importantly, the court found the defendant was not covered under the Himalaya clause.

8.3.2.5 *Mediterranean Shipping Company (Pty) Ltd v Tebe Trading Pty Ltd* [690]

The above case was appealed again in 2008. In essence the appeal was directed at the issues as noted in the above case namely:

1. Did the defendant owe a duty of care to advise the plaintiff if:

   a. The estimated date of departure of the MV "MSC Spain" on voyage from Durban to Jebel Ali was delayed; and

   b. The route of the vessel from Durban to Jebel Ali was changed?

2. If such a duty of care did exist, did the defendant breach that duty with fault so as to incur liability to the plaintiff?

Scott JA, after reciting the important facts again came to the conclusion that *Tebe* knew of the initial delay but was not aware that the vessel returned to port again. The court also referred to the fact that *Tebe* was aware of the term in the bill of lading, namely clause 4 which allowed the carrier to deviate from the

---

689 Ibid., 35-36.
690 2008 (6) SA 595 (SCA).

advertised or ordinary route. Scott JA noted:

> The appellant was not in any way responsible for that deviation. It was furthermore at all times merely acting as agent, either for the carrier or MSC Geneva. By reason of the clauses in the bills of lading, Tebe would have had no claim in contract or delict against the party responsible for the deviation, whether that party was the carrier or MSC Geneva. Unable to recover from the principal, Tebe seeks in effect to circumvent the consequences of the contract by holding the principal's agent personally liable in delict for failing to afford Tebe the opportunity of removing its containers from the vessel on a ground not amounting to a breach of contract on the part of the principal. But agents are contractually bound to protect the interests of their principals. The legal duty that Tebe contends was owed to it by the appellant would therefore be in conflict with the contractual obligation which the latter has to its principal. Even if it were to be accepted that the appellant was negligent, there can be no good reason in my view, given the contractual setting, for the existence of a legal duty on the appellant to take such steps as may have been reasonable to prevent the harm.[691]

The appeal was upheld, and the court found it unnecessary to consider the question of the Himalaya clause.

8.3.2.5. *LTA Construction Ltd v Mediterranean Shipping Company Depots Pty Ltd* [692]

A mobile crane was offloaded in Durban. Due to the delay in obtaining customs clearance the carne was shifted to the premises of the defendant where the crane sustained damage. The issue was again whether the defendant is protected by clauses 17 and 19 of the bill of lading. The initial defence in relation to lapse of time was abandoned as it was made clear to the court that the defendant agreed on an extension.

---

691   Ibid., 604.
692   [2006] JDR 0303 (D).

Clause 17 in effect governed the period of responsibility of the carrier and his agents which was restricted to the carriage operation only. That means that all events during or before loading and after discharge is the sole responsibility of the Merchant.

Clause 18 – Liability of Servants and Subcontractors – expanded clause 17. It specially included stevedores, terminal operators and any other independent contractors.

It noted in the important parts:

> It is hereby expressly agreed that no servant or agent of the Carrier, including any independent subcontractors employed by the carrier shall in any circumstances whatsoever be under any liability whatsoever to the Merchant for any loss or damage or delay of whatsoever kind arising or resulting directly from any act, neglect or default on his part while acting in the course of his employment ... the carrier is or shall be deemed to be acting as agent or trustee on behalf of and for the benefit of any person who might be his servants or agents (including independent contractors) and all such persons shall be deemed to be party to this Bill of Lading.[693]

Hurt J posed the question whether clauses 17 and 18 can relieve the defendant from any obligations. He also noted that clause 18 was a version of a Himalaya clause. He stated that, "the development of the law dealing with Himalaya clauses is concisely dealt with in a judgement by Wilson J in *Santam Insurance Co Ltd v. SA Stevedores Ltd."[694]* Contrary to *Santam Insurance* where South Africa Law was applied this contract was governed by English law pursuant to clause 2 of the contract.

He therefore approached the issue with English law in mind specially relying on the principles put forward by Lord Reid in *Scruttons Ltd*. Hurt J also noted that the plaintiff argued that the defendant could not rely on *Scruttons Ltd* and especially on

---

693   Ibid., 5.
694   Ibid., 7.

clause 18 because:

a) The defendant had not established that the Carrier had the defendant's authority to conclude a contract with the Plaintiff on behalf of the Defendant nor had it been established that the Defendant had subsequently   ratified any such contractual stipulations on its behalf. (3rd of Lord Reid's requirements)

b) The defendant had not established that he has given any consideration, as required by the English law of contract, in return for the contractual protection for which it stipulated in its plea; and

c) The bill was intended to apply only from the time of loading to the time of discharge on to the wharf and its conditions did extend to cover any situations after discharge.[695]

Hurt J addressed the three objections. As to the first one he noted that the defendant worked closely with the Mediterranean Shipping Company for the past five years. He noted that:

> In my view this evidence clearly establishes that either blanket or express authority or implied authority, by the Defendant to the Carrier [was given] to conclude a contract on its behalf.[696]

In relation to the issue of consideration the court simply noted that the ruling in *The Eurymedon* effectively answered the issue of consideration. The court also observed that the dissenting judgments of Lord Simon of Glaisdale and Viscount Dilhorne were effectively dispelled in *The New York Star.* Hurt J specifically stressed the following point:

> Clearly their Lordships were, in this decision, were stressing the importance of commercial efficacy over and above the possible results of too pedantic an approach to legal principle. Accepting that this is the approach dictated by English law, there seems to me to be no reason to draw any distinction between the facts in

---

695   Ibid., 9.
696   Ibid., 10.

this case and those in the *[New York Star.]* [697]

As to the third point the defence argued that the contract of carriage had ended and specifically argued that clauses 5 and 17 were relevant. Clause 5 inter alia noted that discharge to the wharf "shall constitute due delivery of the goods under the Bill of Lading" and clause 17 which is entitled "Period of Responsibility" stated:

> The carrier or his agent shall not be liable for loss or damage to the goods during the period before loading and after discharge from the vessel, howsoever such loss or damage arises.[698]

His Honour did not agree with the partial reading of the clauses by the defence. In particular "clause 17 made specific reference to the contingency that goods might be "in the custody of the Carrier or his servants before loading and after discharge."[699] The court also took note of the *New York Star* where storage before actual delivery was a standard practice and that it was within the contemplation of the Plaintiff and Mediterranean Shipping Company that removal and storage services would be rendered in order to avoid unnecessary charges if the goods are removed by the port authority.

The court granted judgment in favour of the Defendant.

8.3.2.6 MT Fotiy Krylov v Owners of the Mt Ruby Deliverer.[700]

The facts are as follows:

The charterer of the *MT Fotiy Krylov* applied for an order to set aside the arrest of the vessel. The reason for the arrest was the collision between the tug *MT Nikolay Chiker* and the *MT Ruby Deliverer*. The collision – as alleged – was caused by the

---

697   Ibid., 4.
698   Ibid., 15.
699   Ïbid., 17.
700   [2008] (5) SA 434 (C).

negligence of the master/or crew of the *MT Nikolay Chiker*. It was undisputed that the *MT Fotiy Krylov* was an associated ship to the *Nikolay Chiker.* The tug owner was to tow the rig (*Ruby Deliverer*) from Brazil to India or Pakistan. The obligation with regard of getting the rig to its destination fell upon the tug owner.

For the purpose of this discussion the only relevant issue was the argument that the cause of action was time barred and that the jurisdiction clause within the towing contract contained a Himalaya clause. [701]

Clause 19 of that agreement which includes the Himalaya clause reads as follows:

> All exceptions, exemptions, defences, immunities, limitations of liability, indemnities, privileges and conditions granted or provided by this agreement or by any applicable statute rule or regulation for the benefit of the Tug owner or Hirer shall also apply to and be for the benefit of demise charterers, subcontractors, operators, masters, officers and crew of the Tug or Tow and to and be for the benefit of all bodies corporate, parent of, subsidiary to, affiliated with or under the same management as either of them, as well as all directors, officers, servants and agents of the same and to and be for the benefit of all performing parties performing services within the scope of this agreement for or on behalf of the Tug or Tug owner or Hirer as servants, agents and subcontractors of such parties. The Tug owner or Hirer shall be deemed to be acting as agent or trustee of and for the benefit of all such persons, entities and vessels set forth above but only for the limited purpose of contracting for the extension of such benefits to such person, body or vessel.[702]

Furthermore clause 25 also provided that the agreement is governed by English Law and any disputes must be submitted to the High Court of Justice in London and clause 24 provided a one-year time limit to bring suit.[703]

---

701   Ibid., 441.
702   Ibid., 441.
703   Ibid., 442.

Davis J noted that the crux of the issue was whether the defendant performed a service within the scope of the Towcon agreement. If he has then the Himalaya clause becomes effective and he can rely on the protection granted under it. *Santam Insurance* as well as *the Starsin* were noted to explain the effect of the Himalaya clause. Davis J concluded that: ;

> a contract was concluded and that it was so contracted and further that it took place within the context of the broader Towcon agreement that is to fulfil any obligation to provide in assisting tug services.[704]

Considering clauses 19, 24 and 25 the court found for the plaintiff and hence dismissed the action *in rem*.

8.4 Conclusion

South Africa, being a mixed legal system has adopted the Himalaya clauses as developed in England. It is remarkable to observe how the South African courts have applied the Himalaya clause. Lord Reid's principles as noted in *Scruttons* were examined and applied. Arguably South African courts appear to be comfortable to develop their own judgments as demonstrated by the courts in *Santam Insurance* which introduced the Himalaya clause into South African law.

The exemption clause was used in the proper context taking also account of the civil law aspect, namely the principle of *stipulatio alteri*. The issue that The Hague-Visby Rules are central in determining the liability of those who are subject to the Convention was recognised in all judgments. In addition, the judgments relying on English law were properly constructed taking note of all the relevant points which were developed not only in English jurisprudence but what might be termed in the international context.

---

704   Ibid., 448.

The issues where the Himalaya clause applied in South Africa ranged from the usual one-year limitation period and the limitation per package provisions to towage – that is actions in rem - to contract formation and hence to all situation where the Himalaya clause is potentially applicable. Most importantly the principle of commercial efficacy within a contractual setting is a paramount consideration for South African Courts.

Specifically, *Tebe Trading Pty Ltd v Mediterranean Shipping Company (Pty) Ltd* exhibits an outstanding standard of judicial reasoning. Of interest is that the court interpreted the Himalaya clause narrowly. Arguably, due to the negligence and the fact that the respondent was not acting within the confines of the contract the court found that no protection is available under the Himalaya clause and found for the plaintiff. The judgment was upheld in the subsequent appeal by *Mediterranean Shipping Company (Pty) Ltd.*

In essence, the Himalaya clause is not a term which will protect all those connected to the marine adventure but only those who are connected to the contract. The court made it plain that "the Himalaya Clause, [must] be restrictively construed to limit their application to the contract of carriage."[705]

---

705   *Tebe Trading Pty Ltd v Mediterranean Shipping Company* at 35-36.

9

CANADIAN JURISPRUDENCE ON THE HIMALAYA CLAUSE

9.1 Introduction

Canada's legal system is a dual system because in some parts of Canada the common law is entrenched, whereas in the French speaking part the civil law system is followed, specifically the French legal order. For this reason, the Canadian jurisprudence on Himalaya clauses is of interest.

As noted above the Canadian legal system is clearly divided into a dual system that is civil law and common law. However, some overlap arguably is inevitable and, hence, Canadian cases must be viewed not only from a national point of view but rather from the civil or common law perspective. In other words, if a case is heard in Quebec, then civil laws will be applied and if a case is heard in Toronto, common law. Hence, principles which are applicable in Quebec might not necessarily also be relevant in Toronto. Of course, this distinction does not apply to Federal laws, such as The Hague Rules which are applied uniformly across Canada. However, whether civil law of common law is applied the general principle of the Himalaya clause is uniformly applied across Canada relying on "international" jurisprudence, mainly case law which was developed in England and the United States. The first major case occurred in Canada in 1971 but still adhered to the Privity rule.

9.1 Jurisprudence

9.2.1 Canadian General Electric Co. v. Pickford & Black Ltd.[706]

The stevedores negligently stowed heavy electrical equipment on the vessel and it was found that the cargo shifted in the hold forcing the ship to return to harbour. The claim against the ship was settled and this case involves the question whether the stevedores were liable for the damage to the equipment. Ritchie J observed that the stevedores were under a duty to take reasonable care to avoid damage to the goods.[707] This issue was not in dispute but the respondent claimed that they could take advantage of the limitation of damages clause in accordance with the provisions of the Canadian *Water Carriage of Goods Act*, R.S.C. 1952, c. 291 incorporated in the through bill of lading.[708]

Ritchie J pointed out that the stevedores were complete strangers to the contract of carriage and would not be affected by the limitations and would therefore bear full responsibility for the damages. He noted that the law in this regard is fully stated in *Midland Silicones*.

The court first established that the stevedores acted negligently in stowing the electrical equipment and overturned the lower court's decision on this matter. On this issue, the appeal was allowed.

The court was not required to address the point whether the stevedores were covered by the limitations clause, but referring to *Midland Silicones*, it could be reasonably assumed that they were not and the Privity rule was maintained.

---

706   [1971] S.C.R. 41.
707   Ibid., para 6.
708   Ibid.

9.2.2 The Suleyman Stalskiy [709]

The plaintiff sued the stevedores and the shipowner for damages caused to 37 bundles of steel tubing. The plaintiff requested that the stevedores arrange for in-shed storage. The stevedores failed to execute the request and, as a consequence, the tubings were damaged by rain. The plaintiff also asserted that the shipowners had no authority to contract as agents for the stevedores.

Counsel for the defendant admitted that the stevedore was a bailee (or sub-bailee of the shipowner who is the bailee of the goods) for reward of the goods and that the shipowner in the natural course of business engaged the stevedore to unload and store the goods until they were delivered to the consignee. The issue was whether the bailment was for reward or gratuitous, as in the first case a higher duty of care is applied than in the case of gratuitous bailment. The court found that the stevedores were negligent in handling the goods under the bailment for reward.

The next point was whether the stevedores can take advantage of exemption clause 37 which was included in the bill of lading but in very small print. The clause reads:

(Liability of Stevedores and Others)

Without prejudice to any other provision hereof it is hereby expressly agreed that all servants, agents and independent contractors used or employed by the Carrier for the purpose of or in connection with the performance of any of the Carrier's obligations under the Bill of Lading shall in consideration of their agreeing to be so used or employed, have the benefit of all rights, defences, exceptions from or limitations of liability and immunities of whatsoever nature referred to or incorporated herein applicable to the Carrier or to which the Carrier is entitled hereunder, so that in no circumstances shall any servant, agent or independent contractor be under any liability greater than that of the carrier hereunder. It is hereby further expressly agreed that for the purpose of the foregoing provisions the

---

709   (1976) 2 Lloyd's Rep 609.

Carrier is or shall be deemed or acting as agent or trustee on behalf and for the benefit of all persons who are or may be its servants, agents or independent contractors from time to time for the purpose of or in connection with the performance of any of Carrier's obligations under this Bill of Lading and that all such persons shall to the extent be or be deemed to be parties in the contract contained in or evidenced by this Bill of Lading.[710]

The defendant never saw the Bill of Lading until it was surrendered to the stevedore by the client of the plaintiff.

Schultz J noted that the law on this point was proclaimed in *Scruttons Ltd v Midland Silicones Ltd.*. It is sufficient to note Lord Morris who noted that: "there is a clear pronouncement of our Lordship's House that only a person who is a party to a contract can sue on it (*Dunlop Pneumatic Tyres Co v Selfridge & Co Ltd.*).[711]

The defendant relied on the judgement in the *Eurymedon* to the effect that the law has been developed further impairing the principle of law stated in the *Scruttons* judgement.[712] The court went on to quote many statements by the learned judges in the *Eurymedon*.

Counsel for the plaintiff argued that there is no evidence that the carrier had authority from the stevedore to contract as the agent of the stevedore in order for the exemption clause to apply. However, the court noted that the defendant was not a party to the Bill of Lading and hence is liable for the damages.[713] In addition the court read clause 37 literally by stating that the clause covers the "carrier's obligation" and not the defendant's obligation. In essence, the court overlooked that the shipper implicitly expected that the carrier will make the goods available for him to be collected. The literal reading was not – as was coined in

---

710   Ibid., 613.
711   Scruttons Ltd, 385.
712   Suleyman, 615.
713   Ibid., 617.

England - commercially sound. Not surprisingly the court ruled against the stevedore despite the fact that the opinions of judges in the *Eurymedon*, which were quoted, pointed to a different outcome.

The judgement can be explained by the fact that Schultz J noted that he is not bound by the statements of the House of Lords but that the judgement of the Supreme Court of Canada is the determinative law and hence the Privity rule still prevailed.

9.2.3 Eisen Und Metall A.G. v. Ceres Stevedoring Co. Ltd.[714]

The facts were that a container containing nickel scraps was stolen at the terminal in Montreal. The container was left unattended next to a public road and could only be moved by a 25-ton lifter. The only 25-ton lifter belonging to the company was also left unattended in the area with the engines running and the key in the ignition.

This was an appeal from the superior court of Montreal. The court ordered the defendant pay damages to the plaintiff due to gross negligence. The Superior court of the district of Montreal in the first instance ruled that because of gross negligence the defendants were not entitled to the exemption clause and that there was no contractual relationship between the plaintiff and the defendant. Furthermore, the clause was invalid under Quebec and Canadian law. In addition, it was illegal to contract out of the liability resulting from gross negligence.

The Court of Appeal in the Province of Quebec District of Montreal stated the appeal questions a being;

First whether a person who is not a party to a contract are entitled to invoke clauses contracting out of negligence which are stated in the contract to be for their benefit and secondly

---

714   [1977] 1 Lloyd's Rep. 665.

whether clauses of exoneration from liability for negligence constitute a valid defence in the case of gross negligence.[715]

Owen J. noted that the Himalaya clause as expressed in Clause 3 contains three provisions:

1. A stipulation by the carrier that no servant or agent of the carrier or independent contractor employed by the carrier shall be liable for damage resulting from his negligence.

2. A stipulation by the carrier that every exemption in the bill of lading applicable to the carrier shall also be available to his servants or agents.

3. A statement that for the purpose of the clause the carrier is acting as agent or trustee on behalf of his servants and agents (including independent contractors) who are deemed to be parties to the contract evidenced by the bill of lading. [716]

He then went on to indicate that the problems or issues raised against the defendant terminal operator from which the container was stolen can be summarised by the following questions:

1. Was the loss of the container due to the negligence of the defendants?

2. If the loss was due to the negligence of the defendants, are defendants entitled to the benefit of the exonerating clauses?

3. If the defendants are entitled to invoke the benefit of the exonerating clauses in the bill of lading was there gross negligence on the part of the defendant?

4. If there was gross negligence on the part of the defendants do the exonerating clauses afford protection against gross negligence?[717]

---

715   Ibid., 666.
716   Ibid., 667.
717   Ibid., 667.

As to the first issue the court found that indeed gross negligence contributed to the theft of the container as the defendant did not act as a prudent administrator. (*bon père de famille*)

In relation to the second point the court looked at the bill of lading, namely Clauses 3 and 5 which in the court's opinion provide for complete exonerations.[718] Owen J stated the position of the court as follows:

> Taking the clear meaning of the clauses in the bill of lading I would say it was intended by the immediate parties to the contract that the carrier's servants, agents and independent contractors employed from time to time by the carriers should be enticed to the benefit of the non-responsibility clauses in the bill of lading.[719]

The proviso was that such clauses cannot be given effect unless for some reasons they are invalid or illegal. The court consulted leading English, United States and Australian cases and came to the conclusion that, "no series of decisions could illustrate more graphically the importance attached among nations to consistency by their respective courts in the interpretation of the [Himalaya clauses] with far reaching results in the development of the common law."[720]

After coming to the decision that the defendants were entitled to the benefits of the Himalaya clause the third point was analysed. The court agreed with the submission of the plaintiff that the defendant was grossly negligent.

This led the court to the fourth question; was the clause contracting out of liability valid in cases of gross negligence (*faute lourde*). Owen J observed that the defendant failed to provide the care which the least careful and the most stupid person would not fail to give to their own property. He stated the law in Canada as follows:

---

718   Ibid., 668.
719   Ibid., 669.
720   Ibid., 670.

> I have always taken it to be an established principle under our law that a clause contracting out of liability for negligence is ineffective with respect to gross negligence or "faute lourde" on the ground that it is against public order.[721]

The court followed the public policy mandate and hence ruled against the defendant and concluded:

> ... in the present case [the conclusion] is that while the defendants are entitled to invoke in their favour the clauses of non-responsibility contained in the bill of lading such clauses are of no avail because the negligence of defendants amounted to gross negligence or "faute lourde" and it is illegal to contract out of responsibility for gross negligence. [722]

Hence the decision of the lower court was upheld.

9.2.4 Miles International Co. v. Federal Commerce and Navigation Co. and federal Stevedoring Ltd.[723]

This case was heard in the Quebec Superior court. The facts are not complicated. Scrap copper was received by a stevedore for shipment to Montreal. The cargo was shipped in containers and off loaded in Montreal where it was stored for 12 days in an open space. The ship sailed to Rotterdam where the containers were discharged and then sent to Antwerp where it was found that the scrap copper was missing. The disappearance of the copper coils was due to negligence while the goods where in Montreal.

The engagement note, given to the defendants incorporated the clause which was also in the bill of lading. The clause stated as far as relevant:

> Period of responsibility
>
> The carrier or his agent shall not be liable for loss of or dam-

---

721   Ibid., 672.
722   Ibid., 672.
723   [1978] 1 Lloyd's Rep.

age to the goods during the period before loading and after discharge form the vessel.

Exemptions and immunities of all servants and agents of the carrier.

It I hereby agreed that no servant or agent of the carrier (including every independent contractor from time to time employed by the Carrier) shall in any circumstance whatsoever be under any liability whatsoever to the Merchant for any loss damage or delay of whatsoever kind arising or resulting directly from any act in the course of or in connection with his employment, and but without prejudice to this clause, every exemption, limitation, condition and liability herein contained and every right, exemption from liability, defence and immunity of whatsoever nature applicable to the carrier or to which the Carrier is entitled hereunder shall also be available and shall extend to protect every such servant or agent of the carrier acting as aforesaid and for the purpose of all the foregoing provisions of this Clause the Carrier is or shall be deemed to be acting as agent or trustee on behalf of and or the benefit of all persons who are or might be his servants or agents from time to time (including independent contracts as aforesaid) and all such persons shall to this extent be or be deemed to be parties to this contract in or evidenced by this Bill of Lading.

The court first determined the issue of negligence and applied Articles 1053 and 1054 of the Québec Civil Code. Under French law which is in force in Quebec the law distinguishes between negligence and gross negligence. (*faute lourde*). It was found not to be gross negligence because the stevedores took action to prevent a theft. The court noted there was not "a failure to give to the plaintiff's containers while in their possession the care which the least careful and the most stupid person would not fail to give to their own property."[724] The court referred to *Eisen Und Metall A.G. v. Ceres Stevedoring Co. Ltd.* and *The Eurymedon*.

---

724   Miles, 289.

O'Connor J noted that Owen J in *Eisen* followed the ruling of Lord Wilberforce, however, he was urged by council for the plaintiff that the stevedore is not protected because he " is a complete stranger to the contract of carriage, it would not be affected by any provisions for limitation of liability or otherwise contained in the bill of lading. " [725] The judge correctly pointed out to counsel that decisions decided in the courts of Nova Scotia are determined by common law but within the province of Quebec civil law applies "as authorities in Quebec cases … do not depend upon doctrines derived from the English law".[726]

It follows that the defendants' position is that a valid stipulation *pour autrui* was made in Clause 18 pursuant to Articles 1028 and 1029 of the Québec Civil Code. They need to be read together and state:

> Art. 1028. A person cannot, by a contract in his own name, bind one but himself and his heirs and legal representatives, but he may contract in his own name that another shall perform an obligation, and in this case, he is liable in damages if such obligation be not performed by the person indicated.

> Art 1029. A party in like manner may stipulate for the benefit of a third person, when such is the condition of a contract which he makes for himself, or of a gift which he makes to another: and he who makes the stipulation cannot revoke it, if the third person [has] signified his assent to it.

The court noted that there is nothing in the two articles stopping the stevedore taking advantage of the Himalaya clause contained in the Bill of lading.

An issue was raised by the plaintiff whether Quebec law can be applied, and the court was directed to a recent decision where Walsh J noted that the law of Quebec cannot be applied as the contract was entered into in China and Japan. The following statement by Walsh J was considered to be obiter:

---

725   Ibid., 290.
726   Ibid.

> If we were dealing with outward shipment from Quebec where
> the Bill of Lading was issued Article 1029 might then be in-
> voked although I would in any case consider it highly regret-
> table if principles of Canadian Maritime Law which should be
> the same throughout the country could be so interpreted as to
> lead to a different result with respect to a bill of lading made in
> Quebec from that with respect to an identical bill of lading made
> in one of the other provinces. [727]

The court correctly noted that this is impossible as Quebec law needs to be applied and the law cannot be bent for the sake of uniformity. This is obvious as the Canadian like Australian constitution states that contract law is a State matter. In the end, the court found that the stevedores though being negligent were still covered by the Himalaya clause.

9.2.5 ITO-International Terminal Operators Ltd. v. Miida Electronics (Inc.)[728]

A number of calculators were stolen from the ITO Ltd. building while being in their custody. The bill of lading contained a Himalaya clause. One of the issues was whether the Himalaya clause was effective.

In the original hearing Marceau J ruled that ITO could not avail itself of the Himalaya clause as it was not a party to it. However, he noted that Miida, the shipper, knew that a stevedoring firm would be involved and that Miida would derive benefits from it. Hence the shipper was bound by the limitation clause within the shipping contract.[729]

On appeal McIntyre J. observed that he questions whether a Himalaya clause can be effective in Canadian law has not yet been directly addressed by this court despite the great interest

---

727   Ibid., 292.
728   [1986] 1 S.C.R. 752, 28 D.L.R. (4th) 641.
729   Ibid., 746.

it has provoked.[730] He also noted that there is a gap between contractual theory and commercial reality "and it appears that the weight of opinion in commercial circles favours, at least in general terms, the adoption or recognition of the Himalaya clause."[731]

Privity had proved a stumbling block for common law lawyers faced with the proposition that a non-party stevedore could benefit from an immunity or limitation clause in a bill of lading.[732] The Court referred to both the discussions in the *Eurymedon* and *The New York Star* when examining the effectiveness of the Himalaya clause. The court noted:

> There is sound reason to promote uniformity in this field and as great a degree of certainty as may be possible. In the ordinary course of commerce, carriers, stevedores and terminal operators have established practices which are widely followed and generally understood by all concerned. Bills of lading and stevedoring contracts are made in many languages frequently involving different rules and conditions and all must be made operative in the general practice of marine transportation. Himalaya clauses have become accepted as a part of the commercial law of many of the leading trading nations, including Great Britain, the United States, Australia, New Zealand, and now in Canada. It is thus desirable that the courts avoid constructions of contractual documents which would tend to defeat them.[733]

Clause 8 of the bill provided that the carrier will not be liable after discharge of the goods and Clause 18 also provided that after discharge of the cargo, responsibility ceased for the carrier and it imposed responsibility and risks and costs for storage on the shipper or consignee.[734]

Furthermore Clause 7 of the bill provided for the inclusion of

---

730   Ibid., 783.
731   Ibid.
732   Ibid.
733   Ibid., 788-789.
734   Ibid., 791.

ITO as an express beneficiary of all immunities and limitations of liability provisions of the bill of lading and Clause 4 extended it to stevedores.[735]

The court correctly stated the contractual issue:

> Before ITO can have the benefits of the immunities and limitations to which the carrier is entitled to against the claim of Miida, a link must be found between ITO and Miida which would bring ITO into the contractual arrangement between the carrier and Miida, at least sufficiently to enable ITO to benefit from the extension of the immunities and limitations of liability under the provisions of clause 4, the Himalaya clause. [736]

The court followed the reasoning of Lord Reid in the *Eurymedon* in establishing the necessary link.

However, as it was proven that negligence on the part of ITO caused the problem, the court discussed at length whether negligence was covered in the Himalaya clause. The clause does not specially mention "negligence." The question was; "Do the words extend to include it?"

McIntyre J. as a starting point noted that it is a question of construction and the answer must be found in the context of the contract. The carrier, pursuant to the contract, is protected in a specified area namely for the loss of goods and therefore they are wide enough to include negligence. This is reinforced by Clause 18 which states: "... all risks ... incurred by delivery otherwise than from the vessel's side shall be borne by the shipper and/or consignee notwithstanding any custom or the port to the contrary."

The court decided that the Himalaya clause was wide enough to protect the carrier and ITO.

---

735   Ibid., 792.
736   Ibid., 792.

9.2.6 *London Drugs Ltd v. Kuehne & Nagel International Ltd.*[737]

This is not strictly a shipping contract but nevertheless it approaches issues which are equally applicable to any contract of carriage. The facts are simple. London Drugs Limited, the "appellant" delivered a transformer to Kuehne and Nagel International Ltd. ("Kuehne"). The transformer was to be stored first and subsequently was to be installed in the appellants' warehouse facility. The contract of storage included the following exemption clause:

> LIABILITY - Sec. 11(*a*) The responsibility of a warehouseman in the absence of written provisions is the reasonable care and diligence required by the law.

> (*b*) The warehouseman's liability on any one package is limited to $40 unless the holder has declared in writing a valuation in excess of $40 and paid the additional charge specified to cover warehouse liability.[738]

The appellant chose not to obtain additional insurance from Kuehne instead arranged for its own insurance cover. When two employees from Kuehne were told to load the transformer onto a truck and deliver it to the appellant they negligently handled the transformer causing it to topple and cause damage to the amount of $33,955.41.[739] Alleging breach of contract and negligence the appellant brought action against Kuehne and the two employees. The Supreme court of Canada found Kuehne responsible limiting the damages to $40 but found that the employees were personally liable for the full amount. On a subsequent appeal the liability of the employees was reduced to $40. This current appeal had to deal with the argument whether the employees should be completely free of liability.

Iacobucci J delivering the majority judgment narrowed the

---

737   [1992] 3 SCR 299 (Carswell BC 315 (1992).
738   Ibid., para 156.
739   Ibid., para 158.

problem to two issues namely; (1)

the duty of care owed by employees to their employer's customers, and (2) the extent to which employees can claim the benefit of their employer's contractual limitation of liability clause.[740]

It is useful to note the core of the argument first. Iacobucci J stated:

> These comments and others reveal many concerns about the doctrine of Privity as it relates to third party beneficiaries. For our purposes, I think it sufficient to make the following observations. Many have noted that an application of the doctrine so as to prevent a third party from relying on a limitation of liability clause which was intended to benefit him or her frustrates sound commercial practice and justice. It does not respect allocations and assumptions of risk made by the parties to the contract and it ignores the practical realities of insurance coverage. In essence, it permits one party to make a unilateral modification to the contract by circumventing its provisions and the express or implied intention of the parties. In addition, it is inconsistent with the reasonable expectations of all the parties to the transaction, including the third-party beneficiary who is made to support the entire burden of liability. The doctrine has also been criticized for creating uncertainty in the law. While most commentators welcome, at least in principle, the various judicial exceptions to Privity of contract, concerns about the predictability of their use have been raised. Moreover, it is said, in cases where the recognized exceptions do not appear to apply, the underlying concerns of commercial reality and justice still militate for the recognition of a third-party beneficiary right ...[741]

The view of the court clearly indicates that in Canada the Privity rule is not being followed anymore and that the criticism voiced by English judges in the development of the Himalaya clause have been heard and noted. Specifically, the fact that the Privity

---

740   Ibid., para 155.
741   Ibid., para 213.

rule cannot be defended on grounds of commercial reality and injustices is in the forefront of the decision. It is based on the fact that the parties relaying on the contractual clause which after all expressed the wishes of the contractual parties should not be thwarted by legal niceties.

Iacobucci J addressed the issue in relation to the Himalaya clause whether it ought to be recognised as a feature by Canadian maritime law. He referred to McIntyre J writing for the majority who noted that that the major obstacle to the recognition of the "*Himalaya* clause" was the common law doctrine of Privity of contract.[742] The court observed that academic writing already revealed the gap between contractual theory and commercial reality. He noted that:

> the "route" left open by Lord Reid in *Midland Silicones* (i.e. the four-part "agency test") had been applied by Lord Wilberforce, speaking for the majority of the Privy Council, in *The Eurymedon, supra,* a case later affirmed in the Privy Council in *Port Jackson Stevedoring Pty. v. Salmond & Spraggon (Australia) Pty.; "New York Star."* McIntyre J. held that "*Himalaya* clauses" could be effective in Canadian maritime law. His conclusion was largely based on the reasoning of Lord Wilberforce in *The Eurymedon* and the latter's application of Lord Reid's agency "four-step" exception to the doctrine of Privity, especially the fourth step which involves the use of the concept of a unilateral contract in order to show consideration moving from the stevedores to the owner of goods.[743]

The court also consulted the thirteenth edition of Carver which is included as it is a comment made at the crossroads of a full development of the Himalaya clause. Carver noted:

> It will be a happy day when the *Himalaya Clause* and *The Eurymedon* have run their full course. The *Himalaya Clause* has proved to have been a most effective dyke to stem the tide threatening to overwhelm the barrier against incursion on ship-

---

742 Ibid., para 232.
743 Ibid., para 232.

owners' pockets of perils of the sea. But exceptions of perils of the sea can be preserved more thoroughly by simpler and more rational means once it was generally apparent that the fundamental principle of *jus tertii* covers all. It is clearly the available protective principle to apply now to ensure that the will of the parties to a contract of affreightment can simply be secured by saying in the bill of lading what that will is. An omnibus clause, of *Himalaya* vintage, could be devised, but it need no longer go into awkward concepts, which vary as between one country and another such as those of undisclosed agency and deemed (which means non-existent *de facto*) trusts.

England does not stand alone in this matter; the real need to preserve, and possibly improve, the clause at this time stems also from the views already expressed by courts in Australia, Canada and the United States. [744]

Iacobucci J clearly agreed with the comments by Carver as he commented that: "this approach offers a more rational solution to the problem than that outlined by Lord Wilberforce, which compresses the facts into a contractual mould in order to preserve the common law principle of Privity in a situation in which it would appear that it is being rejected."[745] However two basic conditions were laid down by the court in order to relax the Privity bar. The test required that:

1) The limitation of liability clause must, either expressly or impliedly, extend its benefit to the employees (or employee) seeking to rely on it: and

2) The employees (or employee) seeking the benefit of the limitation of liability clause must have been acting in the course of their employment and must have been performing the very service provided for the contract between their employer and the plaintiff (customer) when the loss occurred.[746]

---

744   *Carrage by Sea* (1982), vol 1, 262.
745   London Drugs, para 232.
746   London at para 255.

The court discussed at length whether the doctrine of Privity be relaxed and concluded that it should not be discarded lightly but that there are sound policy reasons why the Privity rule should be relaxed. This was in light of the view of the court that the limitation of liability makes perfect commercial sense as the parties – where relevant – can obtain insurance and hence limit the risk of having to cover damages.

9.2.7 Fraser River Pile & Dredge Ltd. v. Can-Dive Services Ltd [747]

It must be noted that this case in effect does not deal with a Himalaya clause in its true intent but deals with its principle that Privity of contract can - in certain cases such as insurance issues - be circumvented. None of the leading Himalaya jurisprudence was noted or referred to.

The facts are relatively straight forward. Fraser River owned a barge and at the time of loss was under charter to the respondent, Can-Dive. The loss was caused through the negligence of the responded which was never denied. The issue was that Can-Dive contended that he cannot be held liable in what is in effect a subrogated action by the underwriter of Fraser River. The respondent maintained that he was covered under the category of "Additional Insured."[748]

The Insurance clause in question stated:

> It is agreed that this policy also covers the Insured, associated and affiliated companies of the Insured, be they owners, sub-sidiaries or interrelated companies and as bareboat charterers and/or charterers and/ or sub-charterers and/or operators and/ or in whatever capacity and shall so continue to cover notwith-standing any provisions of this policy with respect to change of ownership or management. Provided, however, that in the event of any claim being made by associated, affiliated, subsidiary or

---

747   [1999] 3 S.C.R. 108.
748   Ibid., para 2.

interrelated companies under this clause, it shall not be entitled to recover in respect of any liability to which it would be subject if it were the owner, nor to a greater extent than an owner would be entitled in such event to recover.[749]

Iacobucci J. posed two questions of which the second one is of importance within the context of this book.

> b. Is Can-Dive, as a third-party beneficiary under the insurance policy pursuant to the waiver of subrogation clause, entitled to rely on that clause to defend against the insurer's subrogated action on the basis of the principled exception to the Privity of contract doctrine established by the Court's decision in London Drugs?[750]

The court in essence followed the decision in *London Drugs*[751] where a principled exception to the common law doctrine of Privity of contract was introduced.[752] The Supreme court held that the reasoning in *London Drugs* was not limited to a master servant relationship but also where there was an unconditional intention that a third party should benefit from the contractual terms and that the act of the third party conformed to the scope of the exemption clause. In essence, the court was guided by the need to determine the intention of the contracting parties and asked two questions:

> Accordingly, extrapolating from the specific requirements as set out in London Drugs, the determination in general terms is made on the basis of two critical and cumulative factors: (a) did the parties to the contract intend to extend the benefit in question to the third party seeking to rely on the contractual provision; and (b) are the activities performed by the third party seeking to rely on the contractual provision the very activities contemplated as coming within the scope of the contract in general, or the provision in particular, again as determined by reference to the

---

749   Ibid., para 5.
750   Ibid., para 20.
751   London Drugs Ltd. v. Kuehne & Nagel International Ltd. [1992] S.C.R. 299.
752   Fraser River, para 24.

intentions of the parties?[753]

Iacobucci J. found that both requirements for relaxing the doctrine of Privity were met. Importantly he noted that, "the corollary principle is equally compelling, which is that in appropriate circumstances, courts must not abdicate their judicial duty to decide on incremental changes to the common law necessary to address emerging needs and values in society."[754]

9.3 Conclusion

Canadian courts – as any other courts in the common law system - increasingly looked at commercial reality and the intention of the parties in contractual settings as a guiding principle when the Privity of contract principle is not a solution in commercial settings. However, it must be noted that the Privity rule was still discussed as late as 1992 in relation to the application of the Himalaya clause.

Iacobucci J, introducing the "principled exception" test made sure that in common-law Canada, third parties will be permitted to benefit from the Himalaya clauses if and when they meet the two-part test as noted in *London Drugs*.

It can be argued the Himalaya clause is the forerunner of an important change in the development of the common law. Of particular interest (as noted above) in Canada, specifically in the French speaking provinces, the French principle of *faute lourde* is applied which in essence "trumps" a perfectly validly drafted Himalaya clause. Care must be taken when Canadian law is applicable to ensure that the clause is well drafted taking account of this principle.

Specifically, the question of negligence played a crucial part in *Eisen Und Metall A.G. v. Ceres Stevedoring Co. Ltd.* In contrast

---

753   Ibid., para 32.
754   Ibid., para 44.

to other jurisdictions, the Canadian court recognised a principle of *faute lourde* (gross negligence) which took precedence over the otherwise valid Himalaya clause. *Faute lourde* is a French concept and obviously used in Canada where French law is still applicable, but it is not a common law principle. In the words of Walsh J decisions decided in the courts of Nova Scotia are determined by common law but within the province of Quebec civil law applies "as authorities in Quebec cases ... do not depend upon doctrines derived from the English law".[755]

In sum, there is an overarching principle which can be found in both the French speaking and English speaking parts of Canada in relation to the Himalaya clause, namely that the principles as developed in England, the United States and Australia to a lesser degree are valid in Canada. However, the principle of *faute lourde* will override the Himalaya clause as it is against the public policy of the French speaking provinces only.

---

755   Ibid.

10

SIGNIFICANT HIMALAYA CLAUSE JURISPRUDENCE IN SELECTED CIVIL LAW COUNTRIES: GERMANY, SOUTH KOREA AND THE PEOPLE'S REPUBLIC OF CHINA

10.   Introduction

This Chapter considers the way the Himalaya clause has been applied in selected civil law countries, in particular Germany, South Korea, and the People's Republic of China. As noted in previous Chapters, in civil law countries, the right of third parties unconnected to a contract has been recognised. For example, in Germany, Article 328 of the Bürgerliches Gesetzbuch (BGB) allows a third party to become the beneficiary of an underlying main contract and as a result the independent contractor's liability is the same as the one of the carriers.

As courts in civil law jurisdictions focus attention on academic commentaries, this Chapter, in addition to statutory material, also relies on commentary and jurisprudence where applicable. Jurisprudence in South Korea and P R China is not easily available in English and, hence, merely short descriptions are part of this Chapter.

10.1 Germany: an overview

German law regards the extension of liability as achieved by the Himalaya clause as valid. The inclusion of independent third parties into the exemption clauses of a contract is governed by the Bürgerliches Gesetzbuch (BGB) and the Handelsgesetzbuch (HGB). In this context, Professor Schmidt wrote in 1984 that, "the liability of employees of a contracting party and of third persons is one of the most fascinating legal problems in the German law of obligations."[756] Specifically, the question of exemption clauses and issues dealing with maritime matters are contained in the HGB. Hence, this part will follow the discussion as found in the HGB and by the seminal article by Professor Schmidt. Case law specifically referring to Himalaya clauses is discussed in more detail below.

Commentaries point out that the origin of the Himalaya clause as understood in German law is based on *Adler v Dickson*.[757] However, case law is not as extensive as in the common law.

The issue as noted already above is not whether the Himalaya clause is valid but whether it is necessary and if so, how the extension of liability can be justified legally.[758] Importantly, courts have ruled that even absent express limitation clauses, employees by implication enjoy the same rights as the contracting party. The German High Court even extended the limitation to "whenever the circumstances of the case seemed to justify this result."[759] However, courts have not extended the limitation to stevedores; Schmidt in a sense predicted in 1984 that, "it is quite likely the German courts would extend a carrier's liability limitation to a stevedore even if the Himalaya

---

756 Karsten Schmidt, *The Himalaya Clause under the Law of the Federal Republic of Germany*, ETL 1984, 675.

757 See Dieter Rabe, *Seehandelsrecht*, 4. Auflage 2000 § 607a HGB Rn 9; Herber, *Seehandelsrecht* 1999, 207.

758 Schmidt, (n756) 677.

759 Ibid., 678 quoting BGH 28.4.1977.

clause is not stipulated."[760] Simply put, the validity in favour of employees was beyond doubt but to extend the principle to independent contractors was less obvious.[761] However, a reliance on § 328 BGB by analogy would allow the court to construct an implied protection beyond employees to other third parties such as stevedores.[762]

Professor Schmidt summed up the issue of the application of limiting liability in the German legal system by noting:

> If a limitation of responsibility is not expressly extended to third persons a contractual explanation of "Himalaya effects without Himalaya clause" is a difficult task. The legal doctrine in Germany tempts the courts to justify "Himalaya effects without Himalaya clause" by means of contractual interpretation incorporating tacit premises (erganzende Vertragsauslegung) But this method of construction can only be justified as a means of completing the contractual relationship in accordance with the implied will of the parties. In the final analysis, this must be considered an objective legal problem, i.e. a problem of legislation or of "development of law."[763]

This is exactly what happened 30 years later. Many of the relevant §§ in relation to liability and hence exemption clauses have been revised on 25 April 2013. The former § 607(a)(2) HGB (old) has been deleted and the revised § 508 HGB is now in force. § 508 HGB has introduced some substantial changes but has retained the general line unscathed in its first paragraph. § 436 HGB, in force as of 1998, is still in force, but cedes to § 508 HGB the latter being the *lex specialis*. Specifically, in German law it is important to understand any commentaries, academic writings[764] and jurisprudence in relation to the relevant applicable legislation. From a practical point of view the most

---

760   Ibid., 678.
761   Ibid., 679.
762   Ibid., 680.
763   Ibid., 681.
764   Even today the best and most detailed coverage of the Himalaya clause under German law is still provided by Karsten Schmidt, ETL 1984, 675.

important changes took place in 2013 hence pre-2013 cases[765] (which have not always addressed specifically Himalaya clauses, but also similar exemptions from liability) have to be regarded with caution, but can generally still contain valuable guidelines, particularly with regard to the admissibility of contractual relief. Hence, some pre-2013 jurisprudence has been included in this Chapter.

The importance of being aware of the changes § 508 HGB brought about is illustrative, though § 607a HGB (old) as some kind of pre-2013 version of § 508 HGB did not mention any limitations of liability and merely noted that any claim against a carrier or any other person must be heard in the court of the "home-harbour" of the carrier or carriers, However, the revised § 508 HGB in its title notes that it is relevant in relation to liability of the "peoples" (an old fashioned, 19th century expression for "employees") and crew of the carrier. In effect, it has been completely rewritten and enlarged.

The HGB in relation to exemption clauses distinguishes between trade in general and maritime trade. As an example, § 436 HGB is discussed as it can also affect multimodal contracts.

10.2 German Legislation

10.2.1 § 436 HGB

§ 436 HGB protects all those who are employed within the business (Leute) of the freight forwarder against damage to or loss of goods as well as delay in delivery.

In effect, this rule allows all those who are engaged within the freight forwarders business or independent third parties and

---

765   BGH 07.07.1960, II ZR 209/58, VersR 1960, 727; OLG Hamburg VersR 1960, 607; OLG Hamburg Hansa 1970, 615; OLG Hamburg, 07.11.1974, 6 U 157/3 VersR 1975, 801.

their employees the same protection as he would have had.[766] In essence, this article affords the same protection as a properly drafted Himalaya clause. The commentary specifically notes that a sub-bailee is also protected under § 436 HGB.[767]

The legislation is directed at claims where the employee, independent sub-contractors and sub-bailees are not party to the contract. However, this § does not apply if the damage or loss is due to negligent or wanton disregard to the possible outcome of the action. In other words, if an employee could not have been unaware that his action can cause damage or loss, he is not protected by § 436 HGB. This article also includes the destruction or loss of shipping documents as well as delivery of goods to a person who is not in possession of a bill of lading.[768] Furthermore, the right to sue is not only limited to the shipper and the original consignee but also to parties in possession of a bill of lading pursuant to § 434(2) HGB. However, § 434(2)(2) HGB restricts the right to protection if the freight forwarder did not have authority from the shipper to send the goods and if the goods went missing before delivery takes place.

There is a significant difference between the German and English position in relation to exemption clauses. The German legislation – unlike the English position – does protect the owner of the goods against negligent and careless conduct by third parties irrespective of the wording of the exemption clause.

10.2.2 Liability in relation to sea carriage.

The default position in relation to liability for loss or damage is contained in §§ 498 to 512 HGB. § 498 HGB notes that the carrier is responsible for all damage to and loss of cargo

---

766 Herber, *Münchener Kommentar zum HGB*, 3. Auflage 2014, § 508 HGB Rn 1 to 11.

767 Ibid.

768 Ibid., Rn 1 to 11.

from the time he took over the goods until they are delivered. This rule also provides that he is not liable for damage or loss if he used the relevant duty of care and the ship is cargo- and seaworthy. Furthermore, § 501 HGB states that the carrier is also responsible for damage and loss caused by employees and ship's crews as well as any person the carrier engages in the execution of the carriage contract. Arguably, therefore he is responsible for the action of all of those who perform any duty during the taking over of goods until their delivery pursuant to § 498 HGB. Himalaya clauses are mentioned in the commentary as being relevant not only in the general part (§ 436 HGB) but as far as shipping is concerned in § 508 HGB.

10.2.2.1 § 508 HGB

This rule protects employees and crew from liability as they can rely on, or find protection under, the main contract between shipper and carrier. However, there is a limitation as also noted in § 436 HGB, namely that the protection is waived if the damage is caused through negligence or wilfulness and if the damage could have been foreseen by a reasonable person. It follows in essence the regulations as found in the Hague-Visby Rules, Art. 4bis(2) but is stricter.

The protection is only available – that is restricted - to those who are directly engaged in the carrier's business which includes the ship's compliment whether they are under the direct control of the carrier or the shipowner. It should be noted that the pilot is not included as he is protected by his own limitations of liability regulations. The protection is also extended to loss of or damage to documentation such as the bill of lading and includes any claims against delivery to a person who is not entitled to it. This rule is not protecting independent contractors (like stevedores or subcontracting actual carriers) and their employees. This is regulated in § 509 HGB. The starting point is that the independent contractor is liable to the shipper unless there is a direct contractual relationship including exemption clauses. Simply put, the subcontractor is able to rely on the main contract between the carrier and the shipper.

The carrier, therefore, through a Himalaya clause can extend his protection and limitations to independent contractors. The Commentary specifically notes that the exemption clause in favour of third parties is generally effective if the third party or independent contractor is in "specific proximity of the main contract" which is generally the case when sub-bailment is an issue.

There is no current jurisprudence available relying on the current § 508 HGB simply because this rule has only been recently introduced. Some select cases relying on the Himalaya clause and similar contractual devices will be discussed below.

10.3 Jurisprudence

10.3.1 BGH 07.07.1960, II ZR 209/58, VersR 1960, 727

The facts in this case deal with inland shipping on the Lahn River. Barge transport was necessary as the steel construction was too large to transport by road. The relevant clauses were those which are regularly in use on the Rhein River and the related canals. These clauses were well known in the trade as they were essentially in use for the last four hundred years.

The clause – as far as relevant – noted:

> The carrier and his employees as well as the owner and employees of the towing vessel are not liable for damages caused to the goods in the navigation of the vessels or handling of the goods.

While loading three steel pieces each weighing about 20 ton onto the barge all went well. The problem started when the barge moved most likely due to the waves which were created by a passing barge. The vessel tipped, the cables broke and the barge sunk. The problem was that old cable was used which caused the walls to fall and hence caused the ship to sink

The plaintiff maintained that the sinking of the barge was due to the negligence of the owner or crew of the barge.

The court noted that there was no contractual relationship between the crane operator and the owner of the goods (HGB 432(2)), hence, there is a question whether a duty of care is owed to the owner of the goods. The issue was that the carrier was negligent in allowing old cables to be used. He ought to have realised that the cables were too weak. Furthermore, the barge did not have adequate wires on board. The court found that the defendant was liable as he did not exercise due care and diligence in handling the goods.

However, the question was to whom did he owe that duty. In answering that question the court noted that the contractual relationship was between the freight forwarder and the defendant. The owner of the goods was a third party. In essence, anybody who is a bailee has a duty of care in handling the goods in their possession.

The court then turned to clause 20, the exemption clause between the freight forwarder and the owner and posed the question whether the carrier can take advantage of the protection offered by Clause 20. The court argued that the clause did not only protect the freight forwarder but also the carrier (BGB 328). The court stated the purpose of clause 20 was that it was not only applicable to the bailee of the goods but also to the sub-bailee. The interpretation of the clause leads to this conclusion and, hence, to the protection of all the participants of the transportation of goods in the inland water trade. In addition, the court took into consideration that exemption clauses are a commercial practice and well known. The court did note that parties to such a contract can exclude third parties from the protection of Clause 20.

Of importance to the court was the fact that the freight forwarder was also an owner of barges and that it was contemplated that the defendant could use his own or other barges. In essence, the court argued that it was irrelevant for the plaintiff whether the defendant or anybody else's barge was used. Of interest is that only HGB Article 432 was referred to as otherwise the BGB was the relevant code.

10.2.2 OLG Hamburg, 07.11.1974, 6 U 157/3, VersR 1975, 801

The MS Behrmann – on a time charter – sunk in a storm with the loss of her cargo. The ship owner also was the captain on the vessel and was the defendant in this action. The Himalaya clause in the bill of lading noted the following:

> All limitations of liability and other provisions herein contained shall insure not only to the benefit of the Carrier, His vessels, Agents, Employees and other Representatives but also to the benefit of any Independent Contractor performing services to the goods.[769]

The defendant stowed by all accounts the cargo properly and proceeded to set sail towards the North Sea. A storm warning was issued while the vessel was still sailing down the Elbe River. During the storm, the deck cargo shifted which caused the ship to sink. The plaintiff argued that the vessel was not seaworthy and, hence, the carrier was liable for the loss.

The first issue was whether the claim was time barred. The court noted that – pursuant to Article 903 HGB - the time starts to run when the delivery of the cargo was due. The court noted that the actual time was not terminable as the ship was due to call in on several ports in England on its way to Sweden. Furthermore, the court also noted that it is very difficult for the plaintiff to work out the exact time when the defendant actually receives the writ as he cannot influence the time the court takes to issue

---

769   Ibid., 2.

the relevant notices. As the parties agreed on a proposed time limit the issue was resolved that the claim was lodged within the allocated time frame.

Referring to Articles 511 to 514 of the HGB and also Article 823 of the BGB the court noted that the defendant breached his duty of care and the cause of the sinking of the ship was due to negligently and inadequately securing the deck cargo,

Furthermore, the defendant also breached his duty of care as he continued his travel despite the bad weather forecast (waves up to 5 meters were predicted with strong winds). It was argued that the carrier should have known that in strong winds and high waves the possibility that deck cargo can shift is very high.

The court stated that the Himalaya clause did not validly protect the carrier form liability but pursuant to The Hague Rules the liability is limited. The carrier could not protect himself due to perils of the seas as the storm was foreseeable and hence within the contemplation of the defendant. As the ship was deemed to be unseaworthy as well as not cargo worthy pursuant to Article 559 HGB the defendant is liable. However, the protection under the Himalaya clause enlivened the limitation clause due under the Hague Rules.

10.2.3 BGH 2. Zivilsenat, 8.04.1977, II ZR 26/76[770]

The question in this case hinged on the issue whether an implied clause a well as a limitation of action clause applies. The contractual carrier who employed another carrier to execute the transport noted in the relevant clause that if third parties are engaged in the transportation of goods the exemption clauses of the third parties are relevant.[771] The court relied on Article 328(2) BGB and also noted that exemption clauses in favour of

---

770   Juris, Das Rechtsportal.
771   Soweit wir Transporte ...durch dritte Unternehmungen ... ausführen lassen, gelten deren Bedingungen ...

third parties can include a clause which limits the time in which a claim can be submitted. It is known in the inland shipping trade that limitation in damage claims is usual and, hence, the plaintiff must have been aware that the defendant must have included exemption clauses into the contract.

10.2.4 OLG Frankfurt, 11.05.2012, 5 U 123/11

A freight forwarder lost a package in his care and could not explain how the package was lost. He was liable for the damage. Not being able to explain how the package could have been lost led the court to believe that the employees acted negligently and should have known that their action resulted in a loss and hence claims for damages.

10.2.5 OLG Köln, 05.09.2014, 3 U 15/14

The facts were that an industrial company intended to have goods sent to Saudi Arabia. A transport company transported the goods to the harbour where they were handed over to the Carrier. The problem was that marks relevant to the sea-voyage were missing. On the same day the carrier received from a different company a consignment to be delivered to India which was also not properly marked. The carrier noted the missing marks and duly notified the relevant parties. The carrier was notified and tasked to undertake the relevant marking; however, they cross-marked with the result that the Saudi Arabian goods ended up in India and vise-versa.

In relation to the cross-marking the court noted that there was no contractual relationship between the shipper and the carrier as the communications were directed through the transport company. The court commented that a contract protecting third parties might have changed the outcome. However, this was of no consequence as the issue in essence was one of limitation of claims which is 2 years.

10.4 South Korea

This section relies on an article written by Hyeon Kim[772] which analyses the Korean Maritime Law Update. Korea is a civil law country hence maritime law is codified and was revised in 2007. The Korean Maritime code in essence is similar to The Hague-Visby Rules. The Korean code, Article 790(1) mirrors Articles III(8) and IVbis(2) by excluding specially the independent contractors. The Korean jurisprudence not surprisingly adopted the Himalaya clause and is now in line with most maritime nations. It should also be noted that Korea introduced the New German Transport Law into its domestic code hence aligned itself closely with European law in relation to allowing third parties to take advantage of a contract.[773]

Of significance to this book is the fact that for the first time the validity of the Himalaya clause was addressed by the Korean Supreme court in 2007.[774] This case followed another famous Korean Supreme Court judgement in relation to on deck loading where the carrier was not allowed to limit his liability by carrying the cargo on deck instead of below deck.[775]

The facts in the 2007 case are relatively straightforward. Goods were shipped from China to Korea. The Chinese company, Fritz Logistics, informed the carrier that the goods were very dangerous and had to be kept under minus 18 degrees Celsius. The carrier did not inform the Terminal operator of the requirements and the goods were stored in a normal fashion, not at the required temperature. As a consequence, the cargo exploded. Two issues required to be resolved namely:

(i)   whether UPS Korea is liable as the carrier and if not, whether

---

772   Hyeon Kim, Korean Maritime Law Update: 2007-Focused on the Revised Maritime Law Section in the Korean Commercial Code, 39(3) *Journal of Maritime Law & Commerce* 2008.

773   Ibid., 439.

774   Case 2007.4.27 Docket No 4943. Korean Case Reports 784.

775   Kim (n772) 433 citing 2006.10.26. Docket No. 2004da27082.

the UPS Korea is liable as the freight forwarder;

(ii)   whether Hutchison Terminal Korea is entitled to invoke limitation of the liability based on the Himalaya clause."[776]

The court did not examine the scope of "the subcontractor" in the House Bill of Lading. The Hutchison Terminal Korea invoked the right vested in the Himalaya clause. The clause includes the wording of "anyone participating in the performance of the Carriage other than the Carrier." The Chinese exporter as the shipper promised the carrier to allow anyone participating in the performance of the carriage to enjoy the carrier's benefit to limit its liability.

The carrier under the House Bill of Lading was UPS rather than KMTC. Hutchison Terminal was an independent contractor of Korea Shipping Co. Ltd. In order for the Hutchison Terminal Korea to enjoy the same benefits as UPS as the carrier, the Court should decide whether it can fall within the definition of "anyone participating in the performance of the carriage."

The Himalaya clause states that the word "anyone" includes subcontractor, stevedores, terminal operator, carriers involved in land, maritime, sea transportation, and the term is not exhaustive. Based on this language, the Court accepted that the terminal operator was a covered person. The Hutchison Terminal Korea acted as an independent contractor of the ocean carrier who is the subcontractor of UPS, as the contracting carrier. Therefore, Hutchison Terminal Korea can be regarded as the sub-subcontractor of UPS.

Hyeon Kim argued that the wording of "terminal operator" in the clause can be of assistance in this case. However, it is not clear whether the carrier and the shipper had the intention to allow the terminal operator to invoke the benefit of the limitation of the liability without contractual relationship with the carrier. The Court should have examined the definition of "anyone" in

---

776   Ibid., 446.

the Himalaya clause more thoroughly. Hyeon Kim argued that, "The U.S Supreme Court's Kirby case will be a good guideline on the issue of the scope of the beneficiary in the Himalaya clause."[777]

10.5 The People's Republic of China

China has recognised the utility of the Himalaya clause and it has been enshrined as a principle in the China Maritime Code (CMC),[778] Article 58 of which states:

> The defences and limits of liability provided for in this Chapter7 shall apply in any legal action brought against the carrier with regard to the loss of or damage to or delay in delivery of the goods covered by the contract of carriage of goods by sea, whether the claimant is a party to the contract or whether the action is founded in contract or in tort.

> The provisions of the preceding paragraph shall apply if the action referred to in the preceding paragraph is brought against the carrier's servant or agent, and the carrier's servant or agent proves that his act was within the scope of his employment or agency. [779]

The familiar view is that a port operator should be regarded as the servant or agent of the carrier and hence "the second paragraph of Article 58 is popularly named as the legalized "Himalaya clause".[780] The argument is that under the CMC Article 58 the phrase "such servant or agent not being an independent contractor" as noted under The Hague-Visby Rules has disappeared. This view is supported by jurisprudence from

---

777   Ibid., 448 fn 60.

778   China has not ratified any conventions in relation to the international carriage of goods by sea, Ch. IV "Contract of the Carriage of Goods by Sea" of CMC is closely modelled on both the Hague-Visby Rules and the Hamburg Rules.

779   https://www.google.com/search?q=china+maritime+code&oq=China+Maritime+Code&aqs=chrome.0.0l2.3063j0j7&sourceid=chrome&ie=UTF-8.

780   Yuzhuo Si: Zuoxian Zhu. On the Legal Status of Port Operators under Chinese Law, 2 US-China Law Review 1 2005, Volume 2, No.7 (Serial No.8), 2.

the Chinese Maritime courts such as in *"Shenyang mining machinery (Group) import and Export Corporation v. Hyundai Merchant Marine (2001)* The Dalian Maritime Court held that Wantong Logistics Company, engaged in the storage operations in the container yards, was the employee of Hyundai Merchant Marine and was entitled the right of defence and limitation of liability of the carriers as stipulated in the Chinese Maritime Code, Article 59(2) and hence could avail themselves of the Himalaya clause. "[781]

Yuzhuo Si and Zuoxian Zhu also argue that the word "servant" under the Chinese civil law possibly qualifies as the subject of a contract of employment.[782] However, this appears not to be the case as *The Interpretation on Carriage of Goods by Inland Waterway Rule and Port Cargo Handling Rule* states:

> It may be easily accepted that the Master, mariner and longshore-man be regarded as the servant of the carrier. But it is incorrect that the port operator is also regarded as the servants of the carrier. If this was a correct conclusion, the carrier would also be regard-ed as the servant of the cargo owner. The world would become simpler if we could treat all persons who supply some labour as servants of the others. However, this is not the fact.[783]

The following conclusion has been offered:

> 1. Under CMC, if some conditions are satisfied, the port operator can qualify as the actual carrier.

> 2. As to providing legal Himalaya clause protection, the legal technique adopted by CMC is distinctive.

> Actually, it solves the Himalaya problem through two different ways:

---

781 Prof. Si Yuzhuo, Dr Zhang Jinlei, An Analysis and Assessment on the Rotterdam Rules in China's Marine Industry fn 16 at p 9. Dalian Maritime University, China.
782 Ibid., 2.
783 Hongjun Ye and Xiaobing Wong, The Interpretation on Transport of Goods by Inland Water Rule & Port Cargo Handling Rule, first edition (The People Transport Press, 2000), 112.

(i)   With respect to the servant or agent of the carrier, paragraph
        2 of article 58 directly stipulates that such persons can invoke
        the defences and liability limits of the carrier.

(ii)   On the other hand, with respect to the independent contractor,
        the person will become the actual carrier if he performs any
        of the carrier's responsibilities for the carriage or transport-
        related services with respect to the goods during the period of
        carrier's responsibility. Then, such independent contractor will
        be directly liable to the cargo claimant according to Article 61
        of CMC, and he and the carrier shall be jointly and severally
        liable subject to some conditions.

        3. When the port operator qualifies as the actual carrier, his
        liability for the loss of or damage to the goods is "statutory"
        under CMC, which is not a tort liability.[784]

Apparently, just through the rule of the actual carrier CMC
elevates the Himalaya clause protection. In effect, it is more
extensive compared to the Hague-Visby Rules. Mainly on this
understanding of CMC, the following conclusion can be drawn:

The port operator under Chinese law shall be treated as the
actual carrier.[785]

10.5.1 Port Operators

The CMC as noted above treats the port operator as the actual
carriers. Considering that there are more than 1400 ports in
China this is significant as in ports many accidents can happen
and, hence, exemption clauses must take care to keep the port
operator in mind.

It appears therefore that the protection of the independent
contracts relies on Article 58 of the CMC and the actual
contractual clause in the Bill of lading. However, there are many

---

784   Yuzhuo Si: Zuoxian Zhu (n781) 13.
785   Ibid.

different opinions among judges, academics and practitioners without reaching a uniform viewpoint. In summary:

(1) The port operator should be regarded as the employee of the carrier under CMC;

(2) The port operator is an independent contractor of the carrier, whose liability is independent of CMC and should be governed by laws of tort;

(3) The port operator should be regarded as the "actual carrier" under CMC.[786]

Court decisions are not consistent either and, in some cases,[787] the port operator was considered to be an employee of the carrier. Others have deemed the port operator to be an independent contractor.[788] In China, the courts have not yet accepted that the port operator is the actual carrier as seen in *Fujian Dingyi Food Co Ltd v Guangzhou Container Terminal Co Ltd*.[789]

Simply put, any shipper or carrier unloading or loading goods in a Chinese port will need to pose the question whether the port operator will be most likely considered to be the actual carrier. To that effect he is subject to the statutory liability as described in Ch.IV of the CMC. This issue will determine how the exemption clause needs to be constructed.

10.6 Conclusion

German commentary and legislation note that protection for unconnected third parties is properly enshrined in law and hence arguably a Himalaya clause is not really of much assistance.

---

786 *Zuoxian Zhu*, The Legal Status of Port Operator under Chinese Law, Journal of Business Law, 8, (2011), 737, 737.

787 As an example, see *Fujian Dingyi Food Co Ltd v Guangzhou Container Terminal Co Ltd* [2004] Guang Hai Fa Chu Zi No.111.

788 Qingdao Maritime Court Judgment: [2001] Qing Hai Fa Shi Zi No.73; Shandong Province High People's Court Judgment: [2001] Lu Fa Jing Er Zhong Zi No.17.

789 Guangdong Province High People's Court Judgment: [2004] Yue Fa Jing Er Zhong No. 287.

However German courts are aware of English jurisprudence specifically, or perhaps only, *Adler v Dickson*.

But the important difference between the common laws and German application of the exemption clauses is that negligent and gross misconduct negates the effects of the clauses and, hence, liability will accrue. Arguably – to put it in other words – the common law approach is rather technical in nature as it is irrespective what and how the damage was caused as long as the protection is defined in the Himalaya clause The civil law, on the other hand, does put responsibility on both parties to act within proper commercial standards and importantly protects those parties which are in "specific proximity of the main contract."

This Chapter, in considering relevant developments in South Korea and the People's Republic of China, has also demonstrated that emerging maritime nations are not yet fully integrated into the current settled view that the Himalaya clause, properly drafted, can support sub-contractors which are not directly linked to the contract. As currently the Chinese silk road, the Belt and Road project, is creating new harbours in countries which do not have an extensive maritime legal culture such as the new port in Pakistan and many others in Africa, the challenge to protect all participants in the supply chain will not be insignificant. Arguably, the absorption of extra cost not only in the transport and other associated charges but also insurance costs will need to be carefully assessed.

It is argued that care needs to be taken when transporting goods which have a connection to emerging markets which were not exposed to the Himalaya clause. Importantly the overland route that is the rail route from Europe to China can create new challenges specifically if United States law is the governing one and the *Kirby* decision were followed.

11

THE HIMALAYA CLAUSE: THE DISCUSSION

11.1 Introduction

This Chapter discusses the utility of the Himalaya clause referring to jurisprudence and to scholarly writing. In particular, the question "where next" will be discussed referring to questions and issues such as:

- Statutory Solutions.

- Can the Privity rule be amended?

- Is an extension of the agency ruling a better solution?

- Other principles lending themselves for further development.

- The issue of the drafting of dispute resolution clauses.

11.2 The utility of the Himalaya Clause

A discussion of the utility of the Himalaya clause is not new and can be traced back to Midland *Silicones Ltd. v. Scruttons Ltd.*[790] Viscount Simonds noted:

> For to me heterodoxy, or, as some might say, heresy, is not the more attractive because it is dignified by the name of reform. Nor will I easily be led by an undiscerning zeal for some ab-

---

790   [1962] A.C. 446, 467-468.

stract kind of justice to ignore our first duty, which is to administer justice according to law, the law which is established for us by Act of Parliament or the binding authority of precedent. The law is developed by the application of old principles to new circumstances. Therein lies its genius.

No doubt the history of the Himalaya clause reveals that some judges viewed the abandonment of the Privity rule as heresy, whilst to others it exemplifies the genius of English law in developing legal concepts specifically taking into consideration commercial realities. In addition, the issue of conformity with civil law also played a role.

The function and application of the Privity rule in the common law world attracted much criticism not only in academic but also in judicial circles. Lord Diplock argued that the Privity rule is "an anachronistic shortcoming that has for many years been regarded as a reproach to English private law."[791] Lord Steyn years later also commented:

The case for recognizing a contract for the benefit of a third party is simple and straightforward. The autonomy of the will of the parties should be respected. The law of contract should give effect to the reasonable expectations of contracting parties. Principle certainly requires that a burden should not be imposed on a third party without his consent. But there is no doctrinal, logical, or policy reason why the law should deny effectiveness to a contract for the benefit of a third party where that is the expressed intention of the parties. Moreover, often the parties, and particularly third parties, organise their affairs on the faith of the contract.[792]

As some of the above cases have demonstrated, the 1970's was the most crucial time in the development of the Himalaya clause, not only in England but worldwide. The two seminal cases namely *Satterthwaite* and *The Eurymedon* - the first one holding

791   *Swain v. The Law Society* [1983] 1 A.C. 598, 611.
792   *Darlington Borough Council v. Wiltshier Northern Ltd.* [1995] 1 W.L.R. 68, 76 (C.A).

more or less onto the Privity rule, the second one advancing the Himalaya clause – feature prominently in judgments in many jurisdictions. The "powerplay" between the Privity rule and the Himalaya clause has been occupying many courts. To that end, two cases should be included into the discussion of these issues, namely a Canadian case[793] and a Kenyan case which are discussed here[794] The two cases demonstrate this tussle between the old and new view on the implementation and construction of exemption clauses.

11.3 Lummus Co. Ltd. v. East African Harbours Corporation

A crude oil tower had to be shipped from Liverpool to Mombasa. When the tower was lowered onto the wharf, the sling broke and the tower was damaged. The defendant, the harbour authority, claimed protection under the bill of lading and the East African Harbours Regulations.

Clause 29 of the bill of lading stated:

> It is hereby expressly agreed that all servants, agents of the carrier (including any independent contractors from time to time employed by the carrier) shall in any circumstances whatsoever be under any liability to the shipper, Consignee or owner of the goods or to any holder of the Bill of Lading for any loss, damage or delay of whatsoever kind arising or resulting directly or indirectly from any act, neglect or default on his part while acting in the course of or in connection with his employment and, but without prejudice to the generality of the foregoing provisions in this Clause, every exemption, imitation, condition and liberty herein contained and every right, exemption from liability, defence and immunity of whatsoever nature applicable to the Carrier or to which the Carrier is entitled hereunder shall also be available and shall extend to protect every such servants, agents of the Carrier or independent contractors acting as aforesaid and

---

793   *The Suleyman Stalskiy* (1976) 2 Lloyd's Rep 609.
794   *Lummus Co. Ltd. v. East African Harbours Corp.* (1978) 1 Lloyd's Rep. 317.

for the purpose of all the foregoing provisions of this clause the Carrier is or shall be deemed to be acting as agent or trustee on behalf of and for the benefit of all persons who are or might be his servants or agents from time to time (including independent contractors as aforesaid) and all such persons shall to this extent be or be deemed to be parties to the contract in or evidenced by the Bill of Lading.[795]

The Harbour regulations equally limited the liability of the defendant. Sheridan J noted that the defendant was grossly negligent and that he was in breach of a regulation by not testing that the ropesand also failed to work within the safe working load. The court then focused on the exemption clause but did not follow the ruling in *The Eurymedon*. Sheridan J did note that *The Eurymedon* was persuasive authority, but he nevertheless held that he was not bound by the decision. The reason was that he preferred to follow domestic precedent.[796] He also appeared to prefer the dissenting judgment in *The Eurymedon* by Viscount Dilhorne who noted:

> Anxiety to save negligent people from the consequence of their negligence does not lead me to give an unnatural and artificial meaning to the clause and a meaning which the words it contains do not bear. To give effect to the appellants' contentions appears to me to surrender to the anxiety to which Fullagar J referred, a surrender which cannot be justified simply by labelling the bill of lading a commercial document. It is no more a commercial document than a consignment note for the carriage of goods by rail or road and it should not be forgotten that ordinary members of the public as well as those engaged in commerce send goods by sea as well as overland.[797]

Of interest is that Sheridan J noted that the exception clauses in the both cases are identical but he nevertheless, at least by implication, found that the Privity doctrine is still in command. Interestingly, he did not comment on the fact that he preferred

---

795   Ibid., 317-318.
796   IbId., 322, He also noted jurisprudence from Uganda and Aden.
797   The Eurymedon (n270) 543.

a domestic rule which was not mandatory over a contractual clause. It appears that he simply followed domestic jurisprudence and hence the Privity principle. In addition, Viscount Dilhorne appears to have omitted the fact that a bill of lading is a contract irrespective whether it is the same or different to a consignment note. If the bill of lading would not be a contractual document, what would then govern the interactions between the parties? The surrender of the Privity rule indeed has been fought hard and the Privity rule has lost the battle and now arguably the war.

However, this does not mean that further discussions on the merit of the Himalaya clause are not worthwhile. Additionally, it is not an accident that the "genius" of the Himalaya clause as noted by Viscount Simonds in *Midland Silicones Ltd. v. Scruttons Ltd.*[798] has not only been confined to shipping cases. Just one example is noted, namely *Norwich City Council v Harvey and another.*[799] A subcontractor was employed by the main contractor and the issue was one of damages caused by the subcontractor due to negligence. The question was to whom a duty of care is owed. Clause 18(2) of the main contract stated relevantly that also any subcontractors, servant or agents are subject to the same conditions as noted in the main contract. The court – dismissing the claim - held:

> ... although there was no direct contractual relationship between the plaintiff and the second defendant, since they had each con-tracted with the main contractor on the basis that the plaintiff had assumed the risk of damage by fire, there was no sufficient-ly close and direct relationship between them to impose on the second defendant any duty of care to the plaintiff in respect of such damage, and the mere fact that there was no Privity of contract between them did not make it just and reasonable that such a duty should be owed; that the first defendant owed the plaintiff no duty greater than that owed by the second defendant; and that; accordingly the plaintiff had no cause of action against

798   [1962] A.C. 446 at. 467-468.
799   (1989) 1 W.L.R. 828.

the defendant.[800]

Both *Midlands* and *The Eurymedon* were cited but were not the main jurisprudence in the decision taken by the Court of Appeal but of significance is the fact that the Privity doctrine was rejected in favour of "just and reasonable" criteria.

11.4 The Himalaya clause – where next?

Tetley in 2003 argued strongly against the ever-increasing influence of the Himalaya clause. He specifically pointed out that, "the Himalaya clause is an ingenious, short-term solution to a difficult problem, but is a solution which raises infinitely more problems than it solves."[801]

If Tetley was correct that the Himalaya clause is only a short-term solution - arguably having confidence in the international judiciary – one would see that the Himalaya clause is by now superseded by a different solution better suited to maritime adventures. However, this has not happened; instead we can see different models emerging which are in essence not superior but simply different to the Himalaya clause. In essence, they aim to have the same purpose, namely to protect unconnected third parties.

This leads to the second question: what is exactly the problem the Himalaya clauses have raised? The issue has always been how far should exemption clauses give protection to persons involved in the maritime adventure. Arguably, the issue is that persons who are not party to the underlying contract are able to be protected through the main contract which has been viewed as encouraging third parties not to exercise due diligence in the handling of goods. It ignores the basic principle that persons who negligently cause damage to goods are not held

---

800   Ibid., 828-29.
801   Tetley, (n13) 6.

responsible. One solution has already found favour in Canadian civil law cases where gross negligence negates the protection under the Himalaya clause. If this would be an issue in common law, courts would have taken up this solution but hey have not. Arguably therefore it is not a pressing shortcoming of the clause.

Tetley furthermore argued that Lord Goff seemed to have missed this important point when reviewing the Himalaya clause in *The Mahkutai* with a confusing declaration.[802] Lord Goff stated (emphasis added):

> In more recent years the pendulum of judicial opinion has swung back again, as recognition has been given to the undesirability, especially in a commercial context, of allowing plaintiffs to circumvent contractual exception clauses by suing in particular the servant or agent of the contracting party who caused the relevant damage, thereby undermining the purpose of the exception, and so *redistributing the contractual allocation of risk which is reflected in the freight rate and in the parties' respective insurance arrangements.*[803]

However, reading it closer and within the context of the judgment Lord Goff correctly stated that the pendulum has swung back in favour of plaintiffs to sue servant and agents, that is all those who are not directly party to the underlying contract. But subsequent judgments have swung the pendulum back again to protect all those parties named or associated within the maritime venture - that is – the courts gave force to the Himalaya clause.

However, Lord Goff's view that in essence the Himalaya clause redistributes *"the contractual allocation of risk which is reflected in the freight rate and in the parties' respective insurance arrangements "*[804] is open to different opinions. From an insurance point of view the Himalaya clause increases the risk as a third party unconnected to the contract entered into the

---

802   Ibid., (x).
803   The Mahkutai, (n71) 661.
804   Ibid.

protection of the contract. There is no redistribution of risk at all. As a matter of fact the insurance companies would need to insure the same risk but with several parties hence increasing their earnings. Furthermore, if other parties took out insurance there is merely a shift of insurance but not a reduction. Tetley argued that:

> ... theft and pilferage continued in epidemic proportions in the Port of Montreal until finally stevedores and terminal operators were held responsible for negligence by the Quebec courts. Thereafter, losses were considerably reduced, insurance premiums of shippers and consignees as well as stevedores and terminal operators were reduced, and the port experienced a surge in traffic.[805]

The question therefore is how to deal with third party benefits considering that shipping is a transnational legal issue and harmonisation of rules is desirable. Domestic and international rules have taken note of the problem. In Canada, several court judgments explored where the limitation of the Himalaya clause lies. In particular a right was established that a limitation of liability agreement has no effect in a case of gross negligence as noted above already.[806] In *Marubeni America Corporation, v. Mitsui O.S.K. Lines Ltd*[807] Marceau J despite agreeing with the judgment in *Eisen* nevertheless also agreed that the defendants were covered by the exception clause. He specifically stated that:

> The general obligation of prudence and diligence required by the Civil Code cannot include all the duties that a cargo handling firm might have to assume in its capacity of a commercial undertaking within a framework of a contract. On a purely delictual level, plaintiff has failed to prove fault within the general meaning of the law.[808]

---

805   Tetley, (n13) 40 fn 6.
806   *Eisen Und Metall A.G. v. Ceres Stevedoring Co. Ltd.* [1977] 1 Lloyd's Rep. 665.
807   1979 Carswel Nat 37, [1979] 2 F.C. 283, 96 D.L.R. (3d) 518.
808   Ibid., 2.

At this stage Canada appears to be the only mixed law country where gross negligence in effect "trumps" a well written Himalaya clause.

In the United States two cases are indicting that judicial creativity is still in play. Both in *Sompo* and *Kirby* the court extended the liability past the sea leg and included rail transport as well. It is revolutionary because:

> it reverses the terms of the "land-nonmaritime" to "sea-maritime" equation. Under the new test, the presence of a significant land component in a multimodal transport is not enough to make the contract "nonmaritime." The mixed sea-and-land contract will be considered nonmaritime only if the sea component is "insubstantial."[809]

In essence, the development in the Himalaya clause specially in the United States has extended the beneficiaries from those performing maritime operations to non-maritime one such as Rail operators. In so doing the court assumed Federal rights over what used to be a domestic issue (state agency) covered under the Carmack[810] rule. Some commentators argue though that this decision was wrong by stating:

> but to strip Carmack away from inland rail and motor carriers operating on U.S. soil, so they can obtain the ocean carrier's benefits under a Himalaya clause, is simply untenable and unjustifiable, in my view. The Supreme Court should not have given Carmack its own preferred meaning based on a so-called policy of uniformity via contract. This is wrong because uniformity is actually a fiction in intermodal shipments, and cannot be achieved by contract clauses, as these are subject to change according to party agreement.[811]

Arguably the objection is too much based on domestic interests and does not take into consideration that the Himalaya clause

---

809   See also *Kirby,* 395, (n585) 2004 AMC at 2713.
810   Carmack Amendment, 49 U.S.C. § 11706 (2006).
811   P. Talbot, 43 *Journal of Maritime Law & Commerce* (1) 2012, 36.

has in effect achieved uniformity. What the courts are doing is simply extending the "commercial reality doctrine" and hence it does make sense to include the transport from seller to buyer as the underlying object can be covered with one properly drafted clause. However, this controversy – if it was one – has been put to rest in *Kawasai Kisen Kaisha Ltd v Regal-Beloit Corp.*[812] Regal-Beloit clearly delineated between pure domestic and a mix of domestic and overseas transport as found in *Kirby*. First the court noted that interstate carriers are not permitted to deviate from the Carmack Amendment.[813] In so finding the court did not suggest that COGSA trumps the Carmack Amendment but rather it is never triggered when cargo arrives under a through ocean bill of lading from overseas as seen in *Kirby*.[814]

> According to the *Regal-Beloit* Court, the Carmack Amendment is not triggered when a domestic rail carrier accepts such imported cargo. Instead, the Carriage of Goods by Sea Act (COGSA) of 1936 can apply to both the ocean and inland legs of a multimodal import shipment. Thus, the Court's most recent decision gives further imprimatur to the use of *Himalaya* clauses' in through ocean bills of lading to extend COGSA's application to subcontracting overland carriers who participate in a portion of the shipment's overall multimodal transportation.[815]

The conclusion which has been reached by commentators is that the Himalaya clause in particular in maritime matters allows third parties amongst other things to enjoy the package limitation and the one-year delay for suit of The Hague-Visby Rules as well as bestowing on all third parties the same rights that a vessel owner has under the law. Tetley though argued that the cost of abandoning the Privity rule is that, "the door is left open to incongruity, abuse and, at times, injustice to

---

812   130 S. Ct. 2433, 2010 AMC 1521 (2010).
813   130 S. Ct. at 2441.
814   D. Cammarano, Impacts of the Supreme Court Decision in *Regal-Beloit:* Exporting Import Litigation, 85 *Tulane Law Review.* 1207 2010-2011, 1207.
815   Ibid., 1208.

persons who have contracted in good faith."[816] The point is that extending the protection to third parties arguably has the effect that parties who were never in the shipper's contemplation have the same rights as contractual parties. Conversely, of course, a shipper ought to know that independent contractors are parties to the supply chain and the bill of lading reflects this fact.

It is clear that in the United States *"Regal-Beloit* also creates opportunities for clever drafters of bills of lading and potential new carrier defences."[817] As the inland rail transport is linked as multimodal transport to the sea carriage documents both sides of the bill of lading as well as any other contractual clauses of sea and land transporters ought to be looked at. *Regal-Beloit* makes it clear that any forum selection clause in an ocean bill of lading cannot be avoided even if they are trying to sue the domestic railroad. In addition:

> It may now be possible for a bill of lading to mandate a short-ened time bar, just as in *American Road.* It would be unwise to blindly rely on COGSA's one-year time bar or Carmack's two-year time bar, as they may not apply. If an ocean bill of lading calls for a shortened time for filing suit, the prudent step is to comply if possible.[818]

In addition – and perhaps obviously – carriers should always review their bills of lading depending on the circumstances and in response to court decisions. *Kirby* and others have in effect made a change of exemption clauses a mandatory task specially if multimodal contracts are involved. Conversely, if a ship carries export goods to another country a different bill of lading needs to be drawn up as the inbound bill of lading will not cover the risks. It appears *Regal-Beloit* applies with equal force to both railroads and truckers, and therefore both will need to review their transportation agreements and documents to ensure

---

816   W. Tetley, (n13) 40.
817   C. Enge, Intermodal Cargo Claims After *"K" Line v. Regal-Beloit,* 23 U.S.F. Mar. L.J. 118 2010, 2011, 155.
818   Ibid., 156.

the desired legal regime covers the shipments in question.[819] As Enge cautions:

> Because *Regal-Beloit* removes Carmack coverage for inbound intermodal land carriage and replaces it with nothing, it is not clear what law applies if the bill of lading is silent or unclear. Limitations of liability will continue to pose challenges. These issues cut both ways, as sometimes a weight-based limitation under Carmack may exceed COGSA's package limitation, and sometimes not. In *Regal-Beloit,* COGSA applied by contract, not automatically by law.[820]

The *Kirby, Sompo and Regal-Beloit* decisions have a great impact on the Himalaya clause. Arguably, there is no uniformity in the content of the clause anymore as commercial facts, namely the way business is done changes not only between countries but also within a jurisdiction. The only real benefit of the Himalaya clause is that it overcame the restrictive nature of the Privity rule. In that aspect uniformity has been achieved.

11.5 The Himalaya clause and arbitration

Something needs to be said briefly in relation to the inclusion of an arbitration clause into a contract. All the cases discussed above have been litigated because no arbitration clause had been included. The Court of Rotterdam, 18 March 2015 ("Rio Taku")[821] had to deal with this issue. Besides a valid Himalaya clause, the Bill of lading also included an arbitration clause which stated:

> "39. ARBITRATION CLAUSE
>
> Any dispute arising out of or relating to this Bill of Lading shall exclusively be referred to Arbitration in London (sic) before a panel of three Arbitrators, one Arbitrator to be nominated by the

---

819 Ibid., 159.
820 Ibid., 161.
821 Rechtbank Rotterdam, 18 March 2015 (ECLI:NL:RBROT:2015:2617).

> Carrier and the other by the Merchant, and a third by the two
> so nominated. (…) The proper and exclusive law of this Bill of
> Lading shall be English law.'

The Himalaya clause did not explicitly mention jurisdiction and arbitration, but it entitled the subcontractor to "all defences, liberties, exemptions and immunities from and limitations of liability". The question was whether this included the arbitration clause.

The Court of Rotterdam correctly noted that an arbitration clause is a term which only binds the parties to the contract and not any other third party, unlike the Himalaya clause. The arbitration clause benefits merely one party. It is a mutual agreement under which both parties agree which tribunal shall have jurisdiction. Hence, the Court of Rotterdam was competent to hear the case based but on the rules of Dutch private international law. In effect, the court followed the ruling of the Privy Council in *The Makhutai*.[822] The solution is to include the arbitral clause into the Himalaya clause hence making it applicable to all parties covered by the Himalaya clause.

11.6 Statutory Solution

As noted above, The Hague-Visby Rules or amended Hague Rules do not offer any protection to independent contractors. Protection is limited to servants and agents of the carrier under contract and tort.[823] There is a rich and fertile literature on The Hague-Visby Rules; this literature will not be reviewed here. However, for the sake of completion, a brief comment will be made in relation to the Hamburg and Rotterdam Rules. They are not yet ratified by important maritime nations and are of little significance at this stage.

However, of interest to this book is the question who does

---

822   This case has been discussed above.
823   Article IV bis (1) and Article IV bis (2) of The Hague-Visby Rules.

qualifys as a carrier under COGSA. To that end *Fortis Corp. Ins., SA v. Viken Ship Mgmt.*[824] is instructive. The facts are simple: rust damaged steel coils by exposure to seawater. The central issue in this appeal was:

> whether a ship manager charged with providing a Master, offi-cers and crew, and performing various other ship-management tasks for the shipping vessel qualifies as a "carrier" under the Carriage of Goods by Sea Act (COGSA).[825]

COGSA defines a carrier as follows: "The term 'carrier' includes the owner or the charterer who enters into a contract of carriage with a shipper." The defendant asked the court not to interpret the definition of carrier in formalistic way but to endorse a functional approach. In essence, the question is similar to the one asked with regards to the perceived conflict between the Himalaya clause and the Privity rule.

The problem in relation to this issue is: has the entity in question performed:

> a function traditionally carried out by a carrier even if, due to the advances in the shipping industry in the seventy-plus years since COGSA was enacted, it does not meet the traditional view of what qualifies as a carrier under the Act.[826]

This approach did have some academic support as "It could be argued that interpretation of the Act should reflect the policy behind it and evolve to cover vessel management companies acting in the role traditionally played by carriers."[827]

> In the end, the court noted - relying on *Herd* – that the functional approach is foreclosed, and that the manager is not a carrier under COGSA.

However, this does not mean that managers are not protected

---

824   AS, 597 F.3d 784.
825   Ibid., 786.
826   Ibid., 790.
827   K. Baldwin, 35 *Tulane Maritime Law Journal*, 2010-2011, 398.

or can be protected under COGSA as shipping parties simply extend the coverage of COGSA by adding provisions to the bill of lading such as "extending the COGSA regime to any and all agents or independent contractors who participate in the shipment of goods under a particular contract."[828] Another option is to expand the definition of a COGSA Carrier.[829] However, this is not possible by attempting to change the definition within a Convention as it would require new ratification processes. The best solution – as noted above – is simply take note of this issue and adjust the Himalaya clause accordingly

11.7 The Hamburg Rules

The Hamburg rules provide the same protection as the The Hague-Visby Rules, but the only variation is that the rules do not specifically exclude independent contractors.[830] The position of the independent contractor therefore is not clear. Article 1(2) defines "Actual carrier" as meaning "any person to whom the performance of the carriage of the goods, or of part of the carriage, has been entrusted by the carrier, and includes any other person to whom such performance has been entrusted." This leads to the suggestion that any third party could potentially be included in the definition of 'carrier'. However, the Hamburg Rules do make a distinction between an actual carrier and carrier under article X which notes:

> 1. Where the performance of the carriage or part thereof has been entrusted to an actual carrier, whether or not in pursuance of a liberty under the contract of carriage by sea to do so, the carrier nevertheless remains responsible for the entire carriage according to the provisions of this Convention. The carrier is responsible, in relation to the carriage performed by the actual carrier, for the acts and omissions of the actual carrier and of

---

828   Ibid., 792.
829   See K. Baldwin, (n827) 389.
830   Article VII(2) of the Hamburg Rules.

his servants and agents acting within the scope of their employment.

2. All the provisions of this Convention governing the responsibility of the carrier also apply to the responsibility of the actual carrier for the carriage performed by him. The provisions of paragraphs 2 and 3 of Article 7 and of paragraph 2 of Article 8 apply if an action is brought against a servant or agent of the actual carrier.

It will be of interest to discover how courts will apply the Hamburg Rules in connection with the protection of third parties. Though 34 countries have ratified the Hamburg Rules, none of the important shipping countries have become parties to the Rules.

11.8   The Rotterdam Rules[831]

The latest Convention, The Rotterdam Rules, dealt in more detail with the issues of liability.

In relation to the limitation of liability Article 4 notes:

Article 4 Applicability of defences and limits of liability
- **1.** Any provision of this Convention that may provide a
defence for, or limit the liability of, the carrier applies in any
judicial or arbitral proceeding, whether founded in contract,
in tort, or otherwise, that is instituted in respect of loss of,
damage to, or delay in delivery of goods covered by a contract
of carriage or for the breach of any other obligation under this
Convention against:
(a) The carrier or a maritime performing party;
(b) The master, crew or any other person that performs
services on board the ship; or
(c) Employees of the carrier or a maritime performing party.
- **2.** Any provision of this Convention that may provide a
defence for the shipper or the documentary shipper applies
in any judicial or arbitral proceeding, whether founded in

---

831   http://www.dutchcivillaw.com/legislation/rotterdamrules.htm.

contract, in tort, or otherwise, that is instituted against the shipper, the documentary shipper, or their subcontractors, agents or employees.

As Backden[832] noted:

> It was the aim of the drafters of the Rotterdam Rules that this provision would avail any person who assists the carrier in performing his duties under the Rules the full protection of rights, defences and limits of liability available to the carrier in the event that such agent or sub-contractor was faced with a claim directly against it.[833]

Importantly, the term "performing party" has been clarified in Article 1(6) which appears to be broad enough to include the independent contractors. "It can be presumed that the drafters sought to give this provision a scope similar to the standard Himalaya clause used in the trade."[834]

Article 1.6 states:

> Performing party" means a person other than the carrier that performs or undertakes to perform any of the carrier's obligations under a contract of carriage with respect to the receipt, loading, handling, stowage, carriage, care, unloading or delivery of the goods, to the extent that such person acts, either directly or indirectly, at the carrier's request or under the carrier's supervision or control.

Importantly the obligation is not centred on the carrier but the goods; the performing party is responsible for the goods before the carrier arrives or departs from the docks. In essence, anybody within the supply chain, dock to dock, is a performing party. Hence, no distinction is drawn between the contractual parties and the independent contractors. Article 18 to that end notes:

---

832   P. Backden, *Will Himalaya Bring Class Down from Mount Olympus? - Impact of the Rotterdam Rules,* 42 J. Mar. L. & Com. 115 2011, at 118.

833   Ibid., quoting Report of the Working Group mI (Transport Law) on the work of its nineteenth session (A/CN.9/621), 21.

834   Ibid., 119.

Liability of the carrier for other persons

The carrier is liable for the breach of its obligations under this Convention caused by the acts or omissions of:

(a) Any performing party;

(b) The master or crew of the ship;

(c) Employees of the carrier or a performing party; or

(d) Any other person that performs or undertakes to perform any of the carrier's obligations under the contract of carriage, to the extent that the person acts, either directly or indirectly, at the carrier's request or under the carrier's supervision or control.

Furthermore, the period of responsibility of the carrier begins "when the carrier or a performing party receives the goods for carriage and ends when the goods are delivered."[835]

As with The Hague-Visby Rules, the Rotterdam Rules also included in Article 59 a limit to the liability of the carriers and the limitation period of two years has also been preserved in Article 62.

Backden correctly notes:

In all maritime legal areas affected by the new Rotterdam Rules, scholars as well as practitioners are considering the changes that the rules may bring about. It is obvious that the systemic alterations such as the omission of the nautical fault, the continuous obligation of the carrier to keep the ship seaworthy and the extension of the carrier's defences to independent contractors will bring consequential changes in the liability of parties under the maritime legal system as we know it.[836]

In sum Himalaya clauses may be of lesser importance as Articles 4.1 and 19.1 of the Rules provide remedies and limitations sought under the Himalaya clause. However, Himalaya clauses will not be rendered void pursuant to Article 79 as they do not

---

835   Rotterdam Rules article 12(1).
836   Backden, (n832) 122.

lessen any liability provided by the Rules.[837] In contrast, Article 79 will render Circular Indemnity clauses void since they result in excluding the third parties from liabilities regulated by the Rules.[838] As the Rotterdam Rules have found no traction yet no definitive answer can be given.

11.9 Contract (Right of Third Parties) Act 1999

Should England be the forum and English law be applicable, the Contract (Right of Third Parties) Act 1999 might be relevant The issue is that third parties are not always able to rely on contractual protection and arguably "failing to give the third-party rights prevents effect being given to the intentions of the contracting parties"[839] The *Contract (Right of Third Parties) Act 1999* was enacted to overcome this difficulty [840] and provides that a third party may "in his own right" enforce exemption clauses in a contract even if he is not mentioned by name but belongs to a class such as stevedores.[841]

It must be noted that the Act does not preclude third parties from relying on rights or remedies arising from other means such as a Himalaya clause. Article 7(1) notes:

> Supplementary provisions relating to third party.**E+W+N.I.**

> This section has no associated Explanatory Notes

> (1)   Section 1 does not affect any right or remedy of a third

---

837   Theodora Nikaki, 'Himalaya clauses and the Rotterdam Rules', *Journal of International Maritime Law*, 17(1) 2011, 20-40, 37.

838   Richard Williams, *The Overall Impact of the Rotterdam Rules on the Liability of Multimodal Carriers and their Sub-contractors*,.9 (unpublished paper submitted to the Eighth Annual International Colloquium held by the Institute of International Shipping and Trade Law, Swansea University).

839   Robert Stevens, 'The Contracts (Rights of Third Parties) Act 1999', *Law Quarterly Review* (2004), 292-323, 292.

840   Stephen Girvin, *Carriage of Goods by Sea*, 2nd edn (Oxford: Oxford University Press, 2011), 138.

841   See s 1(1)(1)(b) and 1(3).

party that exists or is available apart from this Act.

Furthermore, in the context of carriage of goods by sea contracts,

Section 1 confers no rights on a third party in the case of—

(a) a contract for the carriage of goods by sea, or

(b) a contract for the carriage of goods by rail or road, or for the carriage of cargo by air, which is subject to the rules of the appropriate international transport convention[842]

A third party may still prefer to rely on Himalaya clauses – appropriately drafted – which can confer the intended benefits to the plaintiff. If the third party intends to rely on the Act it is essential to state clearly that immunities are conferred to them[843] and that the third parties are identified in the contract.[844]

11.10 Amending the Privity Rule

The issue of third-party rights had attracted the attention of parliaments in Civil law countries, where the rights of third parties has been recognised for a long time. Simply put, contracts for the benefit of a third party are well known and hence do not pose a problem.[845] It must be noted that not unlike in common law countries the basic rule in civil law countries is that only parties to a contract can sue or be sued. Third party rights are the exception. As an example, in Germany the BGB in Article 328 regulates contracts which contain rights and obligations in favour of third parties. What needs to be said is that the stipulator needs to have an interest in providing a benefit to a third party which, in the carriage of goods, has to be financial in nature.

---

842 Third party article 6(5).
843 Section 1(1) of the Contract (Right of Third Parties) Act 1999.
844 Section 1(3) of the Contract (Right of Third Parties) Act 1999.
845 See for example Art 1121 France, Art 1121 Belgium, Art 1411 Italy, Art 1257 Spain, Art 1446 Québec.

However, the problem is that "from the outset, the Himalaya clause and stipulation for another are both conceptually and terminologically incompatible."[846] Tetley suggest three reasons why the Himalaya clause does not fall within the civilian third-party stipulation. First, the Himalaya clause does not confer a direct benefit but rather a negative right, namely protection of being sued. Secondly, the third party is normally not determined and does not signify an assent as required in civil law legislations. Thirdly, "a stipulation for another is an exception and must be interpreted restrictively."[847]

The observation by Tetley might be intellectually correct but they are not measured against the commercial value which is derived by the Himalaya clause. As noted by an Italian Court of Cassation, there is also a benefit for the carrier, not only for the third parties. The carrier can negotiate better terms with his sub-contractors as the Himalaya clause is of direct financial benefit to the subcontractors.[848]

In relation to the *Contracts (Rights of Third Parties) Act* 1999[849] arguably it was not suited to take the peculiarities of maritime issues into consideration as it tries to do all things for everybody and hence an exception to the exception had to be created. In essence, in England as well as in Australia the Act is of no consequence and only reaffirms the uniqueness of maritime law. It will still be a judicial function to either further develop the Himalaya clauses or simply suggest that he law in this area is settled which is unlikely. As a general comment, the views of Hugh Beale give a good assessment of the utility of this Act in general. He noted:

> While it is perhaps too soon to claim that the Contracts (Rights of Third Parties) Act 1999 has been an outstanding success, in

---

846   Tetley, (n13) 31.
847   Ibid., 31.
848   See A. Antonini, *Liability of Terminal Operators, Case History and Case Law*, 2008, 114.
849   As discussed in Chapter XI.

that as yet its use seems to be limited, I think we can say that it has certainly not been a failure. Rather I regard it as useful but still underused.[850]

In relation to the COGSA Rules the original Hague Rules (which originated as standard clauses found within bills of lading) fail to make any mention of the obligation held by the carrier to actually deliver goods. Therefore, the need to draft concise clauses to cover the liability exemptions for all parties involved in the maritime adventure is important. Specifically, to exactly list all third parties under a bill is important taking note of judicial decisions such as in *Norfolk Southern Railway Company v James N. Kirby Pty. Ltd.*[851]

The Rotterdam Rules appear to have overcome this problem under Article 11: "the carrier shall, subject to this Convention and in accordance with the terms of the contract of carriage, carry the goods to the place of destination and deliver them to the consignee."

The Hamburg Rules solve the problem of the Himalaya clause at Article 4 which extends the responsibility of the carrier from port to port, while Article 10 holds the carrier responsible for the acts of the actual carrier, who by the definition in Article 1(2), would include the stevedore and the terminal agent.[852]

The problem with either the Hamburg Rules as well as the Rotterdam Rules is the slow uptake and, hence, the replacement of the Hague Visby Rules as the dominant Convention is unlikely in the near future.

Courts have also redefined the Privity rule which has come under attack not only through the Himalaya clause but in general,

---

850   Beale, Hugh, "A Review of the Contracts (Rights of Third Parties) Act 1999" in Burrows, Andrew and Peel, Edwin (eds) *Contract Formation and Parties* (OUP, 2010) 225-250.
851   543 U.S. 14, 125 S.Ct. 385 (2004).
852   Tetley, (n13) 36.

specifically in insurance matters.[853] However, the Privity rule has and can be circumvented by persons seeking to take the benefits in a contract where they are a third party.

The main circumstances applicable to shipping are, firstly, that the carrier has entered into the shipping contract as an agent of the third party. Secondly, the aggrieved party can claim under tort. It is still considered to be an artificial means to avoid the Privity rule.

11.11 Agency

Lord Reid in *Midlands* as noted above suggested a four-stage test which has been adopted in other cases such as in the *New York Star*. The weak link in Lord Reid's theory is the question of consideration passing from the stevedore to the shipper. The answer is supplied in the *The Eurymedon*, namely "The performance of these services for the benefit of the shipper was the consideration for the agreement by the shipper that the appellant (stevedore) should have the benefit of the exemptions and limitations contained in the bill of lading." [854] This appears to be the law as it stands in the Commonwealth countries as confirmed in *The Rigoletto*. [855]

Professor Tetley is doubtful about the considerations found by Lord Wilberforce for Lord Reid's agency theory and the presumed benefit to society and commerce because it promotes litigation based on technical points.[856] He based his view on the following paragraph by Lord Wilberforce in the *Eurymedon*:

In the opinion of their Lordships, to give the appellant the ben-

---

853   See for example in Canada, *Fraser River Pile & Dredge Ltd. v. Can-Dive Services Ltd.* [1999] 3 S.C.R. 108, [2000] 1 Lloyd's Rep. 199, and in Australia *Trident General Insurance Co. Ltd. v. McNiece Bros. Pty. Ltd.* (1988) 165 C.L.R. 107.

854   The Eurymedon [1975] A.C. 154, [1974] 1 Lloyd's Rep. 534, 539.

855   [2000] 2 Lloyd's Rep. 532.

856   Tetley, (n13) 10.

efit of the exemptions and limitations contained in the bill of lading is to give effect to *the clear intentions of a commercial document* and can be given within existing principles. *They see no reason to strain the law* or the facts in order to defeat these intentions. It should not be overlooked that the effect of denying validity to the clause would be to encourage actions against servants, agents and independent contractors in order to get around exemptions (which are almost invariable and often compulsory) accepted by shippers against carriers, the existence, and presumed efficacy, of which is reflected in the rates of freight. *They see no attraction in this consequence.*" (Emphasis added).[857]

Tetley specifically argues that it is fallacious to state that "the clear intentions of a commercial document," indicates that the benefit of an exemption clause can be given to third parties. It is true to say that third parties are being able to hide their negligence behind a contract to which they are not a party. However, from a practical point of view it is obvious that every shipper knows that a supply chain involves not only the contractual parties but others as well, hence, it is not reasonable to expect the shipper to either make several contracts with all concerned parties or to require the carrier to ask the shippers to enter into various contracts to ensure that any damage to cargo is covered by a contractual clause. It is commercially far easier to have one contract to exist between shipper and carrier and refine perhaps the Himalaya clause. This clause by now should be well known to any shipper and he should be aware of its consequences. The Canadian exception of gross negligence might be a solution. Importantly many judgments deal with the limitation period and/or package limitations as regulated in COGSA, both issues which a shipper can easily overcome by simply taking out insurance. The same is true for any damages caused to the shippers' goods.

857　The Eurymedon [1975] A.C. 154,. 169.

11.12. Further development of Himalaya clauses

Since *Adler* the drafters of exemption clauses have taken note of court decisions and have refined the wording. Third parties normally are involved only outside the tackle to tackle period which is protected by COGSA and hence "a period of responsibility clause" can be of value. Such clauses are often integrated into the paramount clause and may read:

> The provisions stated in said Act [i.e. COGSA] ... shall govern before the goods are loaded on and after they are discharged from the ship and throughout the entire time the goods are in the custody of the carrier.[858]

A further possibility is that carriers include stevedores and terminal operators as a party to the bill of lading or the carrier acts as an agent for third parties. However, this is not a practical solution as the carrier does not wish to extend his period of responsibility nor be responsible for third parties. What can be said though is that carriers and stevedores and terminal operators as a rule do know each other and the reluctance of including third parties into the contract is not as Treitel suggested just a fiction.[859]

11.13. Circular indemnity clause

The Circular Indemnity clause was invented to overcome the "uncertainty about the effectiveness of the Himalaya Clause."[860] In essence, it allows a third party to sue for "the benefit of the agreement" which was developed in *Beswick v Beswick*.[861]

The facts are simple. An agreement was made between two

---

858   Insurance Company of North America v. M/V Savannah 1999 AMC 1029 (S.D. N.Y. 1997).
859   Treitel, F.M.B. Reynolds, Thomas Gilbert Carver, 7.
860   Robert Newell, '"Privity fundamentalism" and the circular indemnity clause', Lloyd's Maritime and Commercial Law Quarterly, 1(Feb) (1992), 97-108, 97.
861   *Beswick v Beswick* [1968] A.C. 58.

people whereby a business was sold and the seller was to be given a sum of money as a consultant for the rest of his life and in clause 2 of the same agreement the buyer agreed to pay a sum of money to the seller's wife after his death.[862]

The point was that the widow was not a party to the contract and hence the principle as noted in *Tweddle v. Atkinson*[863] should stand. But it was observed that:

> If there had been such a fundamental change in the law, the effect of which was to overrule *Tweddle v. Atkinson* by statute the House of Lords in *Scruttons Ltd. v. Midland Silicones Ltd.* could not have shut its eyes to such a point as this, and the only inference to be drawn from that case is that ... [it] was rejected by them.[864]

The court held that:

> the widow, as administratrix of a party to the contract was entitled to an order for specific performance of the promise made by the nephew and was not limited to recovering merely nominal damages on the basis of the loss to the estate.[865]

Circular indemnity clauses have been introduced into bills of lading – and hence as part of Himalaya clauses – as in the seminal case of the *The Elbe Maru*.

A typical indemnity clause would read as follows:

> The Merchant undertakes that no claim or allegation shall be made against any servant, agent or subcontractor of the Carrier which imposes or attempts to impose upon any of them or any vessel owned by any of them any liability whatsoever in connection with the goods and, if any such claim or allegation should nevertheless be made, to indemnify the Carrier against all consequences thereof.[866]

---

862   Ibid., 59.
863   1 B. & S. 393.
864   Ibid., 70.
865   Ibid., 59.
866   *The Elbe Maru* [1978] 1 Lloyd's Rep. 206 at 207.

In *Godina v Patrick Operations*[867] a second sentence was added which reads:

> Without prejudice to the foregoing, every such servant, agent and sub-contractor shall have the benefit of all provisions herein benefitting the Carrier as if such provisions were expressly for their benefit; and, in entering into this Contract, the Carrier, to the extent of those provisions, does not only on its own behalf but also as agent and trustee for such servants, agents and sub-contractors.

It is also prudent to read the circular indemnity clause in conjunction with the definition clause contained in the bill of lading:

> Definitions ... 'Merchant' includes the Shipper, Holder, Consignee, the receiver of the Goods, any person owning or entitled to the possession of the Goods or this Bill of Lading and anyone acting on behalf of any such persons...[868]

Simply put the clause creates a chain of indemnity.[869] When an independent party is sued by the Shipper or endorsee, there are two possible outcomes; the carrier may ask the court for a stay as noted in the jurisprudence above, or he may indemnify the third party and then bring an action against the cargo owner for breach of contract to recover the amount he has indemnified the third party.[870]

As noted in the English and Australian jurisprudence[871] the

---

867   (1984) 1 Lloyd's Rep. 333, 334.

868   Elbe Maru, (291) 207.

869   John F Wilson, Carriage of Goods by Sea, 7th edn (Harlow: Longman, 2010), 257.

870   Nicholas Gaskell, Regina Asariotis, Yvonne Baatz, *Bills of Lading: Law and Contracts*, (London: LLP, 2000), 397.

871   Many other jurisdictions have also approved of the indemnity clause such as *The Nedlloyd Colombo*, [1998] 2 HKLR 53, 60 (Hong Kong C.A.); *Vander Limited v. P. & O. Nedlloyd B.V.*, [1998] HKEC 928 (Hong Kong H.C.). 78 (2004) 267 F.T.R. 115, para. 37 (Fed. C. Can. per Morneau P.), upheld on other grounds, [2005] 4 F.C.R. 441 (Fed. C. Can.). The clause was also upheld in *Bombardier Inc. v. Canadian Pacific Ltd.*, [1988] O.J. No. 1807 (Ont. H.C.), varied on appeal, (1991), 7 O.R. (3d) 559 (Ont. C.A.).

shipper does promise not to sue any third party within the supply chain. Any actions against a third-party result in stay of proceedings subject to the requirements by the courts that the carrier has sufficient interest in the enforcement of the covenant.[872] "Sufficient interest" has been defined as exposing the carrier – who is protected by the Himalaya clause anyway – to a legal liability to the third party. The relevant clause reads that the carrier promised to: "indemnify the third party against any amount which the cargo-owner might recover from the third party."[873]

The issue which occupied the courts was whether the indemnity clause is in breach of Article III Rule 8 of Hague Rules and The Hague-Visby Rules. The court in the *Whitesea Shipping and Trading Corp & Anor v El Paso Rio Clara Ltda & Ors* [874] ruled that none of the third parties in the contract containing the indemnity clause undertook a sea carriage within the definition of The Hague-Visby Rules and hence the clause is not subject to Article III Rule 8.

However, in *The Chevalier Roze*[875] it was clearly stated that the circular indemnity clauses are inapplicable if the sub-contractors perform any operation which is not within the scope of the bill of lading. In this case, the goods were not collected after they were offloaded, and further instruction went to the agent to deliver them to the consignee. The goods were lost during the transport. The question was whether the onward carriage was on bill of lading terms. The court decided it was not and hence the circular indemnity clause does not apply.[876]

However, care must be taken when inserting a circular indemnity clause as under the Hamburg and Rotterdam Conventions the result might be different. Under the Hamburg Rules the situation

---

872   *Gore v Van der Lann* [1967] 2 Q.B. 31.
873   Treitel, F.M.B. Reynolds, Thomas Gilbert Carver, .469.
874   [2009] 2 C.L.C. 596.
875   [1983] 2 Lloyd's Rep. 438.
876   Ibid., 443.

is different. Article 10 expressly regulates liabilities of the actual carrier. The Article states:

> Liability of the carrier and actual carrier
>
> 1. Where the performance of the carriage or part thereof has been entrusted to an actual carrier, whether or not in pursuance of a liberty under the contract of carriage by sea to do so, the carrier nevertheless remains responsible for the entire carriage according to the provisions of this Convention. The carrier is responsible, in relation to the carriage performed by the actual carrier, for the acts and omissions of the actual carrier and of his servants and agents acting within the scope of their employment.
>
> 2. All the provisions of this Convention governing the responsibility of the carrier also apply to the responsibility of the actual carrier for the carriage performed by him. The provisions of paragraphs 2 and 3 of Article 7 and of paragraph 2 of Article 8 apply if an action is brought against a servant or agent of the actual carrier.
>
> 3. Any special agreement under which the carrier assumes obligations not imposed by this Convention or waives rights conferred by this Convention affects the actual carrier only if agreed to by him expressly and in writing. Whether or not the actual carrier has so agreed, the carrier nevertheless remains bound by the obligations or waivers resulting from such special agreement.

Furthermore, Article 23 must be read in conjunction with Article 10.

> Article 23(1) also states:
>
> Contractual stipulations
>
> 1. Any stipulation in a contract of carriage by sea, in a bill of lading, or in any other document evidencing the contract of carriage by sea is null and void to the extent that it derogates, directly or indirectly, from the provisions of this Convention. The nullity of such a stipulation does not affect the validity of the

other provisions of the contract or document of which it forms a part. A clause assigning benefit of insurance of the goods in favour of the carrier, or any similar clause, is null and void.

3. Where a bill of lading or any other document evidencing the contract of carriage by sea is issued, it must contain a statement that the carriage is subject to the provisions of this Convention which nullify any stipulation derogating therefrom to the detriment of the shipper or the consignee.

The effect of Articles 10 and 23 is that a circular indemnity clause is mostly rendered void as it is in breach of the Hamburg Rules. The Rotterdam Rules - as the Hamburg Rules – also question the validity of the indemnity clause. Article 18 states that:

The carrier is liable for the breach of its obligations under this Convention caused by the acts or omissions of:

a) Any performing party.

b) The master or crew of the ship.

c) Employees of the carrier or a performing party; or

d) Any other person that performs or undertakes to perform any of the carrier's obligations under the contract of carriage, to the extent that the person acts, either directly or indirectly, at the carriers' request or under the carrier's supervision or control.

In essence, third parties are not able to be sued as the carrier is directly responsible. Furthermore, Article 79 states that any term in a contract of carriage is void if it directly or indirectly excludes or limits obligations of the carrier under this Convention.

Under the Rotterdam Rules the situation is changed if the contract stipulates a Free In, Out, Stowed and Trimmed (FIOST)[877] term

---

877   In the event of FIOS (Free In Out and Stowed), the freight rate only covers the actual transport. Neither the loading, unloading or stowing of the goods onboard the ship are included in the freight rate. These costs are payable separately, both by the shipper and the recipient.

as described in *The Jordan II*.[878] Article 13(2) notes that the carrier and the shipper may agree that the loading, handling, stowing or unloading of the goods is to be performed by the shipper, the documentary shipper or the consignee. The effect of this Article is that the stevedores are outside the carriage contract and are not a maritime performing party hence the indemnity clause is enlivened again.[879]

However, under the Hague-Visby Rules this term is not an automatic exclusion of liability as the terms specially the word "Free" needs interpreting within the context of the contract. In *the Jordan II* the court noted:

> There are three facets of the cargo operation which have to be considered. Who is to pay for it; who is to carry it out; and who is liable for it not being done properly and carefully. ... There is no presumption that each of these responsibilities should fall on the same party. In other words, if the charterer has agreed to pay for the cargo operation, there is no presumption that he has also agreed to carry it out or be liable if it is done badly.[880]

Tuckey L.J made a clear distinction between paying for a service and being liable for it. The word "Free" therefore does not mean free of risk; it simply means free of cost as the FIOST term is simply a "who is to pay" provision.[881]

The questions whether the charterer (in this case) can be exempt from liability was discussed and it was held that;

> ... nothing would prevent the shipowner making a contract with the shipper on terms that the shipper would be responsible for loading, the receiver would be responsible for discharging and the shipowner responsible for neither ... The Hague-Visby Rule art. III r. 2 simply compelled the shipowner to load and unload

---

878   [2003] Lloyd's Rep. 87.
879   R. Williams, 'The Rotterdam Rules: winners and losers', *Journal of International Maritime Law*, 16 (2010), 191, 199.
880   The Jordan II. (n878) 103.
881   Ibid.

properly if he undertook these functions.[882]

However, clauses 7 and 17 relieved the shipowner from any responsibility unless the shipowner had intervened which he did not.

The circular indemnity clause on its own has many disadvantages. As stated in *The Elbe Maru* the proceedings were a waste of time and costs:

> If the action ought not to be brought, then the court should intervene and stop it rather than allow a series of circuitous actions which ultimately end up achieving exactly what the stay sought would achieve, apart from the disbursement of a quite unnecessary amount of costs.[883]

In any case the carrier is the only person who is entitled to enforce the clause in the head bill of lading; the third parties are not entitled since they are not the party to the contract. The issue is that the carrier needs to co-operate in the litigation.[884]

In recent times, many carriers have combined the Himalaya clause with Prohibition of Suit Clause and a Circular Indemnity Clause, in their standard form bills of lading.[885] In Canada, as an example, this development has been noted in *Timberwest Forest Corp. v. Pacific Link Ocean Services Corp.*[886] Harrington J noted (citations omitted):

> In maritime matters, the courts have always frowned upon efforts to avoid exemption and limitation clauses by suing the opposite party's servants, agents and subcontractors (Elder, Dempster & Co. v. Paterson, Zachonis & Co.,). It has been sound commercial practice, since at least Lord Denning's decision in the Hi-

---

882 Ibid., 88.
883 *The Elbe Maru* [1978] 1 Lloyd's Rep. 206, 210.
884 Treitel, F.M.B. Reynolds, Thomas Gilbert Carver, (n 219),.468.
885 Peter G. Pamel and Robert C. Wilkins Borden Ladner Gervais, LLP, Bills of Lading vs Sea Waybills, and The Himalaya Clause, Presented at the NJI/CMLA, Federal Court and Federal Court of Appeal Canadian Maritime Law Association Seminar April 15, 2011 Fairmont Château Laurier, Ottawa, 21.
886 2008 FC 801, [2009] 4 F.C.R. 496 at para. 69 (Fed. C. Can.).

malaya, to attempt by contract, in one way or another, to protect employees, servants, agents and subcontractors who actually perform a maritime contract. Apart from the Himalaya Clause, maritime law has also developed forbearance of suit and circular indemnity clauses by which the shipper promises not to sue subcontractors and if anyone else does, to fully indemnify the carrier. These clauses were upheld in England in Nippon Yusen Kaisha v. "Elbe Maru". The circular indemnity clause was upheld by Mr. Justice Chadwick of the Supreme Court of Ontario in Bombardier Inc. v. Canadian Pacific Ltd., His decision was varied on appeal so that the Court of Appeal did not have to deal with the clause. [Emphasis added]

More recently, Prothonotary Morneau upheld the forbearance of suit clause in Ford Aquitaine Industries SAS c. "Canmar Pride". His decision was affirmed on appeal, but Mr. Justice Lemieux did not deal with this point. Extending insurance benefits to subcontractors, by express wording, or at least by necessary implication, is well known in the construction industry (Commonwealth Construction Co. v. Imperial Oil Ltd).

This ruling is a good example to bring the Himalaya clause and the circular indemnity clause into focus. This is so as the "rules are evolving, the carrier must be expressly or by implication instructed in some other contract (e.g. the stevedoring contract or the terminal operating agreement) to contractually benefit the third parties contemplated."[887]

Tetley argues that if a circular indemnity clause is valid – and it is as the section above has shown – this would be a good reason to adopt the Hamburg Rules.[888] However this is neither a convincing reason nor a sufficient reason for a ratification of the Hamburg Rules. As at the end of 2019, 34 countries – mainly developing countries – had adopted the Rules. Arguably therefore The Hague-Visby Rules are still the predominant and most important Rules.

---

887   Peter G. Pamel and Robert C. Wilkins Borden Ladner Gervais (n885), 23.
888   Tetley, (n13) 29.

In sum, the mechanism and rationale upon which the circular indemnity clause is based makes it unattractive for the cargo owner to claim directly against the tortfeasor. The reason is that:

> once the cargo owner proceeds against the wrongdoer, the latter will have to compensate the former; this causes the third party/wrongdoer to proceed against the carrier by virtue of an indemnity clause contained in the contract that regulates their relationship (most often, either a contract of employment or of service): the third party will claim from the carrier the amount it compensated to the cargo owner; lastly, the carrier, by virtue of the circular indemnity clause, can seek indemnification from the cargo owner with regards to the amount conferred to the servant (which is the exact amount the servant was held liable for against the cargo owner).[889]

Simply put the Himalaya clause is here to stay for better or worse. At least it can be said that the Himalaya clause is an example where courts and legislations can develop an international uniform rule without the assistance of an international body like UNCITRAL.

11.14 Conclusion

This chapter has demonstrated that an old principle has been adapted to new circumstances. In effect, commercial reality was the guiding force in recognising third party rights As Lord Steyn noted: "there is no doctrinal, logical, or policy reason why the law should deny effectiveness to a contract for the benefit of a third party where that is the expressed intention of the parties."[890] The demise of the Privity rule in shipping contracts arguable is complete. It would be more than unusual if any court would rely on the Privity rule in deciding an exemption clause in a bill of

---

889   University of Oslo, I Blaskovic, Certain legal aspects of the Himalaya clause in the contract of international carriage of goods by sea, 46.

890   Darlington Borough Council v. Wiltshier Northern Ltd. [1995] 1 W.L.R. 68 at 76 (C.A.).

lading. In addition, the Himalaya clause has also found its way into other areas of law, for example into construction contracts.

However, the Himalaya cause as it stands today is not without its critics either. Tetley and others have argued strongly against the utility of the Himalaya clause. Specifically, Tetley argued that, "the Himalaya clause is an ingenious, short-term solution to a difficult problem, but is a solution which raises infinitely more problems than it solves."[891] One of the arguments – and arguably correctly – is that stevedores and other third parties are not protected even if they are negligent. This issue has been resolved by Canadian courts where gross negligence negates the protection under the Himalaya clause One would assume that if common law courts view gross negligence as a problem, they could follow the Canadian approach. However, jurisprudence, or reality, have shown that Tetley was not correct. The best argument one could suggest is that the Himalaya clause is not the perfect instrument and, hence, other methods can or possibly will be additional tools in drafting exemption clauses. The Himalaya clauses have spawned additional legal principles in order to protect unconnected third parties such as the circular indemnity clause.

One of the more often applied principles is the circular indemnity clause. It is often included into the Himalaya clause as it provides a negative aspect to litigation because it is unattractive for the cargo owner to claim directly against the tortfeasor. The simple conclusion to be drawn is that the Privity principle has been "banished" from exemption clauses in shipping contracts.

---

891   Tetley. (n13) 6.

12

CONCLUDING EVALUATION OF THE HIMALAYA CLAUSE JURISPRUDENCE

This book has demonstrated that the Privity rule, which has dominated the development of contract law, has been superseded by a commercially sound recognition that a third party which is not directly connected to the contract nevertheless needs to be protected in a clause exempting everybody within the supply line from being sued.

The Privity rule contains two prohibitions, namely that a party to a contract cannot impose the contractual obligation upon a third party, nor can the third party sue upon the stipulation in his favour.[892] The civil law has overcome the second prohibition already in the late 19th century whereas England continued to adhere to the view that only parties to a contract can sue. However, despite the reluctance to embrace what is commercially sound, England has developed a system which "trumps" the Privity rule. *Adler v Dickson* is deemed to be the start of allowing a third party to take advantage of an exemption clause. This book has sketched the development in England and

---

892   Palmer, (n17) 1-2.

how the principle of the Himalaya clause has found favour in many other systems, specifically in common law countries. But, also in civil law countries, like Germany, where the Privity rule was not applicable, the term 'Himalaya clause' has found its way into the vocabulary of judges. Arguably, the development of the Himalaya clause can be likened to the development of conventions and model laws by organisations such as UNCITRAL and UNIDROIT as:

> Significant benefits exist in having the same rule apply in each jurisdiction whenever a transaction involves more than one legal system. Citing advantages such as certainty, predictability, convenience, and stability, the legal community has recognized the benefits for generations.[893]

Currently, while the Rotterdam Rules are still not ratified extensively, the Himalaya clause is widely in use, as a very efficient tool for restricting liability. This is specially so in light of the lack of an international convention on the liability of terminal operators and the lack of uniformity at the level of national legislation providing protection for such parties.

The question has and always will be whether the exemption clause is properly drafted in order to give all parties the intended protection. To that end, the BIMCO clause has been discussed in this book because it serves as a template for any drafter of a Himalaya clause.

The conclusion is that the commercial, and not doctrinal, approach taken in the Himalaya clause caused the demise of the Privity rule or at least relegated it to a minor rule in the drafting of exemption clauses. The Himalaya clause in shipping contracts is following, perhaps inadvertently, the mandate of the CISG and the UNIDROIT Principles in achieving a harmonised approach to a discreet area of law, similar to the Cape Town Convention. Arguably, cracks are showing in the interpretative model and perhaps the subjective intent as promulgated in the

---

893   Sturley, (n243) 731.

UNIDROIT Principles and Article 8 of the CISG are taken root. It is arguably the fact that interpretations must take note of commercial reality and introduces customary practices. Importantly, because the courts are assuming that the parties knew that the carrier will be contracting independent parties, the subjective approach is at least by implication in use. The subjective approach is best stated by Article 8 CISG:

> (1) For the purposes of this Convention statements made by and other conduct of a party are to be interpreted according to his intent where the other party knew or could not have been unaware what that intent was.
>
> (2) If the preceding paragraph is not applicable, statements made by and other conduct of a party are to be interpreted according to the understanding that a reasonable person of the same kind as the other party would have had in the same circumstances.
>
> (3) In determining the intent of a party or the understanding a reasonable person would have had, due consideration is to be given to all relevant circumstances of the case including the negotiations, any practices which the parties have established between themselves, usages and any subsequent conduct of the parties.[894]

In the United Kingdom, at least the subjective approach has been noted albeit with a yet negative view. Lord Hoffman in *Chartbrook Limited v Persimmon Homes Limited and others*, noted:

> Supporters of the admissibility of pre-contractual negotiations draw attention to the fact that Continental legal systems seem to have little difficulty in taking them into account. Both the UNIDROIT Principles of International Commercial Contracts (1994 and 2004 revision) and the Principles of European Contract Law (1999) provide that in ascertaining the "common intention of the parties", regard shall be had to prior negotiations: articles 4.3 and 5.102 respectively. The same is true of the United Nations Convention on Contracts for the International Sale of

---

894   http://iicl.law.pace.edu/cisg/cisg.

Goods (1980). But these instruments reflect the French philosophy of contractual interpretation, which is altogether different from that of English law.[895]

It can be argued, as has been demonstrated in this book, that both the civil and common law countries have adopted the interpretation of exemption clauses in achieving the same result, hence, arguably the interpretation must be the same or at least similar. The civil law system has no problems interpreting contracts in the light of subjective intent and in situations where the Himalaya clause needs to be interpreted not only has the common law closed the gap with the civil law on third party contracts but arguably has also, perhaps inadvertently, moved away from the parol evidence rule and by implication adopted the subjective approach.

---

[895] United Kingdom 1 July 2009 House of Lords (*Chartbrook Limited v. Persimmon Homes Limited et al.*) [http://cisgw3.law.pace.edu/cases/090701uk.html].

INDEX

Jurisprudence

Australasia

BHP v Hapag-Lloyd Aktiengesellschaft, [1980] 2 NSWLR 572

Chapman Marine Pty Ltd v Wilhelmsen Lines A/S. [1999] FCA 178

Codelfa Construction Pty Ltd v State Rail Authority (NSW) (1982) 149 CLR 337

Dampskibsselskabet Norden A/S v Gladstone Civil Pty Ltd, [2013] FCAFC 107, [2013] 216 FCR, 469.

Darlington Futures Ltd v Delco Australia Proprietary Limited, [1986] 161 C.L.R, 500

Gadsden Pty Ltd v Australian Coastal Shipping Commission. [1977] 1 NSWLR 575

Glebe Island Terminals Pty Ltd v Continental Seagram Pry Ltd, (1993) 40 NSWLR 206

Godina v. Patrick Operations Pty Ltd, [1984] 1 Lloyd's Rep. 333

Herrick v. Leonard and Dingley Ltd and Another, (1975) 2 NZLR 566.

Koompahtoo Council v Sanpina P/L/ (2007) 233 CLR 115

Nissho Iwai Australia Ltd v Malaysian International Shipping Corporation, Berhad, (1989) 167 CLR 219

Nudrill Pty Ltd v LaRosa [No 3], [2011] WADC 178

Port Jackson Stevedoring Pty Ltd v Salmond & Spraggon (Australia) Pty Ltd (1980) 144 CLR 300

Sydney Cooke Ltd v Hapag-Lloyd Aktiengesellschaft, [1980] 2 NSWLR 587

The Bell Group (in liq) Ltd v WestpacBanking Corporation (No 9) (2008) WASC 239,

Toll (FGCT) Pty Limited v Alphapharm Pty Limited, [2004] 219 CLR 167

Trident General Insurance Co. Ltd. v. McNiece Bros. Pty. Ltd (1988) C.L.R. 107

Water Trading Co Ltd.v Dalgety & Co Ltd, (1951) 52 S.R. (N.S.W.) 4.

Wincanton Ltd v P & O Trans European Ltd [2001] C.L.C. 962

Wilson v Darling Island Stevedoring and Lighterage Co. Ltd, (1956) 95 C.L.R. 43

Canada

Canadian General Electric Co. v. Pickford & Black Ltd., [1971] S.C.R. 41.

Eisen Und Metall A.G. v. Ceres Stevedoring Co. Ltd. [1977] 1 Lloyd's Rep. 665

Fraser River Pile & Dredge Ltd. v. Can-Dive Services Ltd, [1999] 3 S.C.R. 108

ITO-International Terminal Operators Ltd. v. Miida Electronics (Inc.) [1986] 1 S.C.R. 752, 28 D.L.R. (4th) 641

London Drugs Ltd v. Kuehne & Nagel International , Ltd [1992] 3 SCR 299

Marubeni America Corporation, v.Mitsui O.S.K. Lines Ltd, 1979 Carswel Nat 37, [1979]

Manderville v Goodfellow's Trucking Ltd, (1999) 44 CLR (2d) 10.

Miles International Co. v. Federal Commerce and Navigation Co. and federal Stevedoring Ltd, [1978] 1 Lloyd's Rep.

The Suleyman Stalskiy, (1976) 2 Lloyd's Rep 609.

Timberwest Forest Corp. v. Pacific Link Ocean Services Corp, 2008 FC 801, [2009] 4 F.C.R. 496

Germany

BGH 07.07.1960, II ZR 209/58, VersR 1960, 727

BGH 2. Zivilsenat, 8.04.1977, II ZR 26/76

OLG Frankfurt, 11.05.2012, 5 U 123/11

OLG Köln, 05.09.2014, 3 U 15/14

OLG Hamburg, 07.11.1974, 6 U 157/3, VersR 1975, 801

United States

Acciai Speciali Terni USA, Inc, v M/V Berane, 181 F.Supp.2d 458 (D.Md. 2002).

Akiyama Corp. of America v. M.V. Hanjin Marseilles, 162 F.3d 571 (9th Cir. 1998)

Caterpillar Overseas S.A. v Marine Transport Inc, 900 F.2d. 714 (4th Cir. 1990).

Collins v. Panama, (1952) 197 Fed.Rep. 983.

Fortis Corp. Ins., SA v. Viken Ship Mgmt, AS, 597 F.3d 784

Great Northern R.Co. v. O'Connor, 232 U.S. 508, 34 S.Ct. 380, 58 L.Ed. 703 (1914).

Herd & Co. v Krawill Machinery Corp, 359 U.S. 297, 79 S.Ct. 766 (1959)

Institute of London Underwriters v Sea-Land Services Inc, 881 F.2d 761, (1989).

Insurance Company of North America v M/V Savannah, New York, December 4, 1997. 94 Civ. 8846

Komori America Corporation v Howland Hook Container Terminal Inc. Westlaw, 1998 A.M.C. 289

Lucky Goldstar v. S. S. California Mercury, 750 F. Supp 141, 1991

Macpherson v Buick, (1916) 217 NY 382.

Mazda Motors of America, Inc. v M/V Cougar ACE, 565 f.3D 573 (2009).

Mikingberg v Baltic S.S. Co, 988 F.2d 327, 1993.

Mori Seiki USA Inc v M.V. Alligator Triumph, 990 F.2d 444 (1993).

Norfolk Southern Railway Company v James N. Kirby Pty. Ltd, 543 U.S. 14, 125 S.Ct. 385 (2004).

Sompo Japan Insurance of America and Another v Norfolk Southern Railway Co, (2014) 907 LMLN 3.

Steel Coils, Inc. v. M/V Lake Marion, 331 F.3d 422 (5th Cir. 2003).

Taisho Marine & Fire Ins. Co Ltd v Vessel Gladiolus, 762 F2nd 1364 (1985).

Hong Kong

Bewise Motors Co. Ltd. v. Hoi Kong Container Services Ltd [1998] 2 HK.I.RD. 645

Singapore

Yusen Air & Sea Service (S) Pty Ltd v Changi International Airport Services Pty Ltd, [1999] 3 SLR (R) 95.

South Africa

Bouygues Offshore and Another v Owner of the MT Tigr and another, 1995, (4) SA 49 (C).

LTA Construction Ltd v Mediterranean Shipping Company Depots Pty Ltd, [2006] JDR 0303 (D).

Management Centre Pty Ltd, [2001] JPL 8954 (D).

Mediterranean Shipping Company (Pty) Ltd v Tebe Trading Pty Ltd, 2008 (6) SA 595 (SCA).

MT Fotiy Krylov v Owners of the Mt Ruby Deliverer, [2008] (5) SA 434 (C).

Owners of Cargo Formerly laden on Board of MV "Mas Tiga" v Confreight Cargo

Santam Insurance Co Ltd v. SA Stevedores Ltd. [1989] 1 All SA 196 (D).

Tebe Trading Pty Ltd v Mediterranean Shipping Company (Pty) Ltd, [2006] JOL 16093 (D).

REFERENCES

Antonini, A. Liability of Terminal Operators, Case History and Case Law, 2008,

Backden, P. Will Himalaya Bring Class Down from Mount Olympus? – Impact of the Rotterdam Rules, 42 Journal of Maritime Law & Commerce, 115 2011

Baldwin, K 35 Tulane Maritime Law Journal, 2010-2011, 398

Baughen, S., Shipping Law, 2004, 3rd ed. Cavendish Publishing

Barnett, K. "The validity of Himalaya clauses-Privity of contract on the brink of collapse?" The International Journal of Shipping Law, 178

Band 4, Wirschaftsrecht III 5. Auflage Beck Munchen, 2002, 1031-32

Beale, Hugh, "A Review of the Contracts (Rights of Third Parties) Act 1999" in Burrows, Andrew and Peel, Edwin (eds) Contract Formation and Parties

Cammarano, D.. Impacts of the Supreme Court Decision in Regal-Beloit:Exporting Import Litigation, 85 Tulane Law Review. 1207 2010-2011

Costabel, A. M. Himalaya Strain?-A Forensic Examination of Norfolk Southern Railway Co. v James N Kirby, Pty Ltd and Doe v Celebrity Cruises, Inc., 29 Tul. Mar. L.J. 2004-2005, 217

Carver on Bills of Lading (3rd ed) Sweet and Maxwell, 2010

Dean M., Removing a blot on the landscape - the reform of the doctrine of Privity. Journal of Business law, 2000, 143

Enge, C. Intermodal Cargo Claims After "K" Line v. Regal-Beloit, 23 U.S.F. Mar. L.J. 118 2010

Furmston M. and G.J. Tolhurst, Privity of Contract, Oxford Press, 2015

Privity of Contract: Contracts for the Benefit of Third Parties Law Com, No 242. 1996

Gaskell, N.Regina Asariotis, Yvonne Baatz, Bills of Lading: Law and Contracts, (London: LLP, 2000),

Girvin, S. .Carriage of Goods by Sea, 2nd edn (Oxford: Oxford University

Press, 2011),

Gurley, G. "the ninth Circuit Breaches Life into a vessel as a Himalaya Beneficiary." 34 Tulane Maritime Law Journal 2099-2020

Hallebecke Jan and Harry Doudorp (eds) Contract for a Third-Party Beneficiary: A Historical and Comparative Account (2008) Brill,

Halstead, R T, Privity of Contract and Bills of Lading: Midland Silicones Ltd v Scruttons Ltd, 1964, 4(3) Sydney Law Review 464

Hare, J.Shipping Law & Admiralty Jurisdiction in South Africa (1999) Juta & Co Ltd., 403. Herber, Münchener Kommentar zum HGB, 3. Auflage 2014

Hyeon Kim, Korean Maritime Law Update: 2007-Focused on the Revised Maritime Law Section in the Korean Commercial Code, 39(3) Journal of Maritime Law & Commerce 2008

Newell, R. '"Privity fundamentalism" and the circular indemnity clause', Lloyd's Maritime and Commercial Law Quarterly, 1(Feb) (1992),

Nicoll, C. "Himalaya clauses and sub-bailment on terms, A default rule set by the US Supreme Court"., Shipping and Trade Law, Vol 5, No 7, (2005),

Nikaki, T. 'Himalaya clauses and the Rotterdam Rules', Journal of International Maritime Law, 17(1) 2011, 20-40

Hongjun Ye and Xiaobing Wong, The Interpretation on Transport of Goods by Inland Water Rule & Port Cargo Handling Rule, first edition (The People Transport Press, 2000),

Palmer, V.The Paths to Privity, Austin & Winfield, 1992,

Pamel P. G. and Robert C. Wilkins Borden Ladner Gervais, LLP, Bills of Lading vs Sea Waybills, and The Himalaya Clause, Presented at the NJI/CMLA, Federal Court and Federal Court of Appeal Canadian Maritime Law Association Seminar April 15, 2011 Fairmont Château Laurier, Ottawa

Özel, Melis "Incorporation of Charterparty Clauses into Bills of Lading: Peculiar to Maritime Law" in Malcolm Clarke (ed) Maritime Law Evolving: Thirty Years at Southampton, Hart Publishing, 2013, 181.

Ulfbeck, V. Multimodal Transports in the United States and Europe--Global or

Regional Liability Rules? 34 Tul. Mar. L.J. 37 2009-2010, 37

Rabe, D. Seehandelsrecht, 4. Auflage 2000 § 607a HGB Rn 9; Herber,Seehandelsrecht 1999

Lord Roskill, Half-A-Century of Commercial Law 1930–1980, Birmingham, 1981

Schmidt, K. The Himalaya Clause under the Law of the Federal Republic of Germany, ETL 1984

Schoenbaum, T J. Admiralty and Maritime Law, 3rd ed. (St. Paul,Minn.: West Group, 2001),

Summers, D. M. Third Party Beneficiaries and the Restatement (Second) of Contracts, 67 Cornell Law Review, 1982

Stevens, R. 'The Contracts (Rights of Third Parties) Act 1999', Law Quarterly Review (2004), 292-323,

Sturley, M. International Uniform Law in National Courts: The Influence of Domestic Law in Conflicts of Interpretation, 27 Virginia Journal of International law, 1987,729, 733

Talbot, P. 43 Journal of Maritime Law & Commerce (1) 2012

Tetley, W. The Himalaya Cause – Revisited, 2003, 9 JIML 40, 42.

Treitel, G. F.M.B. Reynolds, Thomas Gilbert Carver, Carver on Bills of Lading, 3rd ed., London: Sweet & Maxwell, 2011

Yuzhuo Si: Zuoxian Zhu. On the Legal Status of Port Operators under Chinese

Law, 2 US-China Law Review 1 2005, Volume 2, No.7 (Serial No.8),

Williams, R. 'The Rotterdam Rules: winners and losers', Journal ofInternational Maritime Law, 16 (2010),

Wilson, R.John F Carriage of Goods by Sea, 7th edn (Harlow: Longman, 2010),

White, M, Australian Maritime Law (3rd ed),The Federation Press, 2014,

B. Zeller,The Development of a Global Contract Law. Still a Dream? In Eppur si muove: The age of Uniform Law – Festschrift for Michael Joachim Bonell, to celebrate his 70th birthday, UNIDROIT (ed.), 2016

Zuoxian Zhu, The Legal Status of Port Operator under Chinese Law, Journal of Business Law, 8, (2011), 737

www.ingramcontent.com/pod-product-compliance
Lightning Source LLC
Chambersburg PA
CBHW020912210326
41598CB00018B/1842